too MUCH of A
good THING is
Wonderful

September 9, 2000

Steamboat (annual!)

too MUCH OF A
good THING is
Wonderful

For
Christine for
Vicki, for Rita,
for Lois "the Mother" +
for Anna, the
little
one —

Regina Barreca, PhD.

Here's to
laughter across generations
+ to love between
all of you. Gina

XXX

Too Much of a Good Thing Is Wonderful

Regina Barreca, PhD.

Bibliopola Press, UConn Co-op, Storrs, CT, 06269-2019
Distributed by the University Press of New England,
Hanover, N.H. 03755-2048
Manufactured in the United States

Library of Congress Catalog Card Number
00-102357

ISBN 0-939883-06-6

Cover art by Nicole Hollander
Design by Jennifer Weinland

For my uncle, Laurence Barreca,
who taught me through his philanthropic work
that too much of a good thing can be wonderful
--if you spread it around and put it to good use.

A portion of the profits of this book
will be given to
The Connecticut Women's Education
and Legal Fund.

Contents

Growing Up

Body

Domesticity

Anxiety

Acknowledgements

Right up front, I want to thank cartoonist extrodinaire Nicole Hollander for helping persuade those readers who choose books their cover to take this one home. To those editors at The Hartford Courant (especially Steve Courtney), The Chicago Tribune (especially Denis Gosselin), The Orlando Sentinel (especially Wendy Spiraduso), The Cleveland Plain Dealer, The Detroit Free Press, Attache (especially Jay Heinrichs), The Dartmouth Alumni Magazine (especially Karen Endicott), Working Woman, and elsewhere, I offer my thanks for their support and advice--and for publishing these essays in their earlier versions over the last several years. To Suzy Staubach, who made these pieces into a book the way a potter forms clay into a work of art, I offer my sincere gratitude. To the usual suspects--Nancy, Tim, Bonnie, Pam, Rose, Brenda, George, John, Lee, Diane, Tim, Matthew, Lynette, Margaret, Genevieve, Barbara, Roxanne, Faith, Fleur, Gerry, Jane, Kerry, Bob, Hugo, Wendy, and Ami (whose Mom sent her all the clips from The Courant)--thanks from the heart for the inspiration and for taking the time to read. Thanks to my father, Hugo Barreca Sr., for his patience. And to my husband, Michael Meyer, I owe the privilege of knowing that, whatever story I tell, whenever I tell it, I am not playing to an empty house.

Family

My Italian Aunts Taught Me to Dance

My aunts taught me to dance.

There were dozens of them, fat and small in floral print dresses looking like ottomans scattered across the long dark living room in Brooklyn, except they had round smiling or yelling faces. And yet they could dance, gracefully, wildly stamping their improbably tiny feet and flinging one another around the room to juke box music off the cheap red radio. They could have taught me other lessons, like how to cook sweet sausage sauce or how to survive an early loveless marriage, but they didn't. Instead they swung me around the room in a two-armed gesture more often used by longshoremen unloading freight than by dance instructors. But with one another they practiced the intricate moves, raising eyebrows and half-smiling when they got it perfectly right, when fingertips touched just as the music stopped. It didn't have a name, but it was the only dance they knew and the only one I've learned in thirty-nine years.

I learned to dance, and I learned what life had in store. One aunt was married to an uncle everybody called "The Saint" because they apparently lived together for forty years without having sex. "Your uncle Phil is a saint," a random aunt would whisper in a voice silibant as a stage villain's. For my first few years I only knew he was called a saint by these women without knowing why, but when I was about seven they felt I was mature enough to handle the reason behind the title. I still had no idea what they meant but I learned to raise my eyebrows slightly and nod.

This way they kept speaking, thinking for some lunatic reason that I knew what on earth they were talking about, and I kept quiet, silently and secretly remembering what they said because I knew I would need to figure it out later. The way kids from some other families on the block stole and hoarded food under their beds for the middle of the night, I craved and stole these stories, illegal in my ignorance, so that I, too, could get up after midnight and gnaw on them, filling myself up with stuff I could barely grasp or digest but couldn't get enough of.

"Your Uncle Phil is a saint" meant that he didn't bother my Aunt Grace for sex. Now I wonder whether he dressed up in her slips when she wasn't home, or caressed her shoes, or found other like-minded saints in small basement clubs for a slow waltz. But maybe he just liked her company and wanted somebody to make cinnamon toast for him when he came home from driving a truck to and from New Jersey every day. Maybe they did everything except have sex and there are certainly relationships less intimate than that. They slept in tiny twin separate beds, like children at a boarding school, but that still doesn't make it a tragedy. Sleeping in the same bed next to somebody every night doesn't mean you know what they're dreaming, after all.

The story about Aunt Grace ranked right up there with stories about "the change of life." "The change of life" sounded like what what you got back after you bought something with "the bill of life," but after a while I realized that it wasn't currency they were talking about, at least not the way the word was usually understood. It's true, however, that hearing "Your Aunt Clara went through the change early," sounded like she had emptied her pockets prematurely, and that "Teresa never admitted having the change" sounded like Teresa was cheap. Maybe they weren't too far off the mark; maybe blood was the going currency, with soft tissue as the floating bond of matrimony.

I also learned about matrimony and romance from looking at the cousins around me. At sunset the heat and the energy made it seem like everything might explode; these firecracker nighttimes filled my early summers. Humidity in the hot air rose like city incense out of garbage and Evening In Paris. "If you're not married by twenty, then kiss it good-bye," I heard my cousin laugh to his sister, who was sixteen and whom I adored. From the next door over we all heard my great-uncle yell "There ain't no socks that stink like a woman's nagging." The steamy streets were thick with an undergrowth of children tangled in gritty games until way after dark. In this warm darkness my cousin Marie and her friends were future mothers out looking for future fathers.

It was clear to me even then that there weren't decisions to be made, only choices. Choosing by eye color, height or a single noble gesture, they picked boys the way boys picked jobs: taking what offered the most in the long run. Time set boundaries around them like fences. "Nobody has forever," said Marie to me as she ran down the steps in a hurry, "least of all us. You'll see. Wait." I was maybe ten years old, but I tucked the warning away for later. The beautiful shark eyed teenage boy who waited in a car beside the curb seemed Marie's best bet, I thought. His white smile broke through the heat like a wave on a beach.

My Sicilian great-grandmother, well into her nineties, wished Marie luck and said a prayer for her. She'd stay up late, but sleep in intervals, waking to pray, or curse, or make a prediction. Then she'd fall asleep, fall back into her dreams like a small dark pear that had fallen from one the fruit trees that grew, unceremonious and undaunted, behind the house.

This great-grandmother could not imagine a world immune to magic and so she applied magic to her wish that all the women in the family would marry, considering every girl a woman. She lit votive candles that glowed red on every table. She prayed out loud. When the backyard bushes were hung with fireflies shining like rhinestones, she would tell stories about eating figs right off the tree, and talk about how she met her husband when she was only fourteen. He died when he was forty-seven and she was forty-one but she spoke about him like he was just gone to the store for a few minutes.

(When this old woman fell, not like a piece of fruit but like a kitten flung from a rooftop, down two flights of stairs, it was my twenty-two-year-old mother, not one of her own children, who dared to go with her in the ambulance to the hospital. My aunts wouldn't, being more terrified of doctors and places where no one understood your screamed questions than they were of their mother's solitary death. My mother said the old woman looked into her eyes with a full understanding of all that was happening, apologetic for all the others who were too cowardly to be with them. They placed my great-grandmother on a stretcher and wheeled her away, but not before she smiled good-bye to another immigrant imported wife with no way to make herself understood.)

My mother came home saying that the doctors declared that my great-grandmother had the heart of a sixteen year old. This terrified me. Did this happen to other people in our family? Is that why none of my aunts had children? Or had all their children disappeared, given their hearts away? Nothing in me questioned that the young were sacrificed to the old like virgins flung onto ancient volcanoes. I didn't want to ask the question.

There were no long answers in my family, only short ones. Asked why, at seventy-five, one great-uncle moved himself into the attic, moving a staircase away from his wife of forty-eight years, the only answer was "That's where he wanted to live." Asked why Aunt Louise never married, the answer was "She never found the right man" which always sounded as if she had carelessly misplaced him or at least misplaced the map that would lead her to him. There was never a hint that she might not be looking.

The aunts who danced on Saturday evening went to church on Sundays and some went during the weekday, too, to cover their heads in lace and cry. Churches locally seemed filled with women in mantillas weeping and making excuses. The pews also held a few frowning men, making their own excuses, looking more defiant than unhappy when confronting their Maker with their own sinfulness. My talent, clearly, was for breathlessly overhearing things, not minding my own business, and storing away what I did not understand, in order, it seems, to invent interpretations that only coincidentally coincided with the truth.

So that while I did not know specifically for what sins my aunts cried in the brick churches, I figured that these sins must have happened in the past. Surely they were incapable of sinning at their advanced ages. Sinning was a youngster's game, something to look forward to for me, and something to look back on for them. My aunts led complex lives in a simple setting, and I, wrongly, thought I had their story straight before I was even starting my own. I thought their marriages, their loves, their passions, their furies, were diluted by their years and buried by their shapeless flowered dresses. I separated myself from their circles, and found other rhythms strumming beneath my feet.

"My aunts taught me to dance," I said to somebody when I was eighteen and starting college. We'd just finished dancing and I was sorry to lose the feel of his hip against my own. He was tall and pale, and he had dark hair falling over a high forehead. He was as different from everyone I'd ever met as I was from everyone I was meeting. When I looked up at him I felt my stomach contracting, like someone sketching a detailed picture with ice skates on a frozen pond. But what was happening that evening was the beginning of a thaw, of a new season having nothing to do with winter.

Let me tell you about that dance. That was the night I found out that dancing lets you take a stranger and hold him in your arms, and that such holding is one of the best things about it. You move together, however briefly and silently. I was so conscious of my body while I danced with this beautiful boy that my fingers still remember the feeling of the skin on the back of his hands, of the slight pressure of his leg brushing against mine, and the way I felt my mouth forming words for the sheer pleasure of making my lips move so near to his that he must have felt my breath on his throat.

I was glad I wore perfume in my hair, I was glad that my hair was long, and for the first time I was really glad that it was curly because everyone else had straight hair. He could ask "What happened to the girl with the curly hair?" and it would only be me he was asking about. If he asked at all, that is. Who knew what he was thinking? Maybe he was thinking about the girl he came with, a small-faced woman who wore pearls and clean shoes, and who kept an eye out for him while I kept my eye on her.

In my head I told him "dancing with you is a dressed rehearsal, an upright version of a deed with a downside. Threading my fingers with yours as if we are playing a child's game of church and steeple is for me at least only a prelude to the grown-up game. Your leg against mine even in a dance is no game; my hand spread open against your back and feeling the barracuda movements of your shoulder with my fingertips is no mechanical motion, slipping muscle against bone as you maneuver me across a polished wooden floor to music I can hear only the way you hear the sea inside a shell is serious, serious business." I tried to signal this message to him like a lighthouse or a secret agent, tried to make him understand the message through the hieroglyphs of the heart, but he didn't hear.

He heard how I sounded, my voice instead of my arms capturing his attention. "Say that again," he said, dimpling his perfectly smooth cheek, keeping me inside the gravitational pull of his charm. I smiled because I didn't dare not smile in front of handsome man at that point in my life, but I was puzzled and whatever else he was blind to he wasn't blind to my slightly blank look. "Say what again?" I ventured, no doubt fluttering a few eyelashes for good measure; if I was going to look like a fool then at least I could also look like a flirt. "Say 'My aunts taught me to dance.' You have a real New York accent."

I didn't think of myself as having an accent. I suddenly heard myself the way he must have heard me, with a voice like Brooklyn traffic, saying "aunts" as if I were talking about insects instead of relatives. (If I said "We should bring stuff for the aunts at the picnic" it would have sounded like you should bring Black Flag instead of more food. When I tried to say the word differently, saying "Aahnts" I only sounded ridiculous). The boy and I danced together only that one time. He probably went on to dance slowly but not too closely with the girl with the pearls and the New England accent. As for me, I learned to rely, increasingly, on my aunts' advice: life's too short to hold onto a guy who thinks there's only one way to move to the music.

I moved across other dance floors in my day, small flat wooden countries full of miraculous mobility, slipping and regaining my footing, sometimes with a man's arm around me as a prop or a guide, sometimes just part of a circle of strangers or friends, sometimes with my aunts as they made their ways, more and more slowly, to the place where their lessons were learned without being questioned and their lead was followed without hesitation.

They taught me better than I realized. I follow gratefully in the surprising, smiling grace of their footsteps.

The Other Half

I'm half French-Canadian but I don't know very much about that side of my lineage. Because of her death when I was a teenager, information about my mother's family and her own early life was sketchy at best. Very little was written down or documented; she left few traces behind her. There wasn't much to hold onto once she was gone. That I could have kept up with her relatives--my relatives-- is true. I could have made more of an effort to be part of their lives. It seemed to me, though, in the bitterness of my loss and the selfishness of my youth, that it was their job to reach out to me. Whatever the best and worst reasons, the result has been that I have called myself "Italian-American" and have only rarely folded in the information that I am as much "French-Canadian-American" as I am Sicilian.

Recently, however, my French-Canadian roots have been grabbing hold, tugging at me and demanding recognition. One of my graduate students and research assistants, Geneviéve Brassard, waltzed into my office three years ago and spoke in my mother's voice. The lilt of her voice, the sway of certain phrases, the pronunciation of a word here or there, brought back what I grew up hearing at my mother's knee. But with her curly brown hair and dark brown eyes, Geneviéve could pass for one of my Italian cousins; I asked her how she, a Québécois, came to look so Mediterranean. Geneviéve told me that a lot of French Canadians shared our features and explained that what I assumed to be the norm--my mother's fair skin, blond hair and green eyes-- was not. "Many French Canadians look like us," she said, and I realized at the moment that there was an "us" that might include me.

My mother had always declared me to be "a real Barreca" and there was both a compliment and a condemnation in that phrase. Neither my brother nor I looked like we belonged to her. It appeared that we had bypassed the maternal gene pool. Black haired and dark-skinned, we were chips off the old New York block. "If I had another child," she often said, "He would have looked like me,"and the phrase inevitably roused every jealous blood cell in my veins. It felt like she didn't feel she could fully claim us and God knows I wanted to be claimed, but she probably felt justified in lamenting the lack of a newer edition of herself. Mothers sometimes do and life still goes on. She raised us to be Americans--she herself became a citizen because she was very interested in politics and wanted to be able to vote--and never tried to make us feel divided about our loyalties in terms of nationality. But she always defined herself as Canadian, US citizen or not, and saw her life as lived in a kind of exile, without allies or compatriots. She missed her home.

She had copies of Louis Hemon's novel, Maria Chapdelaine, all over the house--I swear there were five or six copies in our home at any one time-- because it was written about the places where she spent her childhood: Peribonka and Chicoutimi, the wilderness of the world around Lac St. Jean. At a used bookstore a few weeks ago, I found a water-stained copy in an English translation and read it. It was brutally sad and oddly beautiful. It pushed all my emotional buttons and then I realized that it was written by the culture that installed them. I felt manipulated and savaged by the writing but that was because it was closer to me than I imagined it might ever get. What did I know of all that, except what I heard thirty years ago? What I knew or didn't know in my head was beside the point--I could remember the smell of the wood burning in the stove of my Aunt Huguette's house in Alma and remember eating a "tarte au sucre"(a brown sugar and maple pie). I knew the places in Hemon's work because the places he described were engraved in some buried part of me. I knew those winters and that sense of despair. Maybe it was passed down through the sinews and the bone, or during sleep or in the womb. But it was there, that knowledge.

And so now when Doris, another erstwhile French Canadian who works in the same building at school, speaks to me about my heritage, I hear her with a difference. I hear in her voice the same echoes I hear in Hemon's writing and Geneviéve's laughter, sounds reverberating against some unexplored parts of my life.

I listen carefully to the echoes, attempting both to follow them forward and trace them back. It is time for me to acknowledge that I am--whatever it means--my mother's daughter.

In All Honesty

I come from a family of accomplished liars. I don't say this by way of apology or warning; I say it as a preface the way somebody else might say "I come from a family of bankers" or "I'm originally from New Jersey." It's a fact, a piece of information, nothing particularly complicated. Honest.

"Never give anybody your real name" could have been the family motto, carved in granite, translated from the Latin or maybe translated into it; nobody worried about the abstract idea of authenticity. Who really cared if our clan's legend was handed down through generations or made up last Tuesday? Lying was the cornerstone, the bedrock, the weaving and shaking but nevertheless enduring foundation upon which the life of my family was built. And here's the tricky part: I'm not sure I'd want to make an argument against lying.

Why settle for fact? Why offer up prose when you can produce poetry? Why not make a story out of ordinary, found incidents, the way certain artists make sculptures out of wrecked cars or fabricate fabulous images out of dirt, blood, and rust? Isn't the most charming person the one who makes you believe you alone are the most interesting person on earth? Does it matter that, strictly speaking, you are about as interesting as bubble wrap? Don't we choose--for our leaders, for our celebrities, for our icons--those who are willing to supply us with a vision; don't we believe in the vision itself rather than checking the eyesight of the one providing the vision for us? So what if the actuality turns out to be slightly different from how you found it; so you changed it. So who cares, so long as you made it better?

You have to have a certain amount of inventiveness, intelligence, and imagination, as well as an excellent memory, to be able to lie convincingly. You need to be able to make what is not real appear real, whether you're a magician making a rabbit appear out of a hat, or a nurse saying that the shot she's aiming for your soft tissue will not hurt. "People have a careless way of talking about a 'born liar,' just as they talk about a 'born poet.' But in both cases they are wrong. Lying and poetry are arts," argued Oscar Wilde. Wilde wasn't one of my ancestors, but obviously he would have felt very much at home.

The importance of practice cannot be unestimated. In my family you could never depend on anybody's being honest, even about the most minor details. You could ask "What did you have for lunch?" in all innocence, just to fill up the time and not because you actually had a burning desire to inventory somebody's daily food-group intake. The man, who had an egg and sweet pepper omelette at noon, would unhesitatingly reply "A B.L.T. on rye with a side of potato salad." It didn't matter at all what he actually ate, you understand, the point was to fudge the truth--that was the important part.

He would need to lie, the young man (or old man, age was never a factor) just to keep in training. What for? Maybe for the big lie he might be expected to make one day, and which might keep him in a job ("I was out of town when they broke into the warehouse"), or married ("Amy? I don't know anybody named Amy. Somebody named Amy calls and all of a sudden I'm a criminal?"), or alive ("Officer, I swear on my mother, I have no idea how Leo died. Anybody can get run over if he walks around at night"). So lying is pretty familiar and familial to me.

But these days lying is more than a family matter: it's a matter of national interest. When we examine the business between Bill Clinton and Monica, for example, or between Bill and Congress, or between _____(insert the name of almost any politician here) and shady figures from their own suspect past, what we're dealing with aren't your ordinary, run-of-the-mill untruths, but a particular subset of finely-tuned duplicities perhaps best called "lies of omission." These are evasions so carefully crafted that the artists themselves don't recognize them as lies, but instead consider them mere variations on veracity. I can comment personally on such matters because I spent my adolescence concocting such lies of omission in order to be considered a "good girl" when, in fact, I was forming rather steamy alliances. The questions my parents asked me when I came home late, ruffled and wide-eyed, were basic and did not include the indelicate search for details and definitions undertaken by Mr. Starr. Let's put it this way: I did not lie to my parents but neither did I suggest that they might try a different angle in their questioning in order to get a fuller picture of my erotic awakening. I suspect that (unlike the inelastic Mr. Starr), they didn't really want to know the details unless it meant something vitally important. So we proceeded, as do many families with teenagers (mine included), to approach such matters on a "need to know" basis.

The truth, however, is that lies have always been with us. Consider, for example, another passage from Oscar Wilde's brilliant brief treatise, "The Decay of Lying: A Protest," written in 1889. One of the characters complains: "Lying! I should have thought that our politicians kept up that habit," to which his companion replies that government officials can never be accused of actually lying--lying being a talent involving resourcefulness and brains. Instead he argues that politicians "never rise beyond the level of misrepresentation, and actually condescend to prove, to discuss, to argue. How different from the temper of the true liar, with his frank, fearless statements, his superb irresponsibility, his healthy, natural disdain of proof of any kind!"

Wilde regards the revelation of the sordid details of our actual lives as terrible because they turn out to be--not heart-rending or shocking or seductive--but supremely vulgar. Listening in on someone's else's intimacies, Wilde implies, wouldn't have you going "Oooooo!" but "Ugh." Having read and--ever so very worse-- heard bits of Starr and Tripp et al we can all too easily agree. People sound, well, really stupid when talking about the unadorned trivia of existence: the typical unadorned discussion of authentic detail is either tacky, nasty, or remarkably boring.

Let's put it this way: just because something happens to be true doesn't make it significant.

This is not to underestimate the fact that certain lies have important functions in our social order. Lies do lots of things: they keep groups together (when everyone believes the same lie), they protect the innocent (that's why Dragnet changed the names, right?), and they help us survive everyday life.

You don't agree with this last point? How about the following defacto truth, a truth universally acknowledged even in the face of possible evidence otherwise: all babies are beautiful. It simply does not matter if your neighbor's new daughter looks like a cross between Winston Churchill and Drew Carey. It doesn't matter if she's unequivocally homely. Just declare that she's gorgeous and don't define what you mean by gorgeous. If, in the interest of credibility, you decide to say otherwise, you're looking for big time trouble. Saying "Goodness, what an intensely objectionable infant" is not the revelation of truth: it is sabotage. It's the sort of remark that's especially unkind if it's true. White lies, like white magic, make things better, not worse, despite the fact that the practitioners in such cases are--technically-- neither scrupulous nor principled. Lies often help you get along without hurting feelings unnecessarily.

The ties that bind can also be viewed as the lies that tie us all together: like a knot in string, a lie can keep things connected. For example, while it was clear that nobody told the truth in my family, it was also made clear that the people you really couldn't trust were the ones outside the family: it was handed down as fact that tradesmen were out to screw you over for every dime, that hairdressers would lie about how your hair would look once they cut it, and that doctors were evil scientists who would operate on you, whether or not you needed it, only because they wanted to put a new wing on their house. (You agreed to see a doctor in my family only if you were ready to die, and since no doctor ever came to the house before a priest was already set up to perform the last rites, it turned out to be true. My relatives saw doctors and then died; that there was a flaw in the causality of the relationship didn't occur to me until much later on.)

More than anybody else, we were warned against the way that people who came into the family through marriage could not be fully trusted. Truth, therefore, was dispensed with great caution and strictly on that "need-to-know" basis I mentioned earlier. The prototype for this model could have been my uncle Mel who would bring his mistress to his sister's house for a drink every Friday evening before they--the illicit couple-- went out for the evening. My aunt would never think to tell her sister-in-law, Mel's wife, what was going on because she just wouldn't understand. The truth as we understood it was that this uncle "really loved his wife and was a good, good husband," that was the accepted version. The little, incidental, small truth of an affair that lasted, oh, eighteen years or so, was simply a piece of information Mel's wife didn't need to know.

That was the logic of the family. And maybe it was a real truth in its own way; maybe more love for his wife lurked beneath his unfaithful hide than any of us could imagine. The search for truth can be compared to a cat chasing her tail: frantic in her pursuit, her quarry nevertheless eludes her; despite the fact that all the world can see it's right there, it remains just beyond her reach. It cannot be possessed because, paradoxically, it is already part of her. You want to know; you don't want to know; maybe the reality of the situation is that you already know. Truth is like nuclear waste: it needs to be dealt with carefully. Sometimes it needs to be buried way, way out of town. And sometimes it should never be uncovered at all.

Kamikaze revelations of truth ("Son, it's time for you to know that you were actually a product of America's first cloning experiment"; "Dear, would you be upset if I admitted that, as part of a youthful indiscretion, I once slept with the Denver Broncos?") are rarely helpful in shoring up a relationship or solidifying a position of trust. I believe we should reserve a certain amount of suspicion for those who would foist upon truths better left unsaid. These are often seriously scary people. Trust me, those who tell you the truth "for your own good" or because they are sure "you'll want to know this, even if it makes you unhappy" are not your best friends. Maybe they're not actual enemies, but your best friends don't pack up trash, hand it to you, and then tell you that you're a better person for managing it.

The reflection that truth is powerful and dangerous is the logic behind many evasions of candor. "Tell all the Truth but tell it slant," cautioned Emily Dickinson, in a poem dealing with the volatility of truth. "Success in Circuit lies." She wasn't one of my ancestors, either, but she would have been welcome at the table (despite her habit of capitalizing letters in the middle of sentences). Ms. Dickinson knew that "The Truth must dazzle gradually or every man be blind," suggesting that, while we depend on the truth, we must also respect its capacity to astound, to startle, and to shake us to the very core of our being. Truth is like a kind of prescription medication: a substance to be used under supervision, for limited duration, and while being monitored by others who can gauge its impact.

While I traffic in the truth, I nevertheless maintain my inherited ability to fabricate. If I lie to keep peace, or fib to make someone feel better, or reassure myself that the world is not as chaotic and unkind a place as it seems to be, am I the sort of liar who deserves punishment and censure? How about if I offer up to the cosmos not so much a lie about what is, as faith in what might be, should have been, could still be? If I pretend to be courageous when I'm terrified, am I lying or am I being brave? If I fake a happy ending, who's to say the world won't believe me, won't catch up with me and make it so? The truth is too big, too finely nuanced, too delightfully or desperately made up of different stories, to be owned by any single soul, or viewpoint, or mouthpiece.

And I wouldn't kid you about this. Honest.

Dialogue

My father, who just had a knee replacement, is staying with us for a couple of weeks. Seventy-five and in (knock on wood) good health, he's a more than welcome guest. In terms of Dad-figures, think of the father in Hal and Frasier rather than Walter Brennan from The Real McCoys. We have have a good relationship, my father and I, and it's evident that Michael likes him enormously. Naturally, much of their daily conversation concerns what they have in common.

They both read various newspapers with keen interest and discuss what's going on in the world. They like The History Channel and much of the historical stuff on A&E (which is often so obsessed with matters relating to WWII and the Third Reich that we refer to it as "the All-Hitler Channel"). What they mostly have in common, however, is me.

You might think I would like the attention. It ain't necessarily so. Much of the conversation between them and about me takes place while I am in the room but is framed in such a way that I am discussed as if I were 1) a life form on another planet; 2) a person on another continent; 3) a person out of earshot; or 4) dead.

Here's the scene: I'm washing the dishes, Michael is clearing up or drying, and my father is sitting at the table. I'm singing along to, let's say, Mary Chapin Carpenter. Knowing all the words makes me overly confident about my accompaniment, given that I cannot hit a correct note even by accident. My father will offer as an opening gambit, "Isn't she very loud?" to which Michael will reply, "Are you kidding? This is nothing . Wait 'til she starts singing to Patsy Cline. I go outside and sit in the garage until it's over."

"Can't you get her to stop?"my father will inquire, with detached but genuine interest, adopting the sort of tone you use when asking a neighbor about a problem with bats. My husband will reply immediately to the question-- and remember, I am standing about two feet away from them-- "Nah, she likes it. It's not a big deal. But it is loud, isn't it?"

Now, you'd expect a 41-year-old woman, somebody who writes feminist criticism, to demand to be spoken to directly, to demand of her husband and father that she be regarded as a fully-participating adult. Forget it. Mostly I participate by adding my laughter or very loud "HA!s" to their conversation. Why don't I make all those other demands? Because I know they're genuinely playing; there's nothing mean lurking in these dialogues. I am indeed loud; this does not come as a surprise to me and my general volume is certainly not a huge shock to the man who raised me to speak up or to the man who loves me for it.

But I know there are vicious versions of these conversations and can declare unhesitatingly that what I witness in my kitchen is different from those attacks on the heart designed to display the power of conspiracy. When, for example, I overheard a man at a restaurant say to his ten or twelve-year-old "Can you believe your mother eats so much? No wonder she's fat. She has no control," I thought about what kind of lesson in the ritual humiliation that boy was learning. I wanted to smack the guy and rescue the woman and have the kid placed in an environment free from emotional snipers. All I could do is make eye-contact with the wife and order a piece of pie for myself, making my request very loudly.

Maybe it came too close to an experience of my own, one that still gives me pain. About twenty years ago, a boy I was dating said in front of me but not to me, addressing instead one of the friends we had just joined at a local bar, "This woman follows me everywhere. How could I tell her to stay home and let me hang out with you? She'd only cry when I got back," I shuddered, thought "I'm outta here. . . ." and broke up with him the next day. It was one of my smarter decisions.

These are the sorts of moments when you need to make yourself heard, whether that takes the form of speaking out or getting out. But for now, in my house, I'll wash as Michael wipes, as my father talks about his youth, or the birds outside, or what was in today's paper. They'll express their affection for each other, and for me, in this funny way, but I'll be happy to accept it, and take the kiss on the forehead it implies.

Most importantly, of course, I will talk to you about them.

On Being A Stepmother

One of the most problematic moments in the world would often appear disguised as the benign question, asked after I've given a lecture, by a nice-enough and genuinely curious woman in the audience: "How many children do you have?"

For a few years I wrestled with this issue, desperately trying to figure out the right response. I cribbed lines from the old movie Goodbye Mr Chips, saying "Every year I have about two hundred children, and all of them are college students." This was a cute enough response (if not actually an acute response. . .) but finally I just started telling the truth: "I have two step-sons, both of whom I adore. They are one of the great joys of my life."

I figured this was the correct answer because it was, after all, the truth. When in doubt, tell the truth, that's my motto (my other motto is "If you can read this, you're too close"). But, in part because I give workshops dealing with personal issues and talk frankly about such intimate topics as "Why Women Hate the Three Stooges" and "Why Women Will Persist in Asking How Much You Love Them While You Are Simply Trying To Watch 'Motor Week'," I find that folks really want to hear me dish the details about my own life. So, on occasion, when I have indeed bared my soul and talked about my two step-kids, I am then asked, with an air of great patience "Do you have any children of your own?"

It's said as if these children, now perhaps better referred to as "these guys," (given their advanced ages of twenty-two and twenty-six), these two step-sons, aren't really part of my life. Trust me: they have been an absolutely central part of my existence since I, and they, were quite young when we all got together. As far as I'm concerned, they are the Real Thing. They are my kids. We've been in each others' lives for more than ten years and if that isn't cause for declaring Reality in a relationship, I don't know what is.

Let me explain. I married their father when they (the sons, not the father) were in their very early teens. Knowing that they had a devoted mother, I never assumed or attempted that role; I knew the boundaries, the unwritten rules that dictated a permanent back-seat in their lives. But I also knew that they liked me, these sons of my husband (a phrase I saw as a compliment, not a curse), and that we enjoyed more than an ordinarily pleasant association.

I saw them go through some pretty tough times at school, drove them where they needed to go, met girlfriends, got over girlfriends, drove them home at two a.m. when they couldn't or shouldn't drive, bought clothes and CDs, took pictures at the proms and graduations, worried over colleges, worried over late nights, worried over phone calls that didn't come--not to mention also worrying over a few that did come: bizarre, late night orations on the nature of reality and love and travel to strange lands. They would ask to speak to me when they phoned, and not out of a sense of duty but from a sense of authentic kinship. We would have enjoyed one another's company whatever situation placed us together; if we'd been standing in line at the Department of Motor Vehicles, waiting for tickets to a concert, boarding a plane, we'd have made conversation and made good use, therefore, of the time and connection.

No, I didn't have the privilege of making them into the strong, smart young men they turned out to be: I give that honor to both their parents, their mother and father, who put in those long and unrecorded hours early on. Surely those times count most profoundly and I bow to their significance. I also give credit to these young men who did not avail themselves of the myriad excuses offered to them, as if at a banquet, to screw up. They went through their bad times, not around them; like good gamblers, they played -- successfully -- the hands they were dealt. None of that had anything to do with me.

But I do give myself credit as a supporting bit player, someone who enters in a middle scene and gets a few good lines, but who nevertheless helps move the action along in a positive way. Someone whose name appears way down in the list of credits, but who does finally merit the recognition of naming. Too bad the name has to be "step-mother,"since the term itself carries such an unfortunate load of emotional and cultural baggage.

The younger son and I had a long and late-night talk about this: why did I have to be his "step-mother"? He was fourteen or so at the time--too old to speak in the language of fairy-tales but not too old to remember the corrupt villainess at the heart of many of them. I said we could come up with another name, if he preferred, but we couldn't find one that worked without sounding like we were from a different galaxy or simply making bad translations from the Latvian ("This is the woman who exists in a maternal role in my life" Yeah, that sounded smooth...). We settled on what the world had ordained, but I remember the shock of being referred to as his "step-mother" when he introduced me to a friend. At first the title sounded as harsh as a whip, as unexpected as a stick lashed across unsuspecting eyes. But his cohort, beyond his years in kindness, said "I'm really glad to meet you" with a smile so real I couldn't believe he hadn't been prepared by my step-son to meet an ally, a compatriot--not a cannibal, not a witch.

The older son introduces me as one of his "parental units" and I like the phrase; it has a hip urbanity that makes me feel pretty fancy. But I've also come to appreciate even that loaded phrase "step-mother." They don't distance themselves as they might if they'd taken palming me off simply as their father's wife, which would diminish the connection that the kids and I have to each other. That they want to introduce me to their tribes at all is a vast and inarguable compliment. That we might well be stuck with the word "step" between us is something I can live with.

They are a step ahead of me, after all, and I am grateful to follow easily in the exuberant and surprising grace of their path.

Saying "Uncle"

I don't think enough good stuff has been said about uncles. It seems to me that there have always been wonderful stories about the complex and often strong relationships between nieces and aunts (albeit with a couple of rotten aunts thrown in--one thinks of Jane Eyre's aunt and shudders). But often uncles are shadowy figures, usually benign but sometimes terrifyingly evil, and occasionally embodying in selected tales every viscous trait known in humanity.

In contrast, my uncles have always been nice guys: funny, smart, quietly supportive, and interesting in their particular visions of life. My Uncle Louie, for example, is one of the funniest men I have ever met-- and that description takes into account those folks I know who get up and do funny for a living. He's in a hospital in Boca Raton tonight as I'm writing this, and I am certain that, no matter how much discomfort he's in, Louie has learned the names of the nurses and is making them smile. The photographs I have of Louie from when he was a young man in Brooklyn are a testimony to his good looks and his athletic abilities (terrific in track and basketball, Louie is the only male Barreca ever to watch a televised sports event and the only one in my family to ask if I watched the UConn men's team triumph over Duke). My father's youngest brother, Louie is a man who has dealt courageously with multiple sclerosis for the last eighteen years and has--perhaps because of the ironic package fate hand-delivered him-- completely perfected the art of the sharply ironic comment, the deftly-turned phrase that sums up the absurdity of life.

He remembers punch lines to jokes and delights in repeating what he's read or heard recently, saving up stories the way some people buy lottery tickets, to make life a little more fun. What have you got to lose?

My Uncle Laurence, one of my father's older brothers, lives not far from Louie in Florida. The photographs of Laurence in his early youth show him against more exotic locations: not Brooklyn, but Venice; not Coney Island but aboard the Queen Mary. Although his destiny took him to different places I also remember Laurence working side by side with my father at what we used to call "The Place," the workshop on West 24th street in Manhattan where they made bedspreads and curtains. Laurence worked there even though he had enough of an income to not need the family business; he made great sandwiches and they'd all eat in the back by the sewing machines. Laurence was and I believe still is a remarkably talented artist; I have watercolors and sketches of his framed in our house and they often evoke comment and praise. In his home, there are fabulous and important pieces of art--he is a collector and patron of the arts--but none of his own work. He is too modest for that. I brag on his behalf in a way he would never permit himself. I seek his praise, sending him clippings and articles about me, shameless in my desire for his approval. When I think he might be proud of me, I am always especially pleased with myself.

I remember with enormous fondness my Uncle Bill, married to my father's sister Regina. Billy lost his wife early--they had no kids-- and so he was often with me for Sunday dinner when I lived in New York. I'd always make him a steak and baked potato; I'd be making a big, beautiful lasagna or roast chicken for everybody else, but Billy only wanted a nice steak and a baked potato. And heavy cream for his coffee; that, too, was essential. And even though it wasn't why he was welcome, he inevitably brought great gifts with him when he'd come to visit. One day he came into the apartment, announcing himself in his voice like Jimmy Durante (he sort of looked like Durante, too) and said "I've brought you what every woman wants." I couldn't imagine what he meant. Wiping my hands on my apron, I sat down at the table as he removed from a paper bag the following items: a full page of first-class stamps, a bottle of Chanel Number 5, and a bag of subway tokens. You know what? He was right: it was the perfect present for a graduate student with no time to stand in line and no money for anything extra. Billy's mottoes were "Never tell anybody your real name" and "Trust everybody but cut the cards." I've discovered that his advice is sound, if not in practice, at least in theory.

There were other uncles, too, ones I saw less often, ones who lived further away or had their own pack of kids to deal with on the holidays. But I hold all my uncles dear to me, grateful for their presence, privileged to be their niece.

Dreams of My Mother

I do not hope to dream of my young, dead mother again. One dream, nights ago, has left me gutted. Naked, with a smile that lit her face, she asked me why I still mourned her when she was now so happy. I can hear myself yelling in my sleep saying how dare you go and be so pleased with yourself, leaving me to clean up. Already denied a complacent aging--she died at 47 and I fear I will, too-- I am also afraid of nightmares now, of the fierce undertow of thoughts too tumbled for sleep. For her own mother she lit rows of red candles in churches of a harsh god. The smell of wax filled my head until I swore I would never grieve in a stone box built by men. Yet I think of her before I sleep.

Weeks before her death she cut herself out of family photographs. Baby pictures show only babies, no smiling mother. Children hold onto empty spaces, seeming silly. Scissors move straight through the middle of some: there's my father in front of the house, alone; there's the tree in the backyard full of flowers with no one underneath it. It is as if she wanted to see, exactly, how the world would look without her. Cutting through those pictures must have been like opening a vein, the sharp point making a furrow right through the past. But still I see her, in the parking lot with the red and blue market behind her; she smiles at me as I carry the packages. We open the car doors, switch the radio on, and drive away.

My mother's stories were more like magic than just the usual household lies. She told a story about her sister seeing the statue of an angel cry in a cemetery on a black-ice day in December when she was a little girl, swearing that her sister swore that the angel's tears themselves turned into black ice on the marble face of a Canadian cherubim, and that her sister, too, started to cry and that her tears were nearly freezing before she reached the doorstep of their tenement building. Why was I told these stories?

Why did I need to hear about a favorite cat who froze to death on the same doorstep? Why did I need to hear about my youngest aunt getting pregnant at fifteen without having her hymen fully broken? I suppose I can understand the telling of that particular story as a warning or a talisman against any early fertility for me, but the other stories of pure unadulterated loss I don't think were fed to me for my own good. They were, at best, stories that needed telling and I was there with nowhere else to go and a foreign mother who had no one else to speak to, and so I heard and she told these tales.

There was never anyone to corroborate what she said. She grew up in the ferocious wilds of northern Québec where--she said--she shot rabbits for dinner with a .22 and where--she said--her grandmother lived happily in a tar paper shack with a husband who changed yearly despite (or perhaps because) of the arctic temperatures, the lonely forests, and the pervasive sense of unexplained exile. She lived her life in translation, my mother, raising her children in something besides a mother tongue. In this she was like her own mother before her who spoke not French Canadian but a mixture that included Indian words, ones my mother could no longer recall, having been embarrassed as a child not to be speaking the customary bastardized language of her peers, themselves speaking a French no one in France could make out anymore than the Sicilian my other grandmother spoke could be understood outside Palermo.

The words traded in these tribes were hand-hewn, uncommon currency, the language of those who could not own a language they didn't make themselves just like they had no right to own clothes they didn't sew or eat food they didn't cook themselves.

I heard about how her own mother, terrified to pathology of

thunderstorms, dragged them all out, all seven kids, into the soaking dark and soaking wet streets to go to a neighbor's house where they all sat under a tin roof listening to the thunder, under the watchful eye of the neighbor's strange adult daughter who would stare without blinking into the eyes of children who could have been hers if she'd been born on a happier day.

Sitting in a house with a tin roof to escape fear of a thunderstorm seemed about as safe as sticking a lightening rod into your mouth from what I understand about electricity, but when I heard the story I just asked my mother questions about herself. "What did you talk about with the neighbors?" "When did your mother decide it was okay to leave?"

What I would ask now is "Why were you forced to wake up out of a night's calm dreaming just to make certain that you would witness your mother's fear and develop a taste for disaster? Is this how it began?"

I very much wish I could know her answers.

Found and Lost

We all leave something behind at every departure. Maybe it's a wadded up piece of gum wrapper, mud from wet shoes, a photograph, an umbrella. Or perhaps what is left is an impression of great happiness or great sadness, real enough that the very walls themselves soak it up like colored paint.

There are some letters I find when cleaning out my elderly aunt's apartment in Queens; these words, nearly indecipherable, are what she left behind: "Tell me when your train arrives so that I might be ready, my bags in the hallway and a coat over my shoulder in the early September evening. Ready." So she wrote to someone so close there was no name on the paper, only the imperative, the intimately demanding words, "Tell me. . . .""

I run my fingers over the ink as if expecting warmth. The paper is brittle and waxen from hands and face powder; the letters from before 1930 are stacked in careful chronology beneath the underwear of an old lady, my aunt, who was always fat, always smelling of vanilla and almond paste. Not perfume. She sent birthday cards, late, written in thick blotched ink. Generous and clumsy, her handwriting was simply an extension of herself. This spidery girl's writing, slanting and sharp, is nevertheless undeniably hers. It is the quality of longing which is so unexpected to me that I read her words with an open mouth. My mind, however, takes longer to open: I cannot believe the young woman who wrote this way became the woman whose sloping shoulder I used to fall asleep against on long rides home from the beach.

These words of hers were prayers against the inevitable. Whether they--
the words, the letters, the feelings-- were returned, or never sent, it hardly
matters. She saw their power fail: they were of no use. My uncle was from
the neighborhood. He had never travelled much. It was not to him that she
wrote; it was not for him that she waited.

She also kept photographs. The only one that I find of myself is from my
first communion. I know that, on the occasion of my first communion, what
I really wanted was to be a bride. I wanted to be given away. The stiff white
fabric of my dress was crisp as new paper. I could hear the sounds made by
my starched slip as I walked down the aisle, watching the head of the girl
before me. My new shoes slid against the marble floor and I worried that I
might fall. The boys were already kneeling, blue suits, bowed heads, hands
clasped and unmoving. One by one they retreated, sat down in assigned
order. I looked through praying fingers, jealous and surprised after it was all
over. There was no miracle. We were all the same, every one. I had longed for
this, and so I began to weep at the injustice of a God who promised that
something would change; who held out arms apparently already full.

I wish now I hadn't expected so much and I most certainly wish they'd
waited until I was happier to snap the photograph. Surely, even indignant
and outraged, I must have had a good time at some point that day. I wish I'd
stumbled across a record of that now lost happier moment.

I go through even older photographs, the ones shoved into manila
envelopes twenty years ago, unlabeled, unsorted. The dust from these
packages rises like a bad smell, the way old dough for old bread would
smell, getting onto my hands, into my hair, all over myself. The edges of
photographs crumble as I touch them. My hands seem to hold such power: I
choose to look at the picture of this man, put his picture down without even
wondering about his name, pick up this group, ask myself questions. I carry
a few of the photographs to one of my two remaining uncles. Whole lives are
summed up by short gruff phrases: "He died before he was thirty-- that
happened then," as if we are speaking of a hundred thousand years ago,
when animals roamed untamed, instead of fifty or sixty years ago. Houses

still stand, after all, where these people were born. It's not like I'm asking about the period of time before the earth's crust cooled, but maybe all time after a certain point becomes geologic. Maybe it's all about weather changes, land shifts, and the movement of continents away from each other. Maybe all times become important once they pass.

In the photograph I remember best, the face of a woman, my age maybe, stares at me like I'm making trouble. I don't recognize her. She is surrounded by infants; they seem to grow like mushrooms all around her. None smile. Dressed in white, this was an event for them; what happened after the camera and the photographer sent them all home? Did the children tear off clean clothes to run and play in alleys and backyards? Or was this a record of a solemn event: the mother's birthday, a child's Communion? Did any of those children feel the way I did? They all sit and stand together and to fit inside the camera's frame they huddle shoulder pressing against shoulder. Only the mother is taller, sitting in the middle. Her children are old or gone by now, what with the many wars since this picture was taken, not to mention everyday dying.

There is another photograph from the 1930s: four young men at the beach, all smiling, arms around one another. They look at a point slightly beyond the camera. They don't picture me.

Radio Voices

The past flutters like wash on the line: noiseless, changing, yet pinned into place. Certain winds blow, move a bit of white linen here, a dress out there, until cloth catches a piece of sun. Who knows why we remember what we remember? Who knows what stories will have to be told?

As a child my mother told me that dreams had uncanny powers: I recall dreams I had when I was six or seven as accurately as I recall a telephone exchange or the call numbers to a favorite radio station. One dream pulls me back to the night time fears like some fierce undertow carries you out past the safe boundaries, beyond where the shores can still be seen. I dreamed of death, even at this early age, but then all children do; talk to a child for an hour, see whether death or heaven or hell does not come up in idle conversation. In this dream I spoke to my guardian angel, who was pale and thin and looked to be not of much use.

"Do you know that some people don't go anywhere," said the angel, shifting transparent wings uneasily, "after they die?" "But I will," I can hear myself say, "I will go to heaven and be with everybody from my class and from my family." "I can't promise anything," said the angel and vanished. I woke up to the familiar dark and the window lit by the benevolent streetlight. I did not cry, nor did I sleep again that night. There was a small old radio near my bed, and I sometimes entertained myself by listening to midnight phone-in talk shows or recorded concerts of complex classical music. This night I carefully moved the radio from the flimsy wooden night table and moved it under the covers with me, as if to draw the human voices closer, to keep everyone safe. There, flannel-protected and warm, the men who answered the questions and the women who asked them all spoke in muffled tones, suitable for the hours between one and five. After five I was alright: the streetlight flicked off. Light came from the sky behind the fat tall trees and only the single star shone in the corner of my window.

That morning I told my dream at the breakfast table. The backyard was full of the day: birds snipped at one another to get the seed cunningly placed so as to provide us with a view of their feeding; noises from the neighbor's garden climbed the trellis with the ivy. I told my mother, word for word, about the dream.

"That's a strange dream. What did the angel look like? Was he like somebody we know?"

"No," I said, picking raisins from my cereal with my fingers and eating them one by one. " No. I'm sure this really was my guardian angel. I just had that feeling. What do you think it means?"

"I don't know. I really don't know."

Perhaps I had never heard an adult say those words before, and perhaps that's why they stand, as a frame to the dream, engraving that morning like an illustration for a bookplate. I looked at my mother who looked out to the backyard and I was more scared that morning than I had been in the night. What was there about a dream that could worry a person once the dream was over?

I don't remember whether I asked any more questions and I don't remember whether any other explanations were given. Part of my past assures me that, kind as my mother was, she must have provided solutions and effected reassurances as she did when large dogs came too near me on the street. But I cannot recall anything else of the morning. I didn't remember the incident for years.

So when I started living alone in my early twenties I started sleeping with the radio tucked under the covers, near my shoulder, under my hair. The first night I was alone I reached over to the shining digital clock am/fm unit, powered not through a macramé of colored wires but by neat batteries, and I could not remember why at first this ridiculous gesture seemed so natural; hearing what seemed like familiar voices, it was only as I grew numbed with sleep that I thought of that dream, with the sterile, embarrassed angel, and remembered those months when I kept a vigil with the radio talk show hosts, waiting for sunrise.

Mea Culpa, Mom

I'd like to apologize to my Mom. This might be tricky, given that she hasn't been "with us," as they say, in going on twenty-five years and getting in touch with the dead is even more difficult than trying to track down an old friend from high school who's changed her last name twice and moved to Brazil. But The Hartford Courant has a wide readership and, hey, who knows? Maybe they get Northeast wherever she is. What I'd like to say is this: Mom, I just didn't know.

I didn't know what it would be like to face middle age. I couldn't imagine what it would be like to wonder whether I'd spent my youth wisely. I couldn't even imagine, back then, what it might have been like for you to live in a foreign country where even your own children didn't speak your language, where the traditional shout from mother-to-kid "I don't know what you're talking about" was sometimes literal. (You did teach us to swear in French, not through lessons but through example of course, and for that I'm grateful. It made getting around Paris with my girlfriends at twenty-one much easier; at least one of us could use persuasive language on the gentlemen who sought our attention by lurching at us as we strolled on the boulevards.)

I used to wonder why you didn't wear lots of make-up like the other mothers but instead wore only black mascara and red lipstick. Now I usually only wear mascara and lipstick when I go out, no longer having the patience for the elaborate troweling on of foundation, power, blush, eye shadow, etc..

That whole process was appealing until I hit my thirties, when I discovered I had better things to do than to curl my eyelashes with a device that was clearly better suited for circumcision than cosmetology.

You used to cry sometimes and I was resentful of your anguish, not because I was genuinely sympathetic but because I needed you to be The Mom at all times. It wasn't fair, I figured, for you to have any angst because, as a card-carrying teenager, I was supposed to have the monopoly on misery. You were cutting in on my turf. You were supposed to bustle about, making things cheerful and easy for everybody, never thinking "How on earth did I get here? What am I doing with my life?" Your vocation was us, I thought, and your voice should have been heard only when you were cooing gently, or offering advice and solace. It didn't occur to me that you were as busy thinking about your destiny as I was thinking about mine. You were the main person in my life for so long that it seemed inconceivable that I wasn't the only one in yours. It didn't occur to me that there were other occupants seated in your imagination.

There were the times I made fun of your cooking, or told you that you were putting on weight, or wore your dresses and (because I was fifteen) looked better in them than you did and mentioned this to you, not to be mean, but simply as a point of information. There were times I asked you to pick me up at school but to park the car around the corner so that no one would see you waiting for me. You did it, too, and your only commentary a wry smile. I see that now for the act of love and understanding it so clearly was. Back then, it seemed to me a simple favor; now it appears to me as a great gift because of everything that underwrote the selfless gesture.

I apologize for lying and saying that I wasn't going to meet a boy at the park when I was, thereby forcing you to follow me, secretly, in order to save me from what you (quite correctly) assumed to be deeds leading to possible ignomy. You hated hearing lies and I hated that you could almost always catch me in the telling of them. You knew me too well, I thought, but now I see that everybody does the same things, that you knew what I was up to because you had been up to precisely the same escapades in your own day (which was not as far back as I then imagined).

I want to say how sorry I am for being so angry for so long at your death that I had to disinherit you, describing myself only as my father's daughter and brother's sister, but rarely as anything of yours. True, all the women in your family preferred their sons to their daughters (part of their culture, their universe, a belief founded so far back it wasn't even examined) and that might have eclipsed what was between us, but it didn't erase it. I am trying to understand us, but it's like playing cat's cradle with one hand or driving while looking only in the rearview mirror.

If you were here, I'd like to think that you and I would sit down with cups of strong coffee and pieces of sweet cake and laugh together, taking each other in and helping each other out.

A Love Story

"I met your father at the beach," my mother would tell me. She would be sitting at the kitchen table, smoking, looking out the window."We were both reading From Here to Eternity. I saw him. Then he looked up and saw me." She had photographs of herself at the beach, long legs for a short woman, dark glasses nearly obscuring small features. Sexy. Disguised. Posed.

"I worked all day at the phone company putting through international calls. It was August, hot, and I came home tired. But when my girlfriend Hèléne who worked at Eton's Department Store called to invite me I just went. But it wasn't really Helene calling, even though it was her voice; it was destiny on the other end of the line that afternoon. I'd been putting through calls from foreign cities all day but that one time, through Hèléne, long distance called me."Here my mother would pause, let out smoke, and look into the distance, even though the distance was limited by the trees that lined our small backyard.

I loved that part about destiny. It made me shiver and close my eyes in a tight smile. It wasn't just an accident, their meeting, their marriage, our family. I loved the sense of sweeping purpose behind it. That the beach could be a place for the chance but still providential collision of human beings, that such a frivolous spot could be the geographic location for the seriousness of my parents' first encounter, awed me.

It was August, after the war. My father had returned from the war in Europe, still surprised to wake up everyday. He'd been the radio man on a

Liberator, his fingertips alive to sounds and pulses in the silent hollow plane. He spent two years making calls to longer distances with shorter messages than the ones that went through my mother. While my mother patched through calls with people crying or gossiping, the messages transmitted to my father came with numbers and pinpoint locations. They were both, my parents, receivers, conduits, channels. They were used by others to get the point across.

In that plane, words, like oxygen, were passed through tubes and wires known to my father but unfamiliar elsewhere. Words would fall like pebbles bouncing off the metal walls in the bomber, so nobody spoke. Not even the man with the mouthpiece. My father's all male, all-silent nighttime world of flying into the skies over Hamburg or Tokyo was different from the noisy life with his mother, grandmother, brothers and sisters in Brooklyn. The sky was not home. He wasn't like other men who loved the sharp cold sense of war's importance. He was relieved when it was over.

Home wasn't home, either, after he returned. He was older, had been other places. Needed to get away every once and a while. A friend had a Canadian cousin and they decided to head up the road to Québec. My father worked in a plastics factory and so did his friend. They didn't talk about much. They didn't talk about what they were doing, or their families, or their girls. Maybe they spoke about some places they had been. Mostly they talked about what they saw from the car windows, the weather, and the news.

Who knows what happened that August? Maybe my father had enough of the girls from the neighborhood, big girls in shiny dresses with starched black curls and snapping gum; he liked my mother's difference. She rejected the chipped-toothed boys who flocked around her mother's boarding house; she liked my father's dark looks. My father's voice scratched at her heart like a pen knife, leaving his initials there. She sent him letters full of perfectly quoted lines from the American movies she went to almost nightly to improve her English. They had long conversations on stolen telephone company time.

They saw one another on weekends, with my father driving five hundred miles after a full work week for a couple of years to go see a French Canadian blond girl with green eyes. Once he called her from a motel in Mechanicsville, New York, because the muffler fell off his car and he had to wait there for a replacement part. My mother cried so hard, he said, that he couldn't bear it, and instead of waiting took a bus, spent only six hours with her, took the bus back to Mechanicsville and then drove back to Brooklyn so he could get to work on time.

That was a long time ago, but I carry the story with me, like change in my pocket, because I like the sound and weight of it, and because it reassures me.

My Brother

I begin with letters from my brother sent to me when I lived in England. I was twenty-one and he was twenty-eight. My father was moving out of the house we'd lived in for ten years. The winds of chaos were whistling right outside the singleframe windowpanes of both of our lives and darkness crouched right outside the door.

"It is Sunday afternoon and I'm sitting in the living room, in our living room, where the white pictureless walls stand listening and watching. They've seen me here before, in this yellow sofa that used to be downstairs which we just brought up here again, years ago where I sat and read mystery stories and did my science homework. God, I loved those mysteries which I used to take out of that old wooden library. I would get so scared I would have to finish the book before I could sleep. I came here for today, hot and humid and disgusting in Manhattan, to taste this pleasure just once more."

"I took the car and drove down and up all the old routes. Past Oak School Number Three where the baseball diamond and basketball courts were empty, where you worked that summer with those little girls, teaching them to play volleyball and to play fair, and where Mike Turner beat me up in 1965. He blew his brains out with a .45 two years ago. And by every old girlfriend's house, by Chrissy's house, Nancy's house, Vicki, all those nights ago. Then by the huge junior high, so overcrowded it looked like a Cecil B. DeMille movie, and then the huger high school with its vast slick lawn and qualified classrooms. Through that old maze of streets and on to Harbor Isle, lovely, unforgettable, the water too blue to mention, by Kenny's house and that little tennis court where his father stood shirtless and sweating, the portrait of a homeowner, just about to put in a new air conditioner."

"I sit in the yard and watch and listen. The squirrel sits on his limb and does not move for one half hour. The yard is rich and heavy and green. I thought of the old cat, how he would walk so deliberately, paw down, next paw down, and come striding out from his jungle, shaggy belly swinging. Daddy made me breakfast, eggs and ham and coffee. I felt good and calm, and the house felt friendly, and the only sort of ghosts were benevolent ones, smiling gently at the passage of time. Dad looked good, his hair strong and white, looking like he always did."

"I hope you are well (I know you are)," my brother ends the letter by writing, "and wish that you could be here, but even more I wish I were there."

We wrote to each other a lot, my brother Hugo and I, my only sibling, the only one who knew what it was like to grow up in our house, the only one who knew what it was like to have our particular mother and father out of all the other mothers and fathers in the world. We sent letters. When we could afford it we had long late night telephone calls, with me inevitably huddled against the wall in some student digs and him in one of his many lower East side, low-profile, low-rent apartments.

We missed each other, not in any sentimental way--ours was not and is not now a sentimental family--but in the way I imagine animals miss their litter mates, the way creatures howling across unfamiliar landscapes for their kin miss one another, longing for the answer of the oldest known voice.

As I said, we are not a sentimental family.

But we are a family. What's left of the core group--my brother, my dad, and myself--constitute a serious family, an undiluted family of three fiercely attached and wildly different people. And, because fate has been kinder to us than any of us deserve, there are also the families we have made with others--families that bring us out of the gritty, undiluted, exhausting nature of sharing a past. I am relieved and grateful for my brother's well-earned and hard-earned happiness; his wife and children are (I tell him) the best thing he's ever done; in comparison, his M.B.A. and recent law degree pale in comparison. I believe that Hugo is relieved and grateful for the life Michael and I have made for each other.

These days we have daytime or early evening telephone conversations, checking in about what is going on, but also checking in--sometimes--about what happened, often years ago, to see whether we agreed on any truth. We remember vastly different childhoods, completely different mothers, for example, so that it is always interesting to compare notes--a process that has necessarily lead to loud and vituperative arguments, with him mad and me crying over the dissonance in our stories. But such things are bound to happen when the stories really matter; dissonance leads to discovery, voices raised can sometimes be those voices calling to each other. I am glad my brother is there to answer the cry.

Big Days

Is it me, or has the whole holiday season become an event most sincerely, most wholeheartedly, most tenderly appreciated in retrospect? Aren't these major holidays best, to put it bluntly, when they are over? Big Days (as in: "Johnny is cranky because he went to the zoo and then to a birthday party. He had such a Big Day") are greatly improved when they're firmly stuck in the past.

It wasn't always this way. As a kid, you await holidays with a wide-eyed, passionate, almost maniacal enthusiasm. Heavy breathing is involved. Days are crossed off calendars with large felt-tip pens. Finally, there is the counting of minutes until the holiday officially begins. Awake all night, mutated into a hyperactive alien being with a transfixed smile resembling one of the creatures from Dr. Suess's Whoville (or, for the less-than-cute, resembling Peter Lorre), you imagine the splendors waiting for you. Maybe this year you'll win first prize: Santa, like Calvin--not Klein, the other one-- will name you one of the Elect and you'll find a trip to Disneyland under the tree. Or maybe you'll have been Nice all year and will unwrap a new Volkswagen Passat. Or a pony.(At least the pony will not be responsible for the sort of television ads whose underlying message is "Darn it. If these rotten kids weren't in the car, I'd be off having an affair with this stranger I just met at a stop sign.") Or maybe Santa went into therapy this year and awarded the best boys and girls what they really need: a whole new set of relatives.

Not that relatives aren't fun--in retrospect. I was remembering with genuine fondness an uncle we used to refer to as "Herman, the Human Meat Thermometer." For three years Herman worked in a supermarket, a fact that naturally made him the world's expert on food preparation. He would stand for hours by the oven and repeatedly open the door, as if signaling to the turkey in a secret code that it should cook. That he reduced the oven's temperature every time he performed this ritual did not act as a deterrent. "It's Christmas. This makes him happy, leave him alone," I was told. So what if dinner was a little late? So what if would have been quicker and healthier to cook the bird with an acetylene torch?Herman was happy.

It was impolite to point out that Aunt Marie conversed with her mouth so full of food she looked like a talking landfill. Nor did one mention cousin Tom's habit of sticking his finger in his ear, twirling it around vigorously, and then gazing with rapt concentration at whatever it happened to capture from its voyage into the interior. "It's Christmas. Leave them alone,"I was told in that hissed whisper used to shut kids up.

The phrase "It's Christmas" (or Easter, or The Fourth of July) was shorthand for "Put your shameful sense of judgment away. It doesn't apply here. If you want to make fun of otherwise perfectly nice people who happen to love you but who also happen to stick their fingers in their ears, you'll just have to wait until you get back to your fancy friends, you ungrateful snob." The holiday season was a time for total immersion in the otherwise bizarre world of family lunacy. You weren't actually allowed to laugh while anything was going on but you laughed your head off once it was all over. It was worth it.

So the best holidays now are the ones that are over, even if they just ended five minutes ago. I don't mean this in a bad way, believe me; I just find that my pleasure derives less from anticipation than from remembrance. Sometimes the most perfectly enjoyable minute of a wonderful day is the very minute it is over. When the tables are cleared, when the dishes are washed, when the locks on the doors have been changed--no, I'm just kidding. But I'm not kidding about the satisfaction, the moment to be cherished and embraced, when the door closes after a party is over. That's when the story about the festivities begins to blossom into the work of art that all shared stories become. The laughter may be an echo, but it is enriched and purified by the distance it travels. So feel free to worry about New Year's Eve, just so long as you are prepared to tell funny stories about it once it is over.

Eat Before You Go

So this smart, funny, ambitious student comes into my office and talks about how her mother wants to bake some muffins for me. Her mother equates food with safety and pleasure. She has told her mother that she really likes the class and the mother's delight and gratitude is shown through the offer of dough--real dough, the good stuff, not just lousy lucre. The daughter is embarrassed by the effusive emotion shown by her mother. I am not; I think the gesture is wonderful, and I understand her mom's desire to feed someone, even if the person in question is someone to whom one is connected only distantly.

This kid is an "A" student, no question about it, but she is afraid that if her mother makes muffins it will seem like a bribe. I tell her that her mother can bring a billion muffins in assorted flavors to the office as soon as I've handed in the grades for the course so that there will be no administrative complications. She nods and accepts the compromise; no muffins during the term, but muffins in a soi-distant future. Everybody's happy, especially me.

To trust someone enough to cook for them is a big issue; to trust someone enough to allow them to cook for you is a matter equally fraught with weighty issues, no matter what your size. Whenever I left the house as a kid to eat at a friend's home I was told in no uncertain terms: "Eat before you go." The idea behind this instruction was twofold: 1). You don't show up at a stranger's table with the kind of appetite that will encourage others to believe you are starved by your own family, kept locked in a basement, and neglected; 2). You don't know what on earth these strange people might serve you. They might give you one piece of ham on a slice of white bread. They might give you radishes as a main course. They might cover their spaghetti with store-bought sauce or serve you only one half of a baked potato. There might not be seconds. You would get pale. You would pass out from hunger. It would be such a shame to do that to these people.

The lesson, therefore, was that you could not be safe when it came to food. You would be in trouble if you didn't eat before you left because either you'd eat too much or there wouldn't be enough to eat. You would disgrace your family in either case because, presumably, if you ate store-bought sauce you would keel over into the Prego on contact.

Therefore you would be force-fed before going out to dinner. You would have "a little snack" at home before having appetizers elsewhere; "a little snack" would involve chicken cutlets, stuffed mushrooms, and/or brasciole. You couldn't actually walk straight because you would be so full but you would waddle off to a neighbor's house and sit down at their table. Of course it would be wildly impolite if you didn't eat everything they served you, too. You ate to be nice; people cooked to be nice (even if they only cooked two baked potatoes for four people); eating and niceness went hand-in-hand, or fork-in-spoon. You ate a little more than you might otherwise; what could it hurt? There is a reason, remember, behind elastized waistbands and belts that can be let out a few notches.

And it strikes me that the idea of being prepared for any event--feast or famine--is not a bad one: that's what the eat-before-you-go policy is about. Nothing can sneak up on you. Nothing can catch you off guard. You don't have to rely on anyone else and you don't burden people by making them assume responsibility for your needs. It's the food equivalent of not needing to be given a lift to work in the morning; it's like not counting on your spouse to type your correspondence or reload ink cartridge for the printer. You're not dependent on someone else's ability to provide what is essential to you which means that when you are offered a gift--a meal, a favor, a lift--you regard it as a wonderful addition to an already replete existence. It's never good to go to someone else "morte de faim" (dying of hunger) literally or figuratively; no matter what you hunger for, this is a good policy.

As for the woman who wants to make the muffins: they will be enormously welcome when they arrive. I'll have one before I go out to dinner.

My Grandmother, A Chicken, and Death

The miracle of death I first had the privilege to witness when I was about five years old.

My grandmother and I, along with a dozen other females of diverse ages, had been waiting about six years for a bus to come down Avenue U in Brooklyn, NY. We'd been marketing--as people then referred to the process-- and now stood in vigilance alongside our string bags, which were lined up next to us on the pavement as if on parade. In addition to the bags of flour, boxes of salt, and cans of olive oil bought for convenience, my grandmother had purchased a live chicken which she held under her arm. This was a Big Deal, this particular purchase. Relatives were coming all the way from New Jersey and the big chicken was a special treat. I had never seen her buy a real live chicken before and although I knew this practice was not actually unusual, I was fascinated by the entire ritual: the selection process, the holding of the bird, the fact of the creature's vitality.

The bird was in her embrace, nestled in the broad expanse of her black cotton sleeve. It seemed calm enough. Resisting the temptation to ask my grandmother if I could try to hold it, I settled for sneaking looks at its eyes. The bird seemed to look back at me and I rather fancied that we had built up a bit of a friendship. I felt sort of proud of the bird and of my grandmother's ability to control and deal with the creature on this warm morning. Other people waiting on line also looked at it and commented on it, some speaking Italian to my grandmother, and smiling at me.

Finally, the bus arrived. Other people got on first; we waited until they were seated. My grandmother, in her seventies at the time, and a slow mover, took her time in moving everything into the vestibule of the vehicle. Only after we had dragged our parcels up the few steps to the little entry platform did the driver notice the chicken. "Lady," he said, with some impatience, "You cannot bring a live bird on the bus.Sorry. I gotta ask you to leave."

I stood, ashamed and shocked, not knowing what to do, afraid of what would come next. We were holding up the bus; other people had important places to go, and there we were, bags and bags of food and a big live bird, standing not quite on the bus and not quite off of it. My grandmother had never been questioned to her face before, at least not in my presence. Hers was the last word on anything; she wielded an authority so supreme it went unquestioned. And this bus-driver had the courage to issue a command! What could possibly happen?

Without a word, and without diverting her eyes even for a second from the face of the driver, my grandmother put her right hand into the cleft of her left elbow and deftly twisted the chicken's neck. It took maybe a one and a half seconds. The chicken no longer filled her arm with its vitality; it was just another grocery item, merely one that had not been packaged at the market. Nothing was special about it anymore. Then my grandmother raised her eyebrows, cocking her head towards the man, as if saying "Now is there a problem?" and the driver shook his head "no"while motioning for us to pass through. Nobody on the bus said anything. My hands shaking, I put coins in the metal and glass box for our fares. We sat down. My grandmother put the chicken into one of the larger bags and brushed off her dress. She looked straight ahead, but she also stroked the back of my neck, as if to reassure me. I loved my grandmother but I was far from reassured by the gesture.

Don't think I didn't eat with a full appetite that night--I was as appreciative of a good meal as ever. The relatives from New Jersey were treated like royalty and everybody had a good time. The next day my aunts made chicken-salad sandwiches with the leftovers.

So much for the miracle of death. One minute the chicken is nestling and making eye contact and small noises and the next minute it's just an ordinary chicken for dinner, head flopping to one side and silent. Death was easy, it seemed; one moment and the whole business was completed.

The miracle of birth would be explained to me only much later and treated with far more shame.

Friends

Other People's Moms

Other people's mothers have been inordinately kind to me; I love them. Yes, I'm pretty nice to them (without, I hope, the kind of creepy-smarmy-niceness characterizing the Eddie Haskell character in Leave It To Beaver) but they've been really nice to me. Extraordinarily kind. Unnecessarily kind.

Maybe this is the key point: seeing kindness as an important and, paradoxically, essential type of emotional extravagance.

When Bonnie's mother, Mrs. Januszewski--known ubiquitously as "Mrs. Jan"-- took time to be nice to my family and me when my mother died, I was overwhelmed. To be honest, I was a little suspicious; she wasn't any particular friend of my parents and didn't know my mother very well. Why should she put herself out? After my mother died, after the long and awful summer that tried us all, we told anyone who asked that we were just fine, that we didn't need anything at all, and, as a matter of course, thanked them for their vague offers of assistance. For most folks, one offer was enough. It was simple. They asked if we wanted help, we answered no, and that was the end of the story.

Mrs. Jan, however, left an enormous casserole dish full of rich, dense food for us with a note saying she was sorry for our loss. Hearing the need in our voices instead of our polite refusal, she didn't show up with the huge dinner in her arms, expecting gratitude and details. Instead she simply left the food, covered, on the porch. We could eat it, throw it away, or send it back; it was clear that the choice was ours.

We devoured it; I remember my father and I sitting at the dreary kitchen table eating as if we'd been lost at sea for months. Which is, of course, exactly what we had been. Bonnie's mom knew that better than we did. Mrs. Jan wasn't looking for things to keep her busy: with a big family of her own and a full-time job, she could easily have let us slip by without a gesture. But she came through and I'm still grateful for the macaroni, for the cheese--for the warmth that had nothing to do with spices or temperature.

While the mothers of various boyfriends along the way were also nice -- I often wished I could stay friends with the parents even after I ditched the guy -- it's the moms of my girlfriends who seemed to be willing to accept the emotional equivalent of a collect call. My college roommate Nancy's mother would pack extra food for me when Nancy came back up to school, burdened with goodies, after a holiday. Years later in New York, Pam's mother Natalie counseled and advised me, telling me the truth when I most needed to hear it. She called me from the intermission of an opera after Pam told her I was thinking of getting a divorce. She wanted to get her good advice to me as quickly as possible, the way you'd hurry to get a snake-bite victim the necessary antidote when every moment matters. Everything she said was right and no one else knew how to say it.

Age has made very little difference: Rose's mother cooks for me, not only making the best eggplant in the universe but putting adorable decorations on the plate's cover. Mrs. Quiello doesn't mind if I'm 41; she knows I love being treated like a kid and that kids like stickers of rainbows and kitties.

Luci's mother, Mrs. Rossi, and I met the day of her daughter's wedding and bonded instantly. She sends encouraging notes and taped me when I was on the Today Show, just as she taped her son-in-law Bob's appearance. It meant as much to me that Mrs. Rossi went through the trouble of working the VCR as it meant for me to be on the show in the first place; her affection lasted longer than three minutes and has had more influence on my life. Annette, a friend from Florida, called the other night to make sure I was getting good medical advice; the last time we were down visiting she made all my relatives sit down and listen to what a newspaper had written about me--just as she would have done for her own kid.

None of these women were obliged in any formal way to be more than cordial to me; in part, this is what makes their acts of emotional generosity both poignant and enduring. On the days when I think most highly of myself, I believe I have become just a little bit like them, that I have a family resemblance to other people's mothers.

All-Time Friends

Rose says that she would give up an organ for a friend. We're not talking specific organs here, just general imaginary organs along the lines of a spleen or, on a slow day, a pancreas. Having worked as a nurse for much of her life, Rose is no stranger to such swaps and so it is not a particularly odd way for her to gauge her relationships. "I would donate for you," says Rose, as very high praise. "I would take a bullet for you" is another one of Rose's lines (she's worked in some pretty tough neighborhoods).

I could measure the precise level of my trust and friendship for Rose when I asked her to read through the journals I kept from high school and college. It was like asking somebody to clip your toenails--a little too intimate for most people, and not exactly putting your best foot forward. But that's what this whole business of letting people into your life is about: not having to do the usual social two-step, but instead following your heart right to their door.

Roxanne says she looks at her relationships and imagines who would hide her and her family had they lived during the Holocaust. Savanna's system is to see with whom she can allow a comfortable silence, not pressured into having to fill up emotional air time. Prue would only let a good friend help her weed out clothes from her closet. My husband says that a real friend is someone who understands that he can read the Sunday paper and yet remain deeply connected to that person. Not to doubt his sincerity, but I think he threw that one in for my benefit. The real way to tell who he considers his best friends is whether he'd let them drive his car.

Telephone calls at any time of the day or night are my friendship index. Let's say the phone rings at three a.m. after I've actually managed to fall asleep. A veteran of many such calls myself, usually filled with shameless weeping, gnashing of teeth, and renting of garments (high rent, too), I remember all too well those long nights of the soul. When I was going through a divorce eight years ago, Pam used to read to me over the phone until I fell asleep. It's no trouble to offer the rescue to somebody else, no big deal at all.

A friend looks after your cranky pets when you're on vacation, not just throwing food at them and running away but making soothing noises promising your return even as the old cat claws absentmindedly at their shoe. A friend picks you up when your car breaks down and bundles you up when you break down, somebody who is willing to find out about AAA or AA when you need it. There's the lunch friend who always offers to split the dessert you want to order to make you feel better about ordering it, and the exercise friend who never parades around bragging about her crunches. (N.B.: The lunch friend and the exercise friend are the same person only in the rarest of cases).

Nancy was my roommate in college and she still knows everything about me, up to and including whether or not I've broken a nail. She still likes me, so we have for twenty or so years survived that test of friendship. We celebrate major holidays together and our families have begun to blend. Pretty soon we're all going to look like each other. Her father yells at me like I was one of his own, and her mother always says comforting things. Tim, Nancy, and her sister Lynette will sit down with us and go over every plan for the renovation of our kitchen; to talk about somebody else's dishwasher choice as if it were a matter of genuine importance is an astonishing act of friendship, one probably deserving a cash prize.

If a friend really needed me, I'd get on a plane that night even though (as far as I'm concerned) I'd be risking immediate death. I'd give them my Charles and Diana coffee cup if they really, really needed it (for example, if they were in a hostage situation). If it would save their lives I'd reveal my pin number, weight, and actual age of consent. I'd even ask my husband to let them drive his car.

Greater tests of friendship are, in fact, easy to imagine: we see them everyday and mostly we rise to the occasion (although I am really hoping to hold onto my spleen for at least a while longer). Good for us; good for our friends.

How Old Are You, Really?

My brother turned 47 in May and was perplexed. "I'm not supposed to be 47," Hugo announced, explaining with exaggerated emphasis that "Dad is supposed to be 47." Unprepared for this mandate, I asked, "How old are you supposed to be?" since it seemed--in the context of this highly illogical discussion--a logical question. "I'm supposed to be around 22." He sounded pretty confident about it. Curious, I asked "And me?" "You're about 12," he answered with alacrity, as if I had always been twelve and always would be.

When I next spoke to my 75 year-old father, I asked him what age he thought of himself as being--was it close to the numerical truth? "Nah," he replied. "Not at all. How old am I in my head? I'm about eighteen, maybe nineteen." That means that my father positions his true self at an even younger age than my brother thinks of himself. My father thinks of my brother as 17, however, and so Dad reserves the right to be the head of the family. He thinks of me as about ten. And believe me, all I could think, as my two family members were describing their vision of me, was this: eleven years of college-- down the drain; all those years spent teaching and writing--forget it. When they think of me, my family pictures me playing with Silly Putty and watching The Patty Duke Show. Terrific.

This is not to say that my father and brother act as if they're teenagers; I am more grateful than I can say to be able to declare that their inner-selves are responsibly and respectably kept well within the confines of "inner." No, this exchange is about the true age of a person, the age one has always been meant to be, the age one works up to and then backs down from. It seems to be a topic some folks have spent time thinking about--certainly more time than I expected. I figured that my husband Michael would laugh or be baffled by the question about how old he pictures himself, but when I asked, he didn't miss a beat, didn't even raise his eyes from the paper. "I'm about fifteen," he said. What could I do but agree?

This morning my friend and assistant Margaret suggested that she was either 22 or 36; I see her as perpetually 23 because that's the age she was when she first walked into my office. I still think she's fairly new to the program even though she's already finished her exams and is now getting ready to start her dissertation. Inevitably, I presume former undergraduate students remain between the ages of 18 and 22, even when they're running their own marketing companies, living in the suburbs, and having baby after baby. They'll mail me photographs of the latest kid and I'll have to shake my brain around to realize that what they're holding in their arms is their own offspring, not their younger sibling.

What is indisputable is this: no member of any population ages faster than other people's children. I'll be talking on the phone with my friend Brenda on Long Island and her daughter will be gurgling happily into the receiver. The next time I call her daughter will have just taken the MCATs. And it's not like I'm out of touch, it's just that a person simply can't keep up. I have no idea what kinds of birthday cards to send: I'll send one with a clown button saying "IT'S MY SPECIAL DAY" to a friend's child only to discover that the child in question will have recently purchased his own marina.

In her 1928 novel, The Hotel, Elizabeth Bowen presents the following declaration: "Isn't it funny that for everybody there seems to be just one age at which they are really themselves? I mean, there are women you meet who were obviously born to be twenty (and pretty at that) and who seem to have lost their way since, and men you do wish you'd known when they were, say thirty, or twenty four, or feel sorry you mayn't come across them when they're forty or fifty-five, and children . . . who are simply shaping up to be pale, sarcastic women of twenty-nine, who won't, once they're that, ever grow older."

Certain wines have a particular moment when they should be poured into goblets, certain fruits have a ripeness that almost begs for the sweet first bite, certain paintings are seen best in an instant of light that passes almost as quickly as it appears. Maybe it's the same with us: maybe there are moments when we are most ourselves and this is what we glimpse when we imagine ourselves as a certain age.

To be honest, I pretty much think of myself as being forty-one. Okay, 40; I shave a year off, not for the sake of vanity but because saying "forty-one" sounds as awkward as when little kids tell you they're five-and-a-half, with the last bit tacked on for show. But maybe that's because in reality I've been forty or thereabouts my entire life; maybe that's why this age is as comfortable for me as a tailor-made dressing gown. I've slipped my arms into my forties and, with a little jiggle here and there for the finer points of adjustment, the years fit just fine.

Do You Like What You Like?

There are two kinds of people in the world: those who like what they like more than they don't like what they don't like and, in contrast, those who don't like what they don't like more than they like what they like. (I know it doesn't seem possible but if you'll just pay close attention, you'll be able to follow what I'm saying. Oh-- I also know there are fifty gazillion types of people in the world, but for the purposes of today's essay we'll say there are two.)

Consider my two cats, Min and Novella. Min, an erstwhile Lower East Side alley cat, is eighteen years old and pretty much hates everything. She likes me, she likes Michael, and she likes food; she tolerates Novella, the adorable interloper. Given her personal history and age, I figure Min is entitled to her sense of universal contempt. She hates our friends and family, she hates the patient and thoughtful folks who look after her when we skip town for a couple of days, and she hates all the loving and caring folks at the animal hospital who have (despite their own feelings) kept her alive all these years.

This makes Min different from Novella, who would have developed a really bad reputation in high school, if you catch my drift, because she will sit on anybody's lap. Sure, she likes us best , but she pretty much loves all humanity, all furniture, all rugs, and most major appliances; she loves the top of the computer (where she sits even as I type these words). She doesn't like thunder and she doesn't like balloons, but that's about it. Novella is a cheap date.

Min doesn't like what she doesn't like more than she likes what she likes;

83

Novella likes what she likes more than she doesn't like what she doesn't like. I love them both unconditionally and unashamedly, and I accept them for who they are.

Which leads me directly to my friends Anita and Marie. Like Novella, Anita is best and most fully known for her appetites while Marie, like Min, is defined most accurately through her aversions. At a big party, Anita will exhibit her characteristic tendency to eat all the appetizers, savoring every bite and murmuring small noises of deep satisfaction, oblivious to the fact that others are beginning to surround her in order to at least see what the food looks like. Anita pretty much enjoys any dish so long as it isn't moving or made from minerals; she is elated around edibles and everybody knows it.

In contrast, Marie will visibly recoil if she is shown any form of foodstuffs she hasn't actually eaten before. She practically faints at the sight of seafood or seafood by-products; she didn't eat seafood as a kid and sees no reason to start now. Marie eats what she knows--meatloaf, mashed potatoes with butter (none of this fancy garlic-and-sour-cream business), iceberg lettuce, and cake. She is flexible in the cake department, however, making those of us who have her over for dinner go wild considering the possibility of whipping up "shrimp-shortcake-surprise" for dessert.

I'm not trying to say that Anita should hire herself out as The Human Goat Girl or that Marie should be known as The Brat That Will Not Be Pleased. But what is significantly different about the two of them is that Anita more completely enjoys what she likes more than she is outraged by what she doesn't like whereas Marie is clearly and unapologetically more horrified by her nightmare foods than she is pleased by her dream foods. And both of them are great people and wonderful friends.

It isn't quite the "glass is half empty" vs. "the glass is half full" because this isn't about basic divisions between optimists and pessimists, or the distinction between those on mood-elevators vs. those who are not. I'd say that most of the characters on Seinfeld or Frasier, for example, base their humor on what they don't like; people love these shows. Artist-types have always been encouraged to torture themselves emotionally, not to mention wreaking havoc on the lives of others, offering proof of how special they are. The tastes of beautiful people everywhere are supposed to be exotic and highly specialized, running more towards organically raised, nurtured, and for all I know, highly educated vine-ripened peppers, whereas others of us are happy with string beans in a boil-n-bag.

As for me, I suspect that I used to be of the Min/Marie camp in my youth--more cautious, on guard, less likely to take risks--but as I fling myself into middle-age, I'm heading into the world of Novella/Anita, where sitting on laps and eating appetizers seems highly adequate compensation for whatever else comes my way.

Who Wants to Date Norman Bates?

When Bonnie was having a sleep-over at my house, we decided that we were old enough to watch Psycho on television. At eleven years old and at eleven p.m., we felt we possessed sufficient maturity, cinema savvy, and sophisticated aesthetic judgment to appreciate Hitchcock fully.

Always (and to this day) more adventurous than I, Bonnie was big-eyed and ready for whatever would appear on the screen. My parents left us alone in the inevitable wood-panelled basement den, where the small Zenith television stood proudly on a t.v. table; imagine, an appliance so important that it had a piece of its own furniture.

Bonnie and I were already in our pajamas and we were eating all the junk food in the universe. My folks were good (or bad, depending on your nutritional perspective) about this: when friends came over, we raided the cupboards. I can still see us with piles of Devil Dogs (seemingly appropriate fare for a horror movie--but I'm puzzled by one thing: how did they come up with "Devil Dog" as a name for a kid's dessert, anyway? We don't sell packages of "Satan's Cup Cakes" or "Lucifer's Jelly Rings" do we?) Bonnie and I had already opened bags of potato chips so greasy you could lube your car with them and bottles of soda so sweet they made your eyes squinch up automatically. In other words, we were two preteens all set for a good time.

I've always been one to scare easily. This remains slightly embarrassing to admit at 41, but it was way, way too embarrassing to admit at age eleven. If Bonnie felt grown-up enough to see this movie and if my parents thought it was okay then I couldn't possibly back down. No way would I "wimp out" (or whatever buzz word we used at that point in historical time to express humiliating apprehensions--I don't think we had "wimping-out" as an option in 1968). I was too scared of appearing scared to act the way I felt.

So we hunkered down, lights off except for the flickering television, the only sounds apart from those created by Hitchcock made by our continuous eating and slurping of Pepsi.

Remember Psycho? Remember how naughty Janet Leeigh seemed by virtue (or its opposite) of the fact that she appeared in her underwear? Forget stealing the money--that didn't brand her as a fallen woman--no, it was the frank display of her undergarments that doomed to her. Remember how nice Tony Perkins seemed initially? I kind of thought he was cute and said as much to Bonnie (as I would continue, for the next twenty years or so, to tell her about apparently nice men who would turn out to be significantly less than terrific relationship material. But I didn't know that then--I only knew Norman Bates's nervousness was sweet and endearing. Now that's scary. . .).

And remember the cardiac-arresting, blood-freezing, terrifying scene when the (stop reading now if you haven't seen the movie because I'm going to give it all away and you need to accept responsibility for your own choices in this case, so please don't read it and then accuse me of spoiling it for you, okay?) camera shows us the hideously deformed and corrupted face and body of the mummified Mrs. Bates?

Yes, this is the climax of the movie. Yes, I understand that without this horrific scene none of the rest of it makes much sense or holds together. But I had decided, you see, to skip the worst scene; I figured out the worst was coming because the good people were going down to the cellar and let's just say they never seem to happen upon a party when this occurs. Scary stuff always happens when main characters go down into the cellar and besides that, the music was already terrifying the heck out of me, and so I asked Bonnie to tell me when it was over and I could safely look again.

Okay, now remember that Bonnie is my best friend. Remember that we're little girls and are renown for playing nicely together. So imagine my surprise when I open my eyes upon Bonnie's all-clear signal and see the close-up of the mummified and empty eye-sockets of the dead lady.

Bonnie and I are still the best of best friends. Not that I completely forgive her-- "forgive and forget" is a great practice, but it's not exactly my motto--but I did learn something important that night. I learned that, despite my fear, I could face the thing that scared me even if I didn't want to; if you have no alternative, you get past whatever it is that's staring at you in the face. You deal with it. Years later, maybe, you can laugh about it; thirty years later it's still funny. But here's the serious lesson: Keeping your hands over your eyes in fear and trepidation of even the worst parts is no way to go through life.

It's a Girl

For a while there the big work-related question facing all of us seemed to be "What color is my parachute?" but now I'm asking a slightly weirder, more intimate question: "What gender is my computer?"

Before you call in the authorities and have me restrained for my own good ("This woman is having an emotional relationship with her computer; give her a serious amount of the medication") let me explain. I tend to develop personal relationships with inanimate objects (I can hear a lot of women muttering "Yeah, so what else is new?" but I'm not talking about guys here, but machines). I have a pretty strong sense of kinship with my computer, but then I also maintain a good working partnership with the microwave as well as an alliance I'd describe as distant but friendly with the photocopier at work.

It's not a huge leap in logic to understand that since we've learned to treat people as if they're machines, we inevitably wind up treating machines as if they were people.

You'll tell me I'm spending too much time alone, racking up too many late nights facing the screen. While this might in fact all be true, the observation in no way lessens my need to figure out whether my computer and I share or are divided by the issues of gender.

Not sex, mind you, but gender; I'm not talking about reproductive functions. Let's put it this way: I'm not talking about hard drives or software. No, what I'm trying to decide is whether my computer would speak in a female voice, laugh with an Ethel Merman roar or a Marilyn Monroe giggle, and whether she understands--really understands--how paranoid I get when she isn't saving often enough. See? I've given it away with these darn pronouns: she's a broad, a chick, a gal--anything but a lady. Sorry--nobody could have lost those five pages of decent, usable prose right before my deadline and still be considered a lady.

I figure that since the suggestions my computer offers me are framed as questions-- "Do you want to replace this file?"; "Do you want to save these changes?"; "Don't you feel for some freshly baked brownies just about now?"-- it must be a feminine creature. My husband's computer, in contrast, threatens and bullies him with phrases along the line of "I'm far from a completed document, you fool. For godssake, how can you stop working now?" My husband's computer doesn't offer kindly directions or beep helpfully to warn of impending crises; it sneers, he insists, when he is about to hit the wrong key and laughs like Vincent Price when he fumbles for the user's manual. It sounds to me like his computer is inhabited by the spirit of Don Rickles. But then he's been known to whack it on the side when something goes wrong whereas I try to talk mine through whatever miserable thing is happening, assuring her that we all make mistakes, letting her know that we'll get through it together. My computer purrs; he swears that his mutters and is capable of genuine and calculated malevolence.

Maybe that explains why our cats sleep exclusively on my PC. My computer and I probably offer a similar kind of warmth, and although I am far softer I sometimes move around too much for their liking. I eat in front of the computer screen without apology, and keep beverages nearby even though I know that I could wreck a year's work if one of these cats decides to dive into my tea from the top of the monitor (a feat which I believe is now considered a Kitty-Olympic sport among felines). My husband, in contrast, respects his computer too much to risk crumbs. Also, I suspect he doesn't want his computer to see his vulnerable and needy side, a side which appears quite distinctly when he's polishing off a bag of Tostidos. At night I cover my keyboard, monitor and hard-drive with a huge piece of flowered chintz;

my husband wraps all his computer's sections with neatly-fitting plastic covers as if he wanted to make sure they were going to remain disease-free through the night. He wants his protected; I want mine cozy.

If my mouse-y girlfriend and I are so close, you ask, then why have't I given her a name? That would be tricky for several reasons: for example, are we on a first name basis, or should I call her Ms. Something-or-Other? But the real reason I hesitate to name the computer is because I know that one day she'll be traded in, replaced by a newer, cooler, faster, more dynamic successor. She'll be farmed out to a friend's kid, or a local school, or even banished completely. I wouldn't do that to a pal, and so our connection remains on a purely professonal basis. Until she offers me a handkerchief when I cry, a shoulder to lean on when I'm distressed, or actually goes out and bakes those brownies, I'm sticking with my real friends.

Desire

I Always Feel Rich When I...

1. Actually have, in the house, totally unused, beautifully packaged light bulbs of the correct voltage to replace ones that burn out.

2. Buy pretty stamps.

3. Use a paper napkin only once. In my family, paper products were considered items of immense luxury and were used--in various ways--until the only thing left of them were a few paper molecules.

4. Use chicken broth from a can instead of making it from a bullion cube. (In case you are tempted to tell me you can only make good chicken broth from real chickens, be assured that I have heard rumors of this in the past and consider such information to be both silly and dangerous).

5. Take a bath. Using all that hot water when I was growing up was considered a confessable sin and so showers were the only option. A bubble bath is still a huge indulgence.

6. Throw away a tube of mascara without digging out the last flakes by employing a surgical instrument.

7. Wear slippers when I travel.

8. Take cabs.

9. Have something framed.

10. Turn off the alarm and go back to sleep.

11. Talk on the phone to friends. I feel even richer when I see them.

12. Donate any amount of time or money to a charity or cause I really believe in.

13. Buy hardcover books. (n.b.: Reading hardcover books in a bubble bath is really spectacular.)

14. Count my blessings, which are too many to count, but the exercise is useful.

15. Stop taking for granted all the quotidian luxuries of everyday life.

I Feel Poor When...

1. I'm in a doctor's waiting room.

2. The house is chilly.

3. I run out of something basic: adhesive tape, shampoo, foil wrap, patience, toilet paper, excuses.

4. Shoes hurt my feet.

5. The car makes funny noises.

6. The phone bill arrives.

7. I'm trying to stick to a diet.

8. I'm lonely or scared.

9. I leaf through copies of Vogue, Architectural Digest, Allure, Travel, or The Nordstrom Catalog, especially when I'm looking at them in a doctor's waiting room.

10. I'm using coupons at the supermarket and there's a line of people behind me.

11. There's a bug in the house.

12. Somebody puts me on call-waiting.

13. I don't understand instructions and need to have them repeated or explained.

14. The printer or my pen runs out of ink--even if I have replacement ink, it always makes me feel nervous.

15. I'm helpless in the time of someone else's need.

Things I Am Convinced Remain Too Luxurious for The Likes of Me....

1. Small, purse-size packets of tissues.

2. Fancy sunglasses.

3. Fruit for dessert at a restaurant. If somebody is paying for dessert, it seems imperative to get chocolate even if you're completely stuffed and want only to avoid food for the rest of your life.

4. Light-colored tablecloths.

5. Pedicures.

6. Really tiny cell phones.

7. Business Class.

8. Nice business cards.

9. Shoe trees.

10. Almost anything breakable costing over twelve dollars.

11. Bottled water that isn't fizzy.

12. Designer aspirin.

13. Designer stockings.

14. Designer toothpaste.

15. Old resentments, dreariness, hate, and envy. These cost way too much over the long haul.

Quest for the Lost Book of Childhood

I'm on a quest. This is not a joke: I've spent an astonishing amount of time during the past month trying to find an old treasure, one meaningful (I fear and hope) only to myself. My hope that its significance isn't universal is born of pure selfishness: I want to locate and possess the treasure. If too many other folks want it, then I won't be able to get my hands on it. That's the trouble with riches, isn't it? There might not be enough to go around.

What is it? There was a book I loved as a child, called (no laughing now, you have to promise, honest, c'mon, cross your heart) yes, titled (wait for it) First Date Stories. It was published by American Girl Magazine in the early 1960s and I bought it with my mother at a local, tiny, wonderful bookstore one summer afternoon when I was about eight years old. We split the cost, which probably meant an expenditure of three quarters from her and three quarters from me. Life was less expensive then, but laying out a buck-fifty in those days still meant that I really must have wanted to take the book home and not run the risk of simply heading towards the library, which was, after all, my natural instinct and habitat. That summer--and for several summers afterwards--I proceeded to read this little paperback book over and over until the pages were falling out of the cheap binding.

I loved the stories. Okay, there were stories I didn't really enjoy in the collection, but I loved them too, out of a sense of loyalty, like relatives, and I read them every once and a while so they wouldn't feel too jealous of the stories I read every day. I think most of them had been published in the 1940s and early '50s--some of them might have even been published earlier--but they echoed every part of my life as if they had been written an hour before I read them. One was about an English girls' school in China, a boarding school where the students competed against each other for grades and for the attention of students from the corresponding boys' school. This story fascinated me for several reasons, the least of which was the exotic setting: I was enthralled by the characters, by the description of unspecified but perfectly articulated tensions between the main characters, by the fact that one girl was willing to sell her soul in order to possess--for a few moments only--the attention of the boy to whom she had been attracted for months. No kissing, no hand-holding, no (God forbid) sexual encounters in these pages, but nevertheless an evocation of passionate intensity dear to the soul of a lonely eight-year old.

And I can't dig up a copy of this damned book. I've looked. We're talking inter-library loan here, and those folks know what they're doing. No dice. Don't tell me about the internet: I've tried everything. Sweetheart, I spent serious time in front of the computer and learned how to use the internet just to be able to locate out-of-print books. I've had successes, true, but they pale in comparison to this one big failure. There was a brief and intense flirtation with a bookstore in Florida, specializing in juvenile fiction (their category, not mine) ; they indicated they had a copy. I ordered it immediately, spent days waiting, panting and wide-eyed by the mailbox, only to discover that they had sold their one copy previously and that their listing of the title had therefore been an error.

How can I describe the sense of heartbreak? You will accuse me of exaggeration; you'll tell me there are other books more worthy of attention. Yes, yes, but this is the one book I want, don't you see? Other, better, more fulsome and satisfying books I know exist, but they are not the objects of my urgent and singular desire. I want what I want, and therein lies my tiny tragedy.

This is not so much a desire to make a critical assessment of the past as it is to rekindle old flames. I want to read again what excited me initially. I want to see sentences that sent my heart racing and my imagination soaring, even if those sentences ostensibly concerned dating rituals in 1948. It wasn't their subjects so much that captured my imagination, but the way the writers constructed their universes.

I was there in a boarding school in China; I was there at a sock-hop in St. Paul, Minnesota. I was there as a student-nurse in Indiana and as a grammar-school teacher on a reservation in New Mexico. Where these writers wrote, I found myself: eager, willing, relentless in my need to draw every fragment of meaning from their words, living out their stories in my mind, loving their landscapes and worshiping their imagined worlds. This wasn't about dating; this was a book about how a girl might live a life.

Is it any wonder I want my own copy?

Writing

When I explained to my father (using the exasperated tone of voice particular to those world-weary souls who have yet to look twenty in the eye) that my college boyfriend was dropping out of school because he "wanted to paint," my father's brief and insightful response was "Yeah? Is somebody trying to stop him?"

It was a good question then and it is a good question now. It's a story I tell everybody who asks me about writing--or any creative endeavor--and it's a story I tell myself when I get stuck and consider complaining about the difficulty of my work. My dad's response, you see, highlights the single most significant element of any generative process: it gets done when you do it. You want to paint? So paint. You want to write? Sit down and put one word after another. You want to make music, sculpt, sing, dance, juggle, or take Pin The Tail On The Donkey to an art form?

Good for you. You probably have a couple of hours each week, so go ahead. Nobody is stopping you. Nice people at any number of retail stores are eager to sell you paper. Everything else is left up to you. Trouble is, many of us want, not to compose a song, but to have composed a song, not to write a book, but to have written a book. The hard part to understand is that it--whatever "it" is for you--doesn't get done when you think about doing it, or when you talk about doing it, or when you get feedback from people about it, or when you spend time wondering how your life will change once you become universally recognized as an expert at doing it. Ask me and I'll tell you writing isn't about tickling the muse or hearing the one true heartbeat of the cosmos, but about meeting deadlines. Most days writing isn't about inspiration. It's about work.

Don't think this attitude hasn't given me trouble. Don't think that being called a "hack writer" by a woman I once considered my friend (this is almost ten years ago now) doesn't cut to an artery still, one that opens up every time I remember her words. She considered herself an artist and defined me as a hack because of our differences in approach; unlike me, she suffered through (usually) rather than enjoyed (usually) the process and (unlike me), she saw herself as a "literary figure."

Not me. I think of myself as someone who hit the jackpot, who got lucky, who won the prize-- not as a cross between Flaubert and Georges Sand (or Nora Ephron and Dave Barry, for that matter) but simply as someone on whom fortune smiled.

After smiling, however, fortune then insisted I work like hell all the time, almost every day, even on holiday weekends. Lady luck doesn't like being taken for granted; she will bestow her favors elsewhere if insufficiently or erratically entertained.

No complaints. I am permitted to tell my stories and hear what people think about them. For this I get small sums of money: it is a miracle. Not enough of a miracle for me to quit my day job (day jobs are Good Things), but ceaselessly astonishing nevertheless. It is not what had been expected of me, this writing and speaking endeavor. The first time I told my family about giving a speech for which I received a fee, my father, smiling in approval, yet again summed it all up when he said "Really? They're paying you to speak? When you were a kid, I would have paid you to shut up."

Until somebody else renews the offer and ups the ante, I'll keep doing the columns, articles, and books. And I'll give anybody who wants to write the same advice: until they make you stop, keep doing it. But I'll also have to explain what I see as the truly tricky part: just because you do it doesn't mean you'll be any good at it. And even if you're good at it, you won't necessarily be successful with it. A person can put words on a page and not be a writer the way I can dance around my house in my nightgown but not be a ballerina. I brush my teeth every day but that doesn't make me a dentist. There's a combination of forces at work and some of them are not benevolent no matter how much we need or beg for their kindness.

So it's simple: you want to write, then write. Yes, it's simple. But don't let anybody tell you it's easy.

To the North

This is a secret love story that has only a little bit to do with secrets and slightly less to do with love. It's about heading through the night with the radio on, moving a big old car towards another country, but only incidentally a story about crossing borders, or erasing boundaries. It's about a lesson learned at college, but not one in the curriculum.

He was a year ahead of me, and had ushered me into the ways of the college when I first arrived, helping me choose the best professors, encouraging me to learn the words to the songs and the ways of this particular world. Protective of me and defensive of the place, he had a tough position to play. Even though we had known each other for years, we knew only those things one knows from classes and meetings; we knew one another casually and intimately at the same time. I knew how much milk to put in his coffee, for example, and he knew I didn't like to call him at his fraternity house for fear of hearing one of the brothers bellow my name up the stairs to him, but I didn't know whether he snored and he didn't know whether I slept in a tee-shirt, a nightgown, or nothing at all. I had occasionally tousled his hair as I passed by him, half reading in the library, and he bought me flowers on my birthday once when everyone else seemed to have forgotten. Knocking on his door late one night, ignoring the noise, I cried to him over the loss of some other man, and he held me at arm's length. And I wondered whether to focus on the fact that I was held, or that I was held at a distance.

We had no anniversaries to share or reason to kiss except to say hello or good-bye after the absence of a vacation, a term away, or parting before a major holiday. We did not kiss. We didn't date. We were friends.

We liked each other, and looked forward to random meetings at the snack bar where we both worked. We were competitive, and each hoped the other would do very well but maybe not better, wincing slightly at being given an A- if the other received an A, and yet we were happy for each other's happinesses: we became better friends after he got a girlfriend at another college because we were positioned on a level playing field. I smiled more deeply into his eyes, and he permitted himself the occasional compliment about my clothes or expression.

His relationship made everything that much easier. He was able to say "My girlfriend and I. . ." in reply to a phrase that included "My boyfriend and I." It was easier for me to hear the possessiveness in the words "my girlfriend" than it had been for me to hear a series of names which I had to memorize and keep steady in my head, like a little ensemble of beauty queens waltzing through my imagination. I was fond of his girlfriend. I didn't know and wouldn't have believed that one of the reasons (but to give us both credit, not the primary reason) I liked her was because in a comparison between the two I felt as if I had a reasonable edge. The girlfriend was adorable, but not quick; she was devoted, which meant she lacked the appeal of an established emotional distance, and the appeal of independence.

But of course the girlfriend was amply compensated: she knew that her new boyfriend snored only when he'd had too much to drink, and only she knew how often he had too much to drink. He'd drink a lot, for example, when the four of us went to a bar called The Bull's Eye every few weeks, although he'd rarely drink too much at those times. She was grateful for his warmth in her bed every night, having loved him for more than two years and having known him for three; he and her sister graduated the same year from a small high school in Rhode Island. She decided not to mind me, I think, and to make a point of encouraging us all to enjoy one another's company.

She liked me and seemed mildly attracted to my boyfriend, making it easier for them to talk; if paired off by default in a social situation or by a seating arrangement, they were not unhappy. Older by two years or so, handsome, witty, and relaxed into his well-deserved sense of pleasure at being in graduate school in Boston, my boyfriend appreciated women with the same delight as he appreciated expensive and contraband cigars: they had been out of reach when he was an undergraduate and would not now pass him by without his admiration.

So we were all right, up to a point.

It was late April, the day of the first big spring picnic a bunch of us always threw before the real parties started at the end of the term. There was still some sneaky snow on the ground, in the shadows, but there were games, lakes, lunches, drinks, laughter, conversation, all making up for the cold. Friendly dogs buzzed knee-high like small planes, wheeling and spinning around people they had never met, confident of approval. The groomed and polished woods by the river sang with invented warmth, and as groups arrived the others made room, expanding into the shade or the sun. We arrived early, packing a picnic basket full of shareable goods: pate, wine, exotic cheeses, and British biscuits. My boyfriend and I each held one handle, carrying the burden between us. The other two arrived later with a cooler full of imported beer in each hand, laughing at the fact that they had to pack them in paper bags in order to disguise them from those acquaintances who had been circling around the bottles like pygmies around a kill.

I sat next to my friend. Wearing a striped tee-shirt and shorts, his battered Converse sneakers made him look even more like a cartoon character than usual. Long fingers were wrapped around a cold beer on this hot day. Dark hair, collar length, just too long or just right, depending where you stood and I was standing right next to him. "I'm sitting too close to him. Will this will make everybody nervous?" I wondered. I didn't move.

I listened to the conversation with less than half my attention. "I've been afraid that I'd been overdoing it lately, that I'd been calling too much or leaving too many messages on his door, telling him too many stories and laughing too hard at his jokes," I calculated, drinking a glass of wine (beer was like skiing, something I knew everybody else liked but the pleasures of which escaped me) and smiling. "But his jokes are a narcotic to me, making the day go faster and my own existence brighter, and I long to tell him what happens to me everyday. Increasingly he's became the receiver of my imaginary conversations, the running commentary of the daily routine is directed towards him." Okay, maybe I thought something simpler: "What happens when you try to be friends with somebody you find attractive? Can you be just friends or is that idea just a joke?"

When I didn't see him and he hadn't returned my phone calls for a few days after the picnic, I started to worry. I stopped him on the way into the library one night and, touching his arm just briefly, asked him whether he was pissed off at me or annoyed or upset or anything. He looked genuinely and welcomingly horrified; his eyes widened and he said no, no, why did I think that? I told him about the not-returned calls and he said that if he didn't call back right away it was only because he was busy but not to think that I'd done anything to provoke that--and then he said "Let's go. We've been in this hick town too long. Cabin fever, stir-crazy early spring: Let's blow this taco stand."

The 1967 Monte Carlo, always parked illegally, waited for action behind the house. We got in and headed north. The signs for towns in northern New Hampshire got brighter as the sun started to set, took on that luminescent quality of unearthly color so that they seemed to shine with their own odd brilliance, white and green in unfamiliar markings. The car had a tape deck, a peculiar piece of luck or else something stolen and installed by a rogue cousin in Providence, and we listened to Steely Dan and Bruce Springsteen and Patti Smith. I sang loudly and off-key but I knew all the words and with the windows down and the volume turned up you could hardly tell I was way off the mark. He had a voice like traffic, rough and low, and he knew all the words, too. The car had those long slick bench seats and before we were at the border I'd dared myself to slide over, tucking myself under the long arm he had outstretched across the back. He didn't seem to notice. We kept singing, looking for luck and signals in the songs. We felt like engines that had lost their driving wheels, we knew that the door was open but the ride wasn't free, and we knew that the night belonged to lovers.

We sang so that we didn't have to speak, and we didn't want to speak because anything we would have said as the white lines moved faster beneath the dark wheels we would have regretted later. It was simple between us, but that didn't mean it was easy. Like knotted string, confused desire complicates what is simple

At the Canadian border we told the skeptical but lazy guard that we were visiting to look at graduate schools the next day, that we had interviews, that we were engaged. He didn't ask questions, which in a way was too bad: the fiction we'd created was an alternative universe, a virtual relationship, a life we could have been living except for the fact that we weren't.

We went looking for a place to eat, walking through the cold clear streets of brightly-lit Montreal, a city awake after dark, just before midnight. He started singing "Mac the Knife," but using only the first line of the song, singing the same words over and over again even though he followed the tune. "When the shark bites, oh the shark bites, and that sharks bites, see the shark bites. . . ." We laughed, and I put my thumb into the belt loop over his hip, feeling the slight limp in his walk from a hockey accident the winter before.   We found a Kosher delicatessen and ate huge smoked meat sandwiches, sharp pickles, and knishes that steamed when you broke them open. We sat at the counter, looking at each other out of the corners of our eyes, and talked to the waitresses in bad French, continuing the fiction we started at the border. We told them we were getting married in June and that we were both applying to graduate school at McGill. They told us which neighborhoods would suit us best. They giggled, conspirators in our elopement plans, and poured coffee into our cups as if it represented their good wishes. We said good-night to them around two a.m. and walked into the now chest-clenching cold of a star-filled night.

We knew our options. We knew there were hotels, we knew there was the Monte Carlo with its bedroom-sized seats. We knew there was the ease of walking hip to hip, despite the difference in height. And we knew it wouldn't work. Not when we had to face each other in the library, at work, at the Bull's Eye's long tables. Not when we still needed to talk about classes, and plans, and a future that included other people.

And so we began the drive back.

It was dawn when the college appeared, Main Street scrubbed white and just waking up . We sat in the car for a few minutes. I intended to leave abruptly, say good-night and go, but instead I sat. I was afraid he wanted me to leave quickly; I thought of asking him to drive around a little more but I knew I couldn't. So we sat and I moved, half-consciously, towards him. There was no music now.

He asked, expressionless, "You staying or going?"

Once said, the texture of the air changed, a shift in the cogs of our working together, something unlocking and then quickly relocking in ourselves. I reached over to put my hand on his and he covered it with both his hands, raised it to his warm mouth and kissed me, on the inside of my palm, briefly. There was no better time to go.

I knew, and he knew, I couldn't have been his girlfriend, couldn't have been softly sweet or constantly agreeable any more than I could have made little quilted pillows or hit a brilliant backhand; I could not do these things. My past was too filled with the tensions of choice to let myself be thinned, like paint, in order to be applied more easily to him. He couldn't have given up skiing and hockey, wouldn't have wanted to compete all day at school and come home only to continue the battle, exhilarating as it was.

We knew that what might have worked had we not been in the same place at the same time wouldn't work because we were linked, not by destiny, but by circumstance. We had the college in common, but we were afraid to find out if there was more. The friendship had to be more enduring, we figured, than any other version of ourselves.

But I wonder now whether that was true.

The friendship buckled, finally, under marriages and kids and distance and these grown-up lives of ours; I don't know where he lives or what he thinks about. And yet there was something put away during that night trip up north, something in self-storage, kept from the wear-and-tear of everyday life, still keeping the edges of it sharp and clear.

Envy

"Envy," said a friend on a cold night over a glass of red wine, "is the one vice everybody has experienced. There are people who aren't gluttons, who aren't greedy, and even some who aren't particularly proud. But everybody," he leaned over the table and lowered his voice to emphasize the point, "everybody has been envious at some time in their life." I knew what he meant, given that the very day on which we were speaking was full of envy for me. Hell, I envied him as he spoke to me, what with his good job and happy family. Then I remembered that I also had a pretty good job and a pretty happy family. Why, when everything is going fairly well, do we still spend time envying others?

What do I envy? Like every women over size ten, I envy women under size ten. Like every worker, I envy other people's bigger offices (complete with more windows with better views), better staff, preferred seating at restaurants over power lunches, and mythically-proportioned expense accounts. I have foreign-language envy: speaking only bad Sicilian and bad French-Canadian (and in these tongues only knowing how to say things you can't say in front of the kids), I routinely envy those fluent in German and Parisian French and Florentine Italian. I envy athletes who play graceful tennis, singers who effortlessly harmonize with Mary Chapin Carpenter, and dancers smooth enough to make George Steinbrenner look like Fred Astaire.

Penis-envy I don't have, although I wouldn't mind some of the benefits awarded to those members: full access to the power structure, political influence, a decent credit line, and the ability to walk into a garage without a mechanic thinking "Oh, good, now I can put that wing on my house" because I have a question about my transmission. (The best story I ever heard as an antidote to Freud concerns a little girl who, when seeing her naked infant brother for the first time, merely commented "Isn't it a good thing, Mommy, that it isn't on his face?"). I content myself with envying those who are richer, cuter, taller, better, and nicer. I even envy those who are less envious, the ones who applaud the accomplishments of their rivals without a tightening of the fist or the heart. That generosity is characteristic of angels, and not even all of them can live up to it: as I remember, Milton's version of the story says that Lucifer took arms against God because of envy, declaring it "Better to reign in hell, than serve in heaven."

My pal, I think, is right: envy is pervasive. Envy is what makes you, when an acquaintance is lustily telling you that she's dating a greek god of a guy, ask "Which one, Hades?" Envy makes you, when a co-worker brags about his son's success on the varsity team, say "How nice. When I bought my new Cadillac last week, my car salesman's assistant had also been a football player." Envy makes you not say "Good for you! You earned it!" even when someone has legitimately, honestly, and sweetly come by some success.

Envy feeds on itself, and is a sort greed with a vengeance. If greed wants what's out there, envy feels a sense of entitlement to what's inside. When Greed and Gluttony want something, they grab it and consume it; Pride says that if it can't have it, then it isn't worth wanting; Envy is destined to be perpetually in a state of longing, howling for what appears just out of reach like a shivering dog baying at the moon. Greed wants money, pride wants fame, and gluttony wants satisfaction, but envy wants above all to breed more envy. Envy grows poor because others gain wealth; envy grows sick because others are healthy; envy grows gaunt watching others eat.

Snow White's stepmother felt envy after asking that effete mirror "Who's the fairest of them all?" and hearing the wrong answer, and every kid whose parent says "no" declares herself a similar victim. "You don't want me to go out Saturday night only because you have to stay home," the teenager yells, and half a parent's heart might hear the truth in this. Iago in Othello was envious, maybe Hamlet was envious of the man who got to sleep with his mother, and certainly The Beach Boys envied The Beatles. The teacher who downgrades the smartass but nevertheless smart student might be driven by envy, and so might the boss who won't give her administrative assistant the raise she earned. "I got it the hard way," sniffs envy, "Why should I make it easier for anybody else?"

Envy isn't jealousy: in Fatal Attraction, for example, we met the mistress who was jealous of the wife and in Disclosure we meet the wife who's jealous of the mistress. These examples highlight the difference between jealousy and envy: the mistress and wife share exactly the same desire for precisely the same man. (These examples also highlight the fact that the Motion Picture Academy should create a category for best actor in a But-Honey-She-Made-Me-Do-It role, and that Michael Douglas should always get that award.) The women circling Douglas like two cheetahs around a kill on The Discovery Channel are jealous of one another and wish to replace one another. That's not the widely-sweeping net of envy, but the hook of jealousy.

The man who is envious of his neighbor's job, in contrast, probably does not want to steal that job away, but instead wants to get a better one. He's envious of the ease with which he assumes his neighbor gets through the day; he doesn't covet his neighbor's wife, particularly, but he might covet his neighbor's 401K plan. If I envy a model's perfect thighs, I am all too well aware that on my body those thighs would look, to put it kindly, out of place. I don't want her thighs, I just wish mine were better; the neighbor doesn't want the other guy's job, but he wants acknowledgement that he is equally accomplished. He wants to be number one, to be best, to be the winner. When only one can be declared a winner, that means that the rest of us are "also-rans," looking on from the sidelines, hoping secretly that the leader will stumble and that their fall will be our big break. It isn't pretty.

Envy is an especially embarrassing vice because it often seems petty. The big sins seem noble; envy creeps around coveting the nobility of a regal vice but never quite making it. When it's not wringing its hands, envy is busy pointing out the spots on the competition's tie. That the spots are there is undeniable, but the glee that envy takes in labeling them gives the game away.

Let's say my actress friend and I go to a movie. If all she can talk about is the awfulness of the heroine's accent, I have a fairly clear sense that her envy is coloring her assessment. I can say in all honesty that I thought the performance good or bad, but she can't. Not if the actress is close to her "type." If I can't stand somebody's essay in a magazine, my husband might lightly point out that my distaste is rather surprising, given that the essayist's style is similar to mine. Of course that's what's getting to me, and he knows it. Someone who loves you doesn't want you to feel envious because it makes everything else in your life seem unimportant. It seems to say "If I only had her unfair advantages, then I'd be happy." Someone who loves you wants to hear "I've got you, so how could I ever envy another person?" This is one reason envy is such a secret vice, and the fact of its secrecy is one of the reasons it is tricky to change.

But I owe a great deal to envy. The first piece I ever sent out for publication I wrote only because a girl I went to college with had two poems printed in a small literary journal that I happened to come across in a tiny bookshop on St. Mark's Place in Manhattan's east village. There I was, flipping through these thin pages after cranking out another paper for graduate school and there was her name in typeface. It tripped some internal alarm signal, her name in print, and all my sirens were immediately set off. I had to do better. For God's sake, I had to do at least as well.

Buying the magazine, I took it home hidden under my jacket as if it were some controlled substance, and I smuggled it up to my typewriter where I read the guidelines for submission like they were the answers to an exam. Which they were, in a way: my test was to be as good as this phantom rival. To make a long story short, I got one poem published, one I wrote that night with my eyes more on her words than on my own. I'm sure she never read it; I no longer have any idea where she is or what she is doing, and I'm sure she never even gave me a quarter as much thought as I gave her. And I only got one poem published. I've never felt quite as if I've caught up. So I keep at it.

In a way, though, I am grateful for the spur of envy that night since it drove me on, took me down the dark road of my own ambition and gave me the necessary gall to toss a typed page on an editor's desk. If I hadn't been so envious I might not have been able to face the blank page. I'm not convinced yet that envy doesn't have something to do with every word that's every been written, and not only by me.

Perhaps fate has arranged for envy to have its best as well as worst uses, and, as is the case with most of fate's arrangements, we can benefit from those very things we are taught to condemn. Without envy we might escape the pain of comparison, but forfeit the vital heat of competition; we might avoid some tingling sorrow, but lose the pleasure of unforeseen accomplishment.

Maybe it's a good thing to think that the grass always looks greener on the other side of the fence. Maybe without that belief, we would only ever focus on the fences, those walls boxing us in and trying to keep us in our place, built as high as they are wide and only climbed at great risk. It's scary to think about getting over them without a reason, and envy can provide a reason--perhaps not a good one, but nonetheless effective.

Envy refuses to allow us to be complacent inside the box of our own making, chides us to move up and out and away into new pastures, across fields of risk. Envy might entice us towards heartbreaking failure or dizzying success, but at least it moves us. That movement, that taking of risk, is what enables us to leave what is familiar and break new ground.

In having such power for good, envy itself is enviable

Lust

Let's face it: when I described a bunch of friends going to a Halloween party dressed as the Seven Vices, didn't you want to see what Lust was wearing? Didn't you want to meet her before you hooked up with Sloth or Gluttony? Lust has a glittering attraction that makes it the starlet of sin. Lust is Billy Ray Cyrus, the construction guy from the Coke commercial, and Sharon Stone. Lust is appealing, basic, and uncomplicated--until it gets adulterated by tricky things such as emotions and perspective.

Or so I've heard. It's inadvisable to appear too well acquainted with lust. It wouldn't look good if I spoke about lust from a really informed perspective, now would it? If I showed pictures and brought out charts and used an overhead projector? (I can sense that one or two of you wouldn't actually mind this. . .). No, I can speak about gluttony, greed, pride, and envy without really causing a raised eyebrow, but if I start talking about lust then where will I be? Thrown among floozies and loose women and dancing girls.

In other words, I'd be pretty much where I already am, and in excellent company as well. So here goes.

Lust can be great. Absolutely fabulous. Terrific. It can get you moving with the thumping persistence of the Energizer rabbit. It can wake you up out of a physical slumber and suddenly remind you of the wonders of the flesh--the sheer joy of having fingertips and eyelashes and skin. Aroused, we can feel as if every single piece of us is being put into play (and as if we can play with every single piece).

Just as every generation thinks its elders sat around carving wheels out of stone while the earth's crust cooled, every generation thinks it invented lust, but that kind of thinking is as cute as it is false. As long as people have been creating music, telling stories, or making pictures, lust has been a primary player. Operas are about lust at least as much as they're about love (consider Carmen); literature is shot through with lust (Chaucer's Wife of Bath is certainly a handful of hormonal longing, and that's just for starters); the greatest art elevates lust, refining it into gorgeous bodies reflecting a benevolent and joyous Maker (see Michelangelo, Carravaggio, and Boticelli, coming soon to a museum near you). Lust isn't confined to the young (see Mrs. Robinson in The Graduate) or the attractive (see the truck driver in Thelma and Louise). We heard stories about it from the nursery onwards. The prince waking Snow White with a kiss has to do with the powers of lust, which is why the wicked stepmother was so aggravated. The big, bad wolf waiting for Red Riding Hood could be a guy with a Harley making his motor purr outside your window. You might have to move off earth if anybody you know sees you get onto the back of that bike, but at the moment it seems worth it.

Lust can pour warmth into a life that has chilled under enforced indifference and resurrect passions once only associated with youth. You realize: Those initial forays into lust, clumsy and amateur as they were, were not half bad, especially for those of us brought up a million years ago (as the earth's crust cooled) when feeling desire didn't mean you had to act it out with a cast of thousands. Far from it.

Remember early lust, that warmth and flush of color that appears like a sunrise when you're just skidding into adolescence? At first I think of CYO dances where you and your partner had to leave enough room in your embrace for the presence of the Holy Ghost. As far as I remember, this strategy only made me think about what might actually happen if we danced up close, which no doubt made the distance as eroticized as any intimacy could be. This was a first, and I think good, lesson about desire. Erotic longing works well with distance; it feeds itself on delay and imagination.

Postponement is most potent; scruples and ceremonies add spice. Given into quickly, lust loses much of its appeal. This is why, in part, some of the best swooning romances exist between two people who barely touch each other: Wuthering Heights' Heathcliff and Catherine, Gone With The Wind's Scarlett and Ashley, and The Age of Innocence's Newland and Madame Olenska all come to mind. (Okay, so what if these novels are all written by women? You think it's only women who writes stories of melting desire dependent on distance? You do? So do I).

Was our prohibition-era lust perhaps the purest--the most exciting, the best--lust of all? I think of Saturday nights when I was seventeen in the long backseat of a car with a handsome, low-voiced boy. I remember kisses that went on for hours and the deep breaths that were somehow as shallow and as far-reaching as a stone skipped across a pond. And I remember being driven home after those kisses--literally, not metaphorically-- and hugged good-night again under the safety of a porch light. Is grown-up desire only an imitation of those moments, or were those steamy-windowed evenings only an intimation of what was waiting for us as adults? Was that a dress--or an undress-- rehearsal, or is this a faint echo?

Those first flash-floods of desires, the trickling, tickling, irritating sensation of awareness can be spectacular. They're right up there with a three-week vacation, a four-course meal, and a five-star hotel. True, lust often coincides with these elements as well. This should not surprise us, given that lust is a luxury (and, like most luxuries, calls for its own form of payment). It's an excess, an outpouring, an overflow, and it usually doesn't overtake you when you're under a deadline, under the weather, or underfed. You can feel lustful watching a healthy young creature saunter across a golden beach, but lustful is not something you feel after waiting forty minutes in the rain for a bus that's late, crowded, and damp.

Lust can be invigorating when it's part of life's healthy vitality, a good old visceral response to make sure all the systems are working. Setting fire to the emotional landscapes of our interior territories, lust can clear space so that great stuff can grow: affection, respect, and the ordinary delights of regulated breathing. (An old Italian saying capturing this process goes something like "Since the house is on fire, let us warm ourselves." This is a proverb about resignation and must be said with a shrug of the shoulders and a slight smile). But it can also burn down the house for no reason except its own consummation.

Because lust can lead to trouble, it has always received bad press. There was a student who, writing about Paradise Lost, discussed the fact that "After the fall, God made Adam and Eve cover their genial organs." Somehow "genial organs," mistake that it was, got it right. We've learned to disassociate our genial organs from the rest of us, to blame them for things that we, of course, would never do. Lust, it seems, frees us from responsibility for our own actions (Augustine called lust "an insubordination of the flesh" calling to mind images of rioting hormones and guerrilla gonads) and turns our sexuality into a foreign set of responses that don't necessarily have anything to do with our real life. It's as if our bodies are controlled by lust's automatic pilot, and that pilot light is too dangerously hot to handle.

As a tangent, or at least a musical interlude, it's worth noting that this not only accounts for Lust's bad rep, but also explains the need for endless country songs saying, in effect, "I wasn't responsible for what my arms/mouth/etc. did to that honey at the honkytonk because they weren't part of me, baby." (Mind you, country songs are nearly unbeatable when it comes to talking about lust. Consider such classics as "If I Said You Had A Beautiful Body (Would You Hold It Against Me?)" and "Shut Up and Kiss Me." Of course rock hasn't done badly, either. Patti Smith belting out Bruce Springsteen's line "Love is an angel disguised by lust" in "Because The Night" is even clearer in its declaration than the more obvious "Love the One You're With").

Lust can be just abrasive enough to polish a dull surface into a shine. But a little lust, like a little drunkenness, goes a long way and should not be encouraged as a habit. And, for anybody feeling a little too easy about their lack of fleshy appetites, it's worth remembering that the bad habits of lust don't necessarily orbit around (non-celestial) bodies. I've known men to lust after cars (which is why centerfolds in Road and Track are very much like centerfolds in Playboy). I've known women to lust after jewelry (it's a diamond, you'll remember, that's a girl's best friend). I've even known kids to lust after video games without using the "L" word but who are nevertheless consumed by a focused, unwavering, and passionate desire few other words dare encompass.

Telling, isn't it, that lust can be applied to things as well as to people? This is the unnerving part of lust: at its scariest, it reduces everything to a mere object, one to be acquired and then discarded when it's used up or when it becomes boringly easy to get all the moves right. Contempt can follow so closely that it sometimes treads on lust's red high-heels. But it doesn't have to; those heels can be kicked up in a dance or thrown off at the end of a long day. Lust can be as much a victory as a vice, as much part of comfortable love as of sizzling intimacy, if we learn how to do it right. And, luckily for all of us, that takes lots and lots of practice.

In My Next Life I
(In No Particular Hierarchical Order) Will:

1. Speak several languages fluently.

2. Lift weights and therefore have highly-toned upper arms.

3. Make excellent Chinese food at home.

4. Read all of Proust.

5. Never cry in public, especially in a fancy restaurant.

6. Eat in more fancy restaurants.

7. Like big dogs.

8. Know which knife to use when eating shellfish.

10. Floss.

11. Never stay up all night drinking cold coffee and stale sandwiches in order to meet a deadline.

12. Polish my shoes.

13. Have enough pillows.

14. Learn to read music.

15. Develop a greater sense of environmental awareness even if it does mean going outside.

16. Do algebra, just to prove that I could.

17. Create a well-organized photo album with pictures correctly dated and identified. No photographs of nameless, blurred, ancient relatives included merely out of guilt.

18. Garden.

19. Learn what every button on the dashboard does without having to push them all in a random sequence in order to find out in an emergency situation.

20. Consider a pear "dessert."

21. Consider an apple an "appetizer."

22. Consider soy products a "food."

23. Back-up all the files on my hard-drive.

24. Label the disks saving all the files on my hard-drive so that I don't have to push them all into the little slot in a random sequence in order to find the important stuff is in an emergency situation.

25. Have fewer emergency situations.

26. Eat a healthy breakfast every morning, including at least one fruit or vegetable.

27. Never run out of seltzer, kitty litter, detergent, or light bulbs.

28. Refuse to eat terrible food simply because it is placed in front of me--e.g.: omelets in airplanes, potato chips at wearisome events, peanuts in bars, muffins at bad breakfast joints, any food item I do not recognize or for which I cannot invent a name.

29. Hand wash garments labeled "Hand Wash."

30. Save scrap paper and actually use it, not merely save it only to throw it away at a later date.

31. Stay up all night telling long stories no family member ever felt safe enough to tell before.

32. Ski.

33. Vacuum my car rugs.

34. Be a better speller.

35. Towel-dry all my glasses.

36. Remember the names of everyone's spouse.

37. Actually enjoy reading books about the old west or the lives of contemporary singers.

38. Quilt.

39. Enjoy flying.

40. Learn to use cartridge pens without getting ink all over my hands, wrists,

and forearms.

41. Learn the tango.

42. Learn the cha-cha.

43. Learn the waltz.

44. Learn to leave my husband alone when he doesn't want to dance.

45. Fall asleep more quickly and dream more creatively. No dreams of being pursued by nameless relatives who are furious over not being included in well-organized photograph album.

46. Wake up with a sense of endless possibility and usually on time.

47. Take better care of those around me and better care of myself.

48. Take it easy.

49. Remember the names of everyone's kids.

50. Remember that we all get only one shot at doing all of this and so should not put off anything until the next life.

Out Of Focus

My old friend Lynette is a hot-shot marketing executive. I can't figure out exactly what she does (people with fancy business jobs usually confound me when they try to explain what fills their days). But I find myself emotionally and intellectually captivated by one particular aspect of Lynette's work: Focus Groups. Perhaps my fascination stems from the fact that so many groups of which I am a member are decidedly unfocused, but whatever the cause I find myself entreating her to tell me what the latest Focus Group project involves so that I can compare my own responses with those of the F.G..

As far as I understand it, F.G.s help folks decide how to produce and market products. It wouldn't be cool, I suppose, to show how ridiculous every human being looks brushing his or her teeth-- sudsing up, swirling, and spitting out, getting water on the mirror, and sucking one's gums--so instead we have commercials showing people talking about toothpaste instead of using it. It's tough, in contrast, to imagine a car commercial where the car is not shown in use .

You'd never show what a woman looks like coloring her hair at home because no one would ever buy the stuff, or what a guy looks like applying athlete's foot medication to either of his athlete's feet because no one would ever watch television again for fear of seeing this action repeated.

So folks in business need to figure out what the rest of us poor souls think, apparently, because there are people in marketing who think it would be just swell to show a guy actually in the process of using dental floss whereas the rest of us know that we would have to give up all dental hygiene (and probably also give up eating) if we ever watched someone on a giant screen really getting into floss-mode.

The information I've received from Lynette, however, has occasionally tripped me up. For example, she recently did a long survey concerning the order in which most people clean themselves in the morning. What is the very first thing you do? Do you face the water in the shower, lifting your kisser to it, or do you turn so that the water hits your back? Do you wash your face before you wash your hair? Do you put the soap into the washcloth before dampening it; do you use a washcloth at all? Which side do you wash first, your right or your left? Do you lather up all at once or bit by bit? Do you keep your eyes open or closed?

Seems simple enough, right? Not for your correspondent here. I no longer know how to take a shower. Suddenly I'm aware of a process that had become so totally ritualized as to be nearly unconscious; I'm like the victim of some alien abduction who has had that part of her mind washed away. I walk into the shower, turn on the water, and stand there like a fool. While I'm busy wondering whether I usually keep my eyes open, windows are fogging. The wallpaper is starting to curl at the edges. My husband is yelling at me to hurry up. As I stand soggy with indecision, I realize this is not a good use of my time, not to mention a real waste of water, but I cannot help it.

Why are questions like Lynette's confusing? Because an astonishingly amount of what we do everyday remains pretty much unexamined. When forced to evaluate our own rituals, we become perplexed by their very familiarity. This is why it's difficult to teach somebody else to drive, or cook, or tie shoelaces.

Not that we haven't become wedded to precisely the way we perform these unspoken ceremonial acts. We'll argue with genuine vigor against those heretical practices used by Others. "If they're not doing it the way we do it, they must be doing it wrong" could be our collective motto--or the title of a new country song.

So what's the lesson in all of this? Maybe we should all be forced (although perhaps not exclusively by marketing professionals) to examine the small rituals of everyday life in order to see what it is, exactly, we spend much of our time actually doing.

Then we might be able to face really big questions, such as "Why do I do what I do?" and "Should I try to do it differently?" "What would happen if, just this once, I wash my hair before I wash my face?" or "How about putting the milk in the cup before I pour in the coffee?" These sorts of questions could lead to ones causing what one writer called "sea changes" in our lives-- enormous, overwhelming emotional, intellectual, and spiritual overhauls. Or they might lead simply to a reaffirmation of our original choices.

But at least we'd be reminding ourselves that we make choices, even when we don't think of them as big decisions, and that each choice influences the course of our lives and the lives of those around us whether we're aware of it or not.

Just don't let the questions--big or small--make you stand, unable to move, in the shower for too long.

Vice

Vice intrigues me. Like all happy families, all virtuous people seem alike; but everyone's sense and practice of vice are interesting in their own way. I find myself thinking of the seven vices in the same way that Snow White deals with her dwarves--with affection, impatience, and a sense of lasting connection. I wouldn't want to live with them, but in cartoon form they're great. Like the seven dwarves, they represent personifications of those things we all find in ourselves--just as we are all occasionally Grumpy, so are we all occasionally Lusty.

Last year a group of my girlfriends went to a Halloween party dressed as the seven deadly sins. They all wore simple black outfits and small white name tags to indicate their own particular vice of choice. There they were, smart funny women in their twenties, thirties and forties (Envy had just turned forty-one and was making full use of every birthday's resentments) representing everything from Avarice to Wrath. Lust wore a tight black dress and flirted indiscriminately, Greed wore an Armani suit and asked for stock tips, Sloth went in her favorite sweatshirt and left gooey plates everywhere. Pride wore a dress with tiny mirrors so that her outfit was a shiny montage of everyone else's and gloated over her glitzy new condo.

In contrast to her pals, Gluttony wore a flowing mumu, stood by the buffet table and delightedly ate her weight in shrimp, miniature meat balls, and sour-dough bread. She ate all the treat-or-treat candies like a ten-year-old. She didn't upset anybody and didn't make anybody's life more difficult.

She laughed and joked with friends and strangers. She had the best time of all. Her friends felt a little cheated. How can you be a deadly sin and have such a good time without making trouble?

It's difficult to imagine how an apparently amateur evil like gluttony got onto a list with big-time sins like envy and greed. Chowing down at the Pizza Hut salad bar doesn't mean anyone else will go hungry that night because of your hankering for croutons. Eating forty-six canapes (without even knowing how to pronounce the word) at a work-related social event is probably better than positioning yourself next to the bar, asking them to fill you up with single-malt scotch and then driving home. If you stuff yourself the worst that will happen is that you will feel as if you could expand enough to fill a rumpus room by merely breathing deeply. But nobody else will be damaged.

After the break-up of an affair isn't it as perfectly acceptable to eat an entire bag of Hershey's kisses in one sitting as it is to rent Brief Encounter and Moonstruck during one trip to the video store? How can it hurt? (By the way, if it's the end of a long-term relationship you are then allowed to eat everything in the house that doesn't move or have a given name since your only secure belief at the moment is that no one will ever love you anyway, pretty much ruling out the idea that you will have to show your naked body to a stranger ever again. When you're facing eternal solitude what's the harm in ingesting an unfrozen Sara Lee cheesecake?)

And the seducers in this crowd are for the most part a little too cute to be regarded as Satan's spawn. Who's there on the sidelines tempting us into gluttony? Betty Crocker? Aunt Jemima? The Keebler Elves? Orvil Redenbacher and his grandson?

These are hardly typical of the villains described to me by the nuns during my wonder years. If anything, the nuns and priests I grew up around were well acquainted with gluttony. A thin priest meant a cheap parish and hinted at spiritual depletion. Having a lean and hungry look was frowned upon in my Italian neighborhood where a girl was considered too skinny if she could make her knees touch. A group of nuns coming down the hallway often looked like a school of killer whales, wide and unstoppable in their black and white habits. If they found out one day that appetites in the kitchen were as punishable as the appetites in the bedroom, there would have been a lot of rending of garments and gnashing of teeth in that group. How could overeating be a sin?

And yet it seems as if we're unwilling to embrace gluttony, even though it's the roly-poly Santa Claus of sin, full of goodies given to us as rewards. No doubt it's because we associate gluttony with incontinence and rapacity. Anything that blurs the clearly delineated boundaries between self-indulgence (giving in to your desire) and self-denial (giving up on ever getting your desire) is frightening to us as a culture. We view self-indulgence with contempt and often confuse self-denial with discipline. "Fat is bad and skinny is good; spending is bad and saving is good; crying is bad and holding back the tears is good: this is the machinery of puritanism that is stalled at the heart of America," says Michael as he eats another cannolli and sips a fully-caffeinated espresso. There's an important distinction to be made between self-denial and self-control but we usually factor it out, as if life were some kind of math problem where we merely need to get to the common denominator. We simplify out the complex relationship between needing, wanting, and getting until we become afraid not only of our own cravings but those of others.

"I don't like a woman who eats too much," shrugs my skinny friend Nick nervously. "Women who always want to snack make me nervous." He says "snack" with the visible distaste most folks reserve for phrases like "eat their young." "They always want something. First it's popcorn at the movies, then a full dinner out, and then she's got you peeling potatoes at the kitchen table for the rest of your life, never letting you go out with your buddies."

I suggest that perhaps he's making a broad jump in connecting a box of Raisinets with the loss of his soul but Nick sees it as a logical, linear and inevitable sequence. He dates women as angular as he is. I imagine at the height of their intimacy it's like two bicycle frames rubbing together but then that's none of my business.

We don't want simply to control rising numbers on a scale, we want to regulate and if necessary suppress our desires. We fear being consumed by our need for consumption. We worry about weight but even more significantly we worry about wanting to eat too much. We fear surplus the way our ancestors once feared deprivation; we fear excess the way our poorer neighbors fear scarcity. We are simultaneously attracted to and repelled by those around us who appear unrestrained in their pursuit of satisfaction. How can they let themselves get away with it?

Roseanne Barr-Arnold was once the queen bee of big women and many once regarded her triumphant sense of excess with a sense of freedom. "She has some mouth on her," declared her fans as well her detractors since she seemed unashamed of what went in or came out of it. Roseanne was powerful because she apparently lacked the blanketing shame that makes us smother our tastes for food, fame, and fast-talk. But that image has changed, what with a new honed-down and hemmed-in version of the star occupying a slightly smaller space on the screen. Ironically enough Roseanne seemed to have nothing to lose when she weighed the most and this made her dangerous and delicious. Now it seems as if she is framed as a glutton for punishment instead of a Rabelaisian barmaid, merely another soon-to-be-divorced again woman who fears that her husband's skinny secretary will eclipse her rightful place in his imagination.

The danger these days for many women and some men is not the buoyant lure of Gluttony but the glittering hook of her sister, Fasting. Women, especially young women, are trying to look like waifs and elfin figures out of a Victorian fairy-tale, which is in itself no dumber than trying to look like a gypsy in 1972 or a suited-up tycoon in 1981, which is what any number of women tried to do, myself among them. But take one look at Kate Moss and you see embodied, literally, a fear of bodies. "When my turkey looks like that I know to throw it away," comments Clara, who is in no danger of being hoisted out on the same grounds. But a number of women, especially teenagers and young women, are in danger of being gluttons of self-denial, packing away hours at Gold's gym instead of ice-cream at Ben and Jerry's with the same sense of senseless abandon as any voracious operatic diva. (Even divas have to be thin now. Too bad.)

Kate Moss is Roseanne Barr-Arnold's opposite, but what she represents is no less excessive. "There's no there there," sniffs Nancy, whose husband traces the outline of her hand with his fingers as she speaks. The men in the group watch on, amused, as we try to convince ourselves that we look fine as we are, Carravaggio's girls if not Reubens'. We are in danger in the nineties of leaping off the cliff of new sins: not gluttony but starvation, not sloth but overwork.

In the final estimation, however, gluttony has as little to do with hunger as greed has to do with want, or rape has to do with attraction. We fear the devouring figure because on some level we recognize the unappeasable nature of the need beneath the act. What we read as their excessive demands sets off alarms in our own regulating systems not because we think they might take something from us but because we're terrified we might become like them. Most of us believe that we have satisfactorily muffled the voice that cries "Feed Me!" or, even more basically, "I Need!" until we hear that voice echoed as if it is merely amplified from inside ourselves. We condemn someone who has "let themselves go" because we're concerned that, given half a chance or a bad day or a lonely night, they might just take us with them.

"If the worst thing you ever do is overeat, then you're a damned saint," said my Aunt Jackie, piling my favorite foods up high. Maybe permission to enjoy food without checking every spoonful has allowed me to remain astonished when I hear my students say "Oh, I was bad today" and by that meaning merely that they ate macaroni and cheese for lunch. I repeat to them what my aunt said and offer them, wickedly, something sweet.

Greed

If our fear of gluttony is the fear of wanting too much, then our fear of greed is the fear of wanting it all. Even the most enthusiastic of gluttons achieves satiation after the eighteenth Whopper or the fourteenth Ring Ding and then falls asleep. Greed never sleeps; the ordinarily greedy make money in their dreams and the successfully greedy make money even while they dream.

Greed is like gluttony--it wants to consume everything around it-- but without the possibility of ever having a full belly. This, of course, makes Greed categorically less fun.

Greed is grabbing all the toys and not letting your kid brother have any. Greed spits on the best piece of pizza so that your sister won't want it anymore. Greed steals the answers to the college exam and dares to be proud of its success. Greed steals your hometown boyfriend just to see if she can. Greed wants cash for Christmas instead of homemade socks. At some point Greed has had a nodding acquaintance with us all.

Greed takes pens from hotels without even thinking "This is the hundred and third pen saying 'Sheraton' I have scattered near telephones in my house." Greed is Imelda Marco's unblinking pronouncement in 1987, "I did not have three thousand pairs of shoes, I had one thousand and sixty." Greed might bring really good wine to the party, but it insists on drinking it immediately; even Greed's gifts come with this sort of price-tag. Everything given is really loaned, and everything is loaned with interest. Greed kills deer after deer for the sheer pleasure of making the hit; greed fishes for the pleasure of the hook and then throws the catch away. Greed sells "We Love The Juice" tee shirts outside the L.A. courthouse as the families of the victims file by. Greed looks astonished when you say that some things aren't worth the price.

Greed wants the best there is and wants it all. Sometimes Greed has to settle, and so we get the joking line about the disgruntled restaurant patron who comes out saying "The food was absolutely disgusting, absolutely inedible, and besides that the portions were too small."

These comments, of course, presuppose that most of us still consider greed a vice; gluttony was a sure bet in terms of guaranteed disapproval, but greed is more dangerous. Gluttony remains an essentially personal vice--as in "I'm a glutton for punishment," or "I'm a glutton when it comes to chocolate"--and involves power only insofar as it relates to food and the self. But greed can easily transcend the self. Nobody really cared if Nero ate every roast oxen in sight, but it was more problematic when he let Rome burn just because he could. Hermann Goering, as a friend of mine pointed out, may have been a glutton when it came to food, but more significantly he was greedy when it came to power. We're playing in a different league when it comes to greed because greed does with power what gluttony does with food--wants it, grabs it, stuffs it away where nobody else can get at it, and eventually incorporates it as a natural part of the self. This is why no one wants to be thought of as greedy; if someone accused any of us of being avaricious we'd silkily mention "sour grapes" sotte voce or we'd simply deny it. We're not greedy, oh no, he's greedy; we're merely comfortable.

"Greed is when other people want more money than you do," declares my brother Hugo. Wendy disagrees, claiming that "Greed is when you're consumed with want for what you already have, whether that's money or attention. Not only can't you get enough of it, you can't even properly enjoy what you've already got. It's like Lynn and her clothes thing." She cites the example of a indubitably greedy friend who offers to buy garments off other people's backs if she thinks she'll look good in the outfit. This is not an exaggeration; she carries an extra tee-shirt in her Coach bag for these occasions, given that she's addicted to blouses and jackets. She has gone up to other women in restaurants and silk has been exchanged for cash. She could clothe all of Finland with what's already in her closets but that doesn't dampen her appetite. Greed, like this otherwise sane enough woman, always wants More. Lynn, who would no more call herself greedy than call herself unfashionable, says that clothes have replaced prey in the hunt of her life and declares that her passion is healthier than being greedy for either men or money.

Ten years ago Lynn would not have even had to justify herself in certain parts of the world. For a while there, Greed was not a problem. Remember the single most poignant signature line of the eighties, when Gecko from Oliver Stone's Wall Street went into his rapturous aria extolling the virtues of avarice, declaring once and for all "Greed is good"? You had the feeling that there were men and women in deliberately and delicately crumpled linen suits writing that line down on their cuffs. (It didn't matter if that wasn't the message Stone wanted to send; Greed screens its ideas as diligently as it screens its calls). Young men in thin yellow ties quoted Andrew Mellon's immortal line "Gentlemen prefer bonds" and laughed; young women in thin yellow suits and fat white sneakers gave one another needle-pointed pillows saying "Nouveau Riche is Better Than No Riche At All."

Greed, after all, is as American as apple pie or baseball--and after this summer's striking of home plate, who would say that baseball isn't about greed? Only in America do we see bumper stickers saying "He who dies with the most toys, wins," not because Europeans or Candians or Africans or Asians are less greedy but because they're less fond of broadcasting it; the bumper sticker, is after all, only partially ironic. A friend's husband wryly suggested, after buying his second new Lexus, that if you have enough toys, maybe you don't die at all. "How can you die when you still have a manufacturer's warranty in your hand?" He smiles when he drives. The last twenty years gave us designer jeans, designer drugs, even designer diners, where you could order nouvelle cuisine meatloaf (nouvelle cuisine, as a friend of mine quipped, being the French term for "child's portion"). We heard that you could never be too rich or too thin and we tried for both, only to discover that if you're rich enough, hey, nobody cares what you weigh and the rest of us are better off just eating cake.

What's tricky, however, is that greed is about wanting instead of necessarily about having. You'll be called greedy if you work overtime and weekends and save obsessively to buy a big house and fill it with antiques, but if you've inherited that big house and the antiques are simply identified as Grampy's set of first editions or Mumsy's matched Degas, then it's okay, and you're not greedy, you're aristocratic. If you're panting after the stuff, having been denied it at an early age, however, then you're lost to avarice as far as this system is concerned. The only thing worse than not having money in some circles is wanting it. What we all needed, evidently, were greedy ancestors who could die and leave us without the taint of desire.

What's most unnerving about greed is the sense of insatiable hunger behind it; where gluttony was only tangentially about a hunger for food, so greed is only tangentially about a appetite for possessions. More accurately greed is about need. We can never assume we understand somebody else's deepest, most passionate, most authentic needs. We look at a Neiman-Marcus laden lady and wonder why she needs yet another cashmere cardigan; we caustically comment on a co-worker's hogging of all the secretary's time. But often we are oblivious to what we ourselves hoard because it never occurs to us that we're stockpiling anything; if questioned, we would explain in all honesty that we take only what we need.

Remember in King Lear when his two mean daughters want to strip him of his very last remaining trappings of majesty? He's moved in with them and they don't think he needs guards. They convince themselves by saying that Lear, used to having everything he's every wanted, doesn't need a hundred, or even a dozen soldiers around him. When they wish to take the final man away from his side, saying "What needs one?" Lear bellows, terrified and suddenly alone, from his inner-most depths "Reason not the need." Lear doesn't need soldiers any more than Scrooge needed silver or Midas needed gold, but it doesn't stop them from wanting it because, in fact, their possessions are the only things that define them. If gluttony says you are what you eat (to which the character in Nicole Hollander's cartoon Sylvia replies "That makes me a Taco Chip") then the greedy are what they acquire. It makes the driver of a red Porsche first and foremost the driver of a red Porsche if that object is the best, most powerful, most compelling thing about him. (Note: It often is).

Not every greedy character is unsalvageable or even unlovable, as Hollywood has shown us. American movies love the greedy tycoon, the miser, the selfish and powerful manipulator out for his own gain. From 1924 and Von Stronheim's Greed (a film version of Frank Norris's 1899 novel McTeague), to Citizen Kane's acquisition of the boxed-up treasures of Europe when all he wanted was paint-peeling Rosebud, to Wall Street, we get a sense that the greedy hero is more misguided than anything else. We want to forgive him or, in rare cases, forgive her. These figures are too much like our own dear selves to consider them terminally wicked.

My favorite greedy film hero is less tragic than his classier peers. When Mel Brooks cast Zero Mostel as Max Bialystock in his 1968 classic, The Producers, he created a flawless portrait of the greedy man who nevertheless remains unequivocally heroic throughout. Max, who was once a fabulously successful producer of Broadway hits, is now a gigolo, giving blue-haired ladies one last thrill on their way to the cemetery. He wears a cardboard belt. He is starving for money and what is most compelling about Max is that he is shamelessly willing to get rich without any hungering after success. Malice plays no role in his endeavors; he just wants the money. He convinces his accountant, Gene Wilder (playing a neurotic Leo Bloom who would make James Joyce proud) to agree to a scheme where they sell 25,000 percent of the profits to a sure-fire flop--a show called Springtime for Hitler-- with plans to leave town with the leftover cash once the show closes.

Listening to Mostel sing the praises of money to thumb-sucking Wilder is a hysterical presage of Gecko's speech. Mostel sings of "lovely ladies with long legs and lunch at Delmonico's," yelling with joyful envy out his dirty office window "Flaunt it, baby, flaunt it" to a man exiting a Rolls Royce. Mostel's appetite is catching. When Zero kisses the piles of money he's conned out of willing fools, fondling the fistfuls of cash saying "hello boys" to all the presidents on the bills, we have Mostel giving voice to the greedy creature inside all of us. When he screams out in complete abandon "I WANT THAT MONEY" we can cheer in a way that we never would have cheered Gecko. Here is greed we experienced as kids waiting for birthday presents that might or might not come; here's greed with a small "g" that comes out of the hard-won experience of uncertainty. We might grab a little too quickly or hold on a little too long or a little too tightly because we're afraid we'll never see such pleasure again. Too much, as the country song goes, just ain't enough.

This is the kind of greed we speak of when we think about lovers being greedy for each other's company, or a mother being greedy for her child's love. We sense in any deep need the temptation for our desires to boil over, like soup. Every woman I know, including myself, is terrified of appearing greedy for affection or approval. The question "Do you love me?" is rarely a request for information, as my brother the lawyer once noted, but instead indicates a greediness of the heart. We pretend to hip aloofness when our scurrying souls are frantically seeking attention. Lovers and mothers, even with a right to their greedy pleasures of love, risk disaffection even as they seek affection.

Money, however, unlike love, often comes to those who spend all their time hunting for it. The robber barons that made America into the world's wallet--Ford, Rockefeller, the Hunt boys, Getty-- didn't get rich by looking sentimentally at pictures of money. They went out and made it--or took it, depending on your point of view and position on the production line--but one way or another they got it. There isn't a buck that won't lie down for the greediest man.

But this isn't to say that a certain greediness isn't a good thing. "Wanting," "desiring," "needing" are the gerunds that made the Western world great. Without the greed of certain collectors, our museums would be depleted;

without the greed for power located in some of the folks on our side, the greed for power on the other side would always win. Without a greed for knowledge, we wouldn't have the discoveries, the vaccinations, the understanding of the world that we take for granted. The process of seeking to attain and secure what your heart wishes for is not a bad impulse, however un-Zen it may be.

Even if our civilization was founded in greed, for most of us greed is usually curiously translated into a better impulse, almost despite ourselves. With our desire for cars and clothes, T.V.s and R.V.s, rings or even racehorses, few of us can be without this vice. And yet we manage to keep our basic decency. We want to make money, but we don't want to be piggish and wasteful; we want to acquire objects, but most of the time we are more than willing to share these with those we love, and even on occasion with those we don't. We want to embrace our heart's desire, and have lots of it, but what's wrong with that?

It might be limiting if what your inner-most heart desires can be summed up by the phrase "Junk Bonds" or can be transcribed numerically, but surely an appetite for getting a lot of what you love has been the cause of much good in the world.

I don't foresee a twelve-step program for the greedy ("Today I will not buy another garment with a Ralph Lauren logo, even at a drastically reduced price," or "Today I will not play Monopoly with real hotels") but there are no doubt ways to make the lives of the greedy better. Maybe we could take up a collection.

Pride

Pride, I am proud to say, doesn't come easily to me. I'm terrible at pride. Shame, guilt, a squirming sense of undeserving-- now those I've got a real talent for; I could teach workshops in "Low Self-Esteem" although nobody would want to sign up for them. If pride is truly the considerable vice everybody says it is--many claim pride is the big original sin, coming before the fall, sort of like winter fashions--then I'm all set for heaven. Saying I'm all set for heaven, however, smacks of boasting and there I am shut out again. Pride, in my modest opinion, is the most confusing of the seven vices.

Writing about gluttony and greed was a piece of cake or money in the bank compared to figuring out the dynamics behind pride. Associated with positive images of self-esteem in everything from sexuality ("Gay Pride") to race ("Black Pride") to employment ("Made With Pride in the USA"), pride is valued by our culture in a way usually reserved for simple pleasures and not complex sins. The fact is we don't have "humility" seminars to bone up on self-effacement and I haven't yet heard of a company bringing in a consultant at a zillion dollars a day to teach the employees to blush shyly at a mention of the institution's success.

America loves pride: we scream "We're number one" at everything from football games to the reclaiming of the Persian Gulf for Kuwait. We've heard that Joe Kennedy told his sons "Show me a good loser and I'll show you a loser," which probably didn't encourage them to get in touch with their soft, vulnerable sides.

We've grown up listening to commercials informing us that we deserve only the best hot dogs (made from the best cow lips, presumably), best mayonnaise (with the most fabulous cholesterol), and best beer (superior to the rest insofar as you can fall down faster with this one than the others). We want to be proud of our pets (First in Show), cars (would you rather show up at your high school reunion in a Jaguar or a Pinto?), and spouses ("Honey, how about wearing that great red tie/skirt/hat/garter belt tonight?"). Thriving on competition and lapping up the cream of others' envy, we've been taught to advertise ourselves by blowing our own horns loud enough to be heard above the rest of the band. Pride waves the baton at the head of the parade, twirling our images of ourselves deftly and catching them in one hand before they fall.

Is this a bad thing? Since it would appear unAmerican to stop waving this little "Hooray for us" flag in my hand, I hardly dare pause to consider. But when I stop the frantic movement and avoid all the cheering, in the vacuum of sound one can hear the pin of self-destruction falling somewhere in the distance. Pride, say the sin scholars, is what led to our being expelled from Eden; Eve was flattered and ate. Adam (like many of his progeny) clearly didn't want to bother making his own meal and so he ate, too. Pride made Lucifer into the bad guy in the first place; declaring in Milton's version of the fall that he'd rather rule in hell than serve in heaven, he went from being merely head chef in paradise to owning the first barbecue franchise. As much as history has sycophantically worshipped at the altar of success, it also delights in the downfall of the great, the boastful, and the powerful.

Act a little too cocky, a little too arrogant, and the dogs of ruin begin yapping at your heels, lead by someone just slightly less cocky and arrogant than you. Act a little too sanctimonious, and not only will the mob eventually rise up against you, but even your best friends will cheer them on. It's tougher to destroy the reputation of someone who says "I'm in it for power and money" than it is to destroy the reputation of someone who says "I'm in it because I have been called to show you all the best way to live your life" and then follows that phrase with "Please make all checks payable in my name."

When Jimmy Swaggart turned out to be, in some folk's opinions, living up to his last name--a combination of "swag" meaning "loot" and "braggart" meaning "television evangelist"--not too many ordinary citizens grieved at his collapse. He had strutted his hour upon the stage full of the conviction of his own righteousness, and when the shrapnel of scandal blew through that facade it made as grand a sound as, say, a pricked balloon. If a regular guy was caught with a babe in a hotel room there would not have been as profound a reaction because the regular guy had not been boasting about personally meeting the obligation for fidelity or purity as one of his selling points.

What are causes for pride in our lives? The easiest pride is the stuff we give away--pride in a child's sweet singing voice or a husband's homemade cake or even a favorite co-worker's success--such pride is downright accessible. But it's harder to be proud of yourself in the right way. And while there are no rights and wrongs in life, there really are rights and wrongs in life--it's like when I tell a student who thinks Danielle Steele is the world's best writer "There's no such thing as a wrong answer-- but if there were, that would be one." There are better ways to be proud of yourself than the guy I knew in college who wore a tee-shirt saying "Yes, I Am Everything You've Ever Hoped For" to which I could only mutter beneath my breath "That's makes you a bag of Snickers and a hundred dollar bill."

There's no telling what will constitute grounds for pride. My cat is proud when she catches a wadded-up piece of paper in one paw, but then so is my lawyer. My niece is proud of herself because she can spell well; I've never been able to spell well and I am proud of that. My aged aunt is proud of the fact that she has never had sex with anyone besides her husband and my rapidly aging friend is proud because she has a new liaison going outside her marriage. You might be proud to own a fur coat whereas your neighbor might wrap an inherited mink in a Hefty bag before throwing it away because she's a card carrying member of PETA. One of the worst feelings in life is to once have been proud of something that later causes you shame: a love affair you bragged about that goes wrong, a career track you ostentatiously discussed that careens into a nose dive, an accomplishment you traded on that suddenly appears meaningless compared to someone else's more substantial or original achievement. And one of the most triumphant moments can occur when something you fear might embarrass you suddenly somersaults and turns into a matter for pride.

Sometimes, it seems, pride sneaks up on us and grabs us by the collar when we least expect it and gives us something--sort of like a pickpocket working in reverse. When I was a graduate student in England many years ago, I did a stint working for the BBC. A producer asked me to appear on a t.v. show that was a sort-of grown-up version of College Bowl with the blush-inducing title "Mastermind." I think it was based on The Manchurian Candidate, but I don't know that for a fact. You sat under a spotlight on a stage and an announcer fired questions at you concerning a special subject and what was cryptically titled "general knowledge." You had to answer as many questions as you could within the space of three minutes. If you didn't know the answer, you had to say "pass" because you risked losing points with an incorrect response--sort of like the SATs, or a criminal trial. The producer explained that the show had been syndicated in eight countries but never made it to the States. Would I consider, he asked, acting as the official American contestant? I had never seen the program, but my British boyfriend of the moment had--and he hissed at me that I shouldn't even consider such a thing. He said, and I quote: "You'll look terribly silly." That, of course, made my decision for me.

I agreed to be Ms. America; I would show him. It wasn't that I was secure in myself or anything good; I just had an instinctive sense that any boyfriend who was so expert at the contemptuous sneer had to be put in his place.

Then I actually watched the terrible, maniacal, sadistic show and was giddy with trepidation. I chose the life and works of the playwright Tennessee Williams as my special subject. When a month or so passed, I showed up with a remarkably bad cold, runny nose and red eyes, fuzzy on cough syrup and mad at the boyfriend who refused to accompany me. I did all right on Williams, but when it came to "general knowledge" I knew almost none of the questions they asked, many of which had to do with American geography which I know almost nothing about, having grown up in Brooklyn. I could not name all the states run-through by the Mason-Dixon Line. I did not know the highest point in Utah (to be perfectly honest, I didn't know that Utah had a high point). I could not for love or money estimate the population of Atlanta. The poor audience members were holding their breath and avoiding one another's eyes in appalled silence as I kept saying "pass" over and over again. Finally the announcer asked me one glorious question:"What kind of animal is a guppy?" and I screamed with unbounded joy "IT'S A FISH!" Instantly there was wild, thunderous applause. They were so relieved that I got one right, that audience, that they forgave me everything. They whistled, they stamped their feet, they were reprieved.

For somebody coming in last in the show, I was shockingly proud of myself. That night I learned that anything worth doing was worth doing badly. If I'd had a greater sense of pride, I wouldn't have done it at all; if I had less pride, I would have backed out as soon as the light went on over my head. Like the baby bear's porridge, for once it seemed that the pride I carried around was just right. It forced me to get through an experience, and yet allowed me to enjoy the adventure of it no matter what the outcome. (My sense of pride that night also prompted me to dump the boyfriend.) Pride didn't get in the way but instead provoked me into accepting a challenge I would have been happier to let slide by, coward of the heart that I am.

Unlike lust or envy, pride seems as much a virtue as a vice. If we are too proud to behave like cowards, or hypocrites, or a cheapskates, then pride has saved us from worse sins; if we are too proud to be vicious, callous, or vengeful, then pride has offered itself to us as the least of all evils, a little bit of possible wickedness injected into our lives the way a little bit of a virus is injected in an inoculation to ward off graver illness.

When Pride shows up like a character out of Edgar Allen Poe's Masque of the Red Death, however, all dressed up and ready to defy mortality itself, then it might indeed be a good time to edge your way out the door. There are usually a number of reliable indications signaling the moment at which Pride runs away with itself. It wasn't a good sign that the builders of the Titanic apparently claimed "God Himself could not sink this vessel," for example, and I for one would have wagged my finger reprovingly at Frankenstein when he was getting ready to create a whole new race of beings to call him master. Interesting to see that the world usually does more than wag its collective finger at those creators of the master race, whether they attempt this with their own community's approval or not. When one group becomes so swollen with pride that it considers itself immune from the slings and arrows of ordinary existence, and so looks to others to carry their burden for them, it appears that the rest of us cannot stand it and so bring the pedestal down. Such is the paradox of pride: a vice that is its own reward.

Sloth

Sloth, or at least my version of it, keeps me very busy. The house is never cleaner, my desk is never tidier, the silver is never so perfectly polished, as when I have a deadline. I'll do everything except the work I'm supposed to do, you see, so that I'm a frantic bundle of random and useless energy when I'm avoiding a specific task. Take this assignment, for example. I've known for , oh, seven months or so, that I need to get these words on paper. And it isn't like I haven't been thinking about the topic; I've been driving my friends mad with hints that I want all their stories along with permission to quote directly. But knowing that I have to sit down in front of this blank screen and begin makes me decide that what I really need to do is give the cat a flea-bath or alphabetize the spice rack. (I mostly rely on basil, garlic, and oregano which made that task incredibly disappointing and which also makes every home-cooked meal taste as if it were delivered by Little Ceasars).

I'm terrified of sloth. More than any other of the cozier, more familiar sins, Sloth I regard as my natural enemy and therefore as the embodiment of my biggest fear.

I'm not kidding now. I'd take a festive feast with gluttony, a steamy night with lust, a stuffed purse from greed, I'd relish a shouting match with anger, compete proudly with pride, and stare down the unblinking gaze of envy and not worry too much about my immortal soul. Maybe I'm overconfident (do I feel a breeze created by heads nodding in unison?), but I still have a feeling that we'll all be waiting in a really long line at the Pearly Gates only to hear the shouts of celebration when somebody yells from the front of the queue "Hey! Good news! Sex doesn't count!"

But what will count, I think, are sins of omission, and I'm afraid these will count big time.

Probably we'll have to account not so much for all the sins we've committed because we're weak or foolish or scared or needy--they'll understand all that, I bet-- but instead we'll have to explain in detail why we just didn't get around to doing all the good we could have done. Somehow the answers "It didn't seem worth it" and "It wouldn't have done much good anyway" or even "I was watching the weather channel" won't cut much slack. It's my suspicion that there will be a lot of forgiveness for everything except wasting the stuff nobody gets too much of: time and talent.

Sloth whispers that you might as well do it tomorrow, that nobody will know if you cut corners here and there to save yourself some trouble, that the world will be the same in a hundred years no matter what you do, so why do anything? Sloth says "Don't strain yourself," "What's the big hurry?" and "Just give me five more minutes." Sloth hits the snooze alarm, hits the remote control, and hits the road when the going gets tough. It's Sloth's responsibility to make you stay up late watching an old movie you've seen before when you know you'll only get all cranky at customers the next morning at work, and it's Sloth's business to make you assume you know enough to pass judgment when all you've done is listen to what others have to say without doing any figuring out on your own.

Sloth cheats on exams, drinks straight from the milk carton, and leaves exactly two sheets on the toilet roll so that it will have to be replaced by the next poor soul who finds out too late that the remaining paper is nothing more than a mirage. Sloth never gets around to RSVPing but shows up at the party anyway.

Sloth slides over to say: "Marry her; she'll make your life easier because she loves you more than you love her. After all, they're all basically the same." It murmurs "Don't contradict him; it isn't worth an argument. He'll only sleep on the far side of the bed."

Sloth does slightly less than the right thing. It doesn't bother returning something to the lost and found but pockets it instead; it doesn't tell the clerk he's undercharged. It's never written a thank you note, sent a birthday card on time, or entertained angels unawares because it all takes too much effort. When other sins get mixed in with sloth they become exponentially more unappealing. Slothful lust dials a 900 number, slothful gluttony eats cold food from the can, slothful pride congratulates itself on a shoddy performance, slothful envy believes everybody else got an unfair advantage, slothful anger screams and hits instead of argues, and slothful greed doesn't leave a tip.

Replacing earned self-reliance with unfounded self-esteem ("I'm good enough, I'm nice enough, and doggone it, people like me"), Slothful folks don't have convictions. They have prejudices. They've memorized a series of pre-formatted responses to the world and choose to label as integrity that which is more accurately called inflexibility. Archie Bunker was slothful; so was King Lear.

Being slothful, by the way, doesn't mean you can't be busy. Some of the busiest people I know have a prize-winning case of the Sloths because they spend all their time by filling the day with evasions from life. They bake their own bread, not because it cuts costs, tastes better, or is fun to do (all sparkling and excellent reasons) but so that they can then complain to the family about all the time they spent doing it which took away from what they really should have been doing--whatever that is. The family maybe likes store-bought bread better, but they daren't say so because the bread-maker has been diligent and has worked hard. But he or she hasn't worked as hard as the kids or the spouse for whom every mouthful is a recrimination. If baking bread is one of your joys and satisfactions, then it is a terrific service to the world around you. If it becomes a way to avoid facing the crisis of deciding what your service to the world actually is, then the bread becomes dust in the hands of the one who makes it and dust in the mouths of those who eat it. Sloth sweeps everything under the rug-- dust, crumbs, lost ambitions, past hopes, once-dear dreams--because who'll know the difference?

And Sloth doesn't only apply to the slobs of the world, some of whom are the least slothful inhabitants of this planet despite scoring low in Dress Code (consider Einstein's unruly hair and unkempt clothes). At the risk of hearing from my grade school teachers, neatness doesn't count. One of the most slothful souls I know is a perfectionist. You want to see a hell of a neat spice rack, then his kitchen is the place to find it. If he can't do something right, then he won't do it at all. Sounds good? On paper maybe, but implementing this motto in life means that he doesn't do much. It's tough to get everything right and easier not to try if you can't permit yourself to fail, make a mess, or lose your place in line. For him, and many others--myself included-- sloth is nothing so much as a thin camouflage for fear.

Maybe this is why sloth seems insidious to me. Indolence and a reluctance to get off my seat and into the world's chaos is a signal of danger to me. Sloth's sirens can call in warm sleepy voices from mossy rocks that can shipwreck your soul. This much I know.

I spent one year of my life indulging in sloth, steeped and swimming in the waters of indolence. I look back on that time when I lived in England seventeen years ago and wonder whether I could have done anything differently. I doubt it. Maybe I was depressed, maybe it was one of those crisis-moments I mentioned earlier, but whatever it was, I couldn't make myself get on with my work or get through the day without focusing on the pointlessness of every single action. Unhappy in love and dissatisfied with my job, I hunted through Camden Town flea-markets and thrift-shops for bargains I didn't really have to make and browsed through stores for things I didn't really need to buy. I read trashy books and watched bad television. The hardest things were falling asleep and waking up. I didn't want to lose the young man I was involved with and so I didn't bring up the fact that our relationship was eating away at my already rickety sense of self like termites at the foundation of a wooden shack. I drank rivers of tea. And yes, you got it, I baked bread.

Rescue came with a letter from my brother who wrote, in response to the note of despair I'd sent him, simply "You can always stop what you're doing." It was the one line written on the blue airmail stationary but it was all the permission I needed. I realized that I could stop doing nothing; I understood at that one astonishing moment that I could begin a voyage home that would also be a journey away from a shadowy life filled with compromises, inertia, and regret. I left town fast, not because the going got tough but because I knew that seductions of sameness were strong. I knew, too, at that moment, that I'd used up my slothful days and that I'd never get to give into indolence for any length of time ever again. That was the bargain I made with myself; living as fearlessly as possible was the price I would pay for escaping what had once laughingly seemed like an easy life. I left the keys on the bed and a note on the door. It was one of the hardest and one of the smartest things I've ever done.

So I'd like to reclaim some of those days when I was twenty-one but they're lost to the long afternoons when I half-napped and looked down the street to see what possible use other people were making of the day. When I have a guilty feeling coming on, I find myself feeling worse about the year I did nothing than I do about anything else I've actually done. And so even on those days when I can't face stringing words together I clean my desk and polish the silver, so as to appease a heaven I believe rejoices in every human action willfully and honestly performed--even if those actions sometimes mean making love, making a profit, making someone angry or envious, making one's self proud, or even making (dare I say?) a devil's food cake.

Romance

Anatomy of an Affair

Infidelity is never unimportant. It matters to at least three people, even if only two of them know about it.

Who is the other woman?

She's the nicest woman you could ever meet; in fact, you might have met her. You might know her fairly well and you might like her a lot without being aware, of course, that she's sleeping with your husband.

She is a nice woman, really. This is the only part of her life that can't be examined, that can't be admired, that can't be discussed out loud. It's the only part of her life she doesn't respect herself for and it keeps her miserable, even when she's happy, because she knows whatever happiness she has stolen is illegitimate. She's not a fool even though she knows she's acting like one.

Educated, polite, and brought up by a loving family, she's not a particularly hot tomato or the kind of woman usually transported across state lines for immoral purposes. Attractive, fun, attentive, and considerate, she is deeply committed to those she loves and that's one of the reasons this tears her apart. One of the things she loves about this man, after all, is the way he treats the ones to whom he is closest.

Not her-- he can't treat her as if she were really in his life after all--but others. His real family, the inhabitants of his real life. If he were an emotional bully or an emotional slob, she wouldn't have been drawn to him in the first place. Those aspects of his life he betrays to be with her are the very parts of him she would never wish him to compromise. So she understands how divided he is, how he feels like a piece of meat being sliced up by a rusty knife, how he feels like he's drowning and suffocating and being eaten alive all at once. He, too, is a decent person, except for this business of loving someone he isn't meant to love.

Holidays are hard, but so is spring and so are winter nights, summer mornings, and long early autumn afternoons. The phone is her lifeline and she has about seventeen different ways of being reached in case some shard of time can be broken off and given to her. She'll take what she can get--not a way anyone would think of her, but in this case it's true. There are codes they use to communicate what can't be spoken or written; these were funny at first but over time they have become as serious as a car crash.

There are impossible nights, intolerable weekends, endless violations of everything she knows about how life should be lived, but they have loved each other for so long now, how can it stop? She starts to worry that he'll die of a heart attack and no one will tell her for days because why would anyone think to call and tell her an incidental piece of bad news about some guy she never knew very well? Or she starts to think about her own final moments. This is the worst.

She can't believe this is her life. Nobody else would believe it either, even the man. It's a tough, rotten, exhausting routine. Nobody chooses it on purpose. This is not a defense of her: she knows better than you that what she's doing is indefensible. Don't ridicule her, and don't think you don't know her. You do.

And as for you, the husband, the lover?

You never, ever wanted it to be like this. You're a good guy, a real contributor to the community, well-liked and well-respected, an excellent father and in many ways a fine husband. You don't do what your father did; you don't come home drunk or raise a hand to your wife. You're not a jerk. You don't spend the rent gambling and never embarrass the family in public. No; you are as different from the old man as possible except that you've started to fool around--but that isn't the right way to talk about it. It was your father's term--"fool around"--but it doesn't apply to you.

Because this isn't fooling around: this is serious business. You love this woman, this other woman. It's not that you don't love your wife; you love her but you're not in love with her. The marriage just isn't enough anymore. You don't want to hurt your wife and you'd rather shoot yourself than hurt your kids.

But you also believe you cannot exist without this new person in your life. It's as if she's giving you mouth-to-mouth resuscitation every time you kiss, it's as if she's keeping you alive and breathing. Sometimes when you're home and the kids have gone to bed, so there are no distractions, you feel like a dog trapped in a closed car on a hot day, like you want to start howling and clawing at the closed windows. It's all you can do to keep the leash on, to be civil, to be considerate, to be what might be considered normal. You count the minutes until you can get to the phone or get into the car and drive away.

All this is made worse by the fact that you know your wife is a terrific woman and that you've been lucky to have been married to her. It's not that she's a big disappointment or that she's any different from what you wanted or expected when you married her thirteen years ago. If anything, the trouble lies with the fact that she is exactly what you expected and you can no longer tolerate the lack of the unanticipated in your life. Is it too much to ask not be greeted by the same complaints, same child-raising issues, same questions about work, same lack of enthusiasm, every night? She doesn't get it. She doesn't know that you're eager to talk to an adult woman, not just somebody's mom, even if she's mom to your own kids. You longed for years for the moment when she'd be able to do something besides change diapers and tell you about what the neighbor's wife's mother-in-law did yesterday. You wanted her to be a partner but now she seems more like your mother than your spouse and it's weird to want to get close to her. So for a while now you've been leaving her alone.

And it's just not natural for a man like yourself to be lonely. You've always had women friends, female colleagues, members of the opposite sex whose company you've enjoyed and whose perspectives and insights you've sought out. It's not like you went looking for something to happen. You were absolutely, totally faithful for years, even in those situations where a lot of other guys would not have been. You've resisted passes, turned down invitations, ignored flirtations, and kept your idea of yourself as a good man and a good husband intact. But at the worst moments, you tell yourself that you're your father's son as well as your mother's and that the old man, in whatever room in hell he inhabits, is having a good laugh.

It's hard to redefine everything about your life. And why should you? You're still a good man, and you're really having a tough time understanding why you're not a good husband. How much has really changed? You and your wife are intimate less often, true, but she seems grateful for the lack of attention. Or at least she doesn't mention it very much. She hasn't actually complained. It was painful when she asked you to buy her sexy underwear for her birthday because you could tell at that moment that she was trying to convey to you her noticing the change in your appetites and that maybe she did miss some of it. But you quickly dismiss this; she probably just read about it in a magazine or one of those ridiculous self-help books she's always dragging home. If she really wanted to help your marriage she should have done it five years ago when you begged her to figure out how to be the woman you fell in love with. You and she even went for a couple of counseling sessions but then stopped, by mutual agreement, because it didn't seem to be getting anywhere. She's put on a couple of pounds, looks more like her mother, hates a lot of your friends, and only wants to talk about stuff you've been over a thousand times.

How can you do this? How can you love this other woman and leave her alone at night while you sit with the remote in your hand and flick through stations until you can bear to go to bed? How can you exist knowing that the woman you sleep next to, whose warm body you still find yourself holding every morning out of habit, is being betrayed? You thought, briefly, that you were doubling the pleasure and possibilities of your life. Now you see that you have done quite the opposite: you have cut them in half. Your whole self is never in one place. One late night, you realize that "remote control" would be a good name for your autobiography. And you realize that among everyone you betray, you betray yourself the most.

And as for you, the wife?

Women who can't attract men like your husband disapprove of men like your husband. He's what you always wanted. You married him--got him, won him, caught him, however you want to describe it--you're his wife. His only wife.

When you're next to him in bed you want to make sure he's not dreaming of someone else. Sometimes if he sighs or moans you want to nudge him with your elbow or kick him, ever so lightly, in the shin. You don't do that, of course, but you look at him so intensely that, even in his sleep, he turns away. This happens even after thirteen years of marriage and three children, all of whom look like him.

Sometimes you worry. You stay awake looking out the window and into your own reflection most of the night. You're worried that, yes, you're his wife, but that other women will be, might be, already are, his lovers. But surely that wouldn't change anything? How can it matter? After all these years, after all you've shared, after everything you've been through, how can it matter? You'll be buried next to each other, you're his only wife, you have children and will one day have grandchildren, how can anything else matter?

You don't even want to let him know how much he means to you. You kid him, tease him, push him away, ask him who else would ever put up with him? But you know that there is a waiting list. Other women would indeed put up with him, even now. He is the cool moon blocking the heat and light of normal affections. He's the penumbra, the licking edge of fire around the black circle of blocking surface in the eclipse. He's the one who usually gets away. You know this even, or especially, when you've got him, even if you've had him for thirteen or even thirty years. Especially.

No wonder your friends disapproved thirteen years ago. They all disapproved, even as they circled him, sniffing around his scent the way wild dogs circle a fierce but trapped animal. Your mother, however, liked him. So did your father, although your father seemed a little suspicious at your good fortune. Your mother drank a little too much at the wedding and told you that you'd have to keep a tight hold on a man like that to keep him home at night. This did not reassure you, but it made you feel good nevertheless. Here, finally, was praise from your mother. You won first place. In your marriage, the most important rite of all, you did better than your mother. Certainly you will have a happier marriage, a more devoted husband, than she managed to have.   Right?

Right?

He saw you and smiled and that was it. You rolled up your sleeves and made a life together. You've done a good job.

So why isn't it easier? Why all these doubts?

The phone rings and when you answer, the person on the other end hangs up. He has a locked drawer in his desk. He has a code to his email that you don't know. He has a bank account without your name on it. Maybe he has a post-office box--just for work, he tells you--but he can get mail there that you can't get hold of. He spends part of each day away, even on the weekends when you've told him over and over he needs to be there for the kids. There are parts of his life you know very little about. He stays up later than you, or goes to bed much earlier. One way or another, you don't fall asleep holding hands and talking over the future the way you once did. He's too tired now, and so are you, and there is mostly silence.

He's pretty much the same age as you but you feel much, much older. You hate to hear yourself nagging or whining or complaining, but you can't help it. You get the feeling that he'd like to walk out on you. To tell the truth, there are days you'd walk out on yourself if you could. You feel like a bully, like a punitive grade-school teacher, like his mother, like a wife from an old situation comedy or even an old-time movie drama.You feel like a wife.

Like a first wife.

Post Valentine's Day Review

Did you get what you wanted?

Now, I don't ask you this question every Sunday morning, do I? So what's special about today? It's the day after St. Valentine's Day! For some of us, this means it should be St. Jude's Day (Patron Saint of Lost Causes) because it is the day that makes you want to gnash your teeth and cry out to the heavens "Oh why did I let myself get suckered into the belief that for once, just once, I'd have a decent Valentine's Day?!" Yes, Valentine's Day is a silly, commercialized, depersonalized, frivolous, and socially daft institution; so what? I was still secretly hoping for a mailbox filled with red envelopes, roses delivered during class, and a huge box of chocolates with an ostentatious ribbon on the outside.

My husband is actually pretty good with Valentine's rituals. I hope it's not only because I start leaving subtle little hints around the middle of January (after he's just breathed a sigh of relief at having remembered my birthday). My subtle hints include huge notes to myself (wink, wink) plastered on the fridge which read something like "Remember to buy Valentine's card for Michael!!" Obviously I'm not looking for spontaneity here, I'm looking for an easy way to keep us both happy. I know women who buy their husbands cards for these husbands to write out and give back to these same women (they better give them back to these same women. . .) but I've never had to go that far. No, Michael does a good job of keeping the Valentine's flame burning, albeit on a back-burner.

Because Valentine's Day is just not a big deal for him. When I talk about it, he regards me with the same indulgent false smile he might use if a nut sat next to him on the subway. What's the big deal? Why do I let myself get manipulated emotionally by Hallmark? Why should cocoa manufacturers worldwide twist my personal life around their collective finger? Why not be content to weave romance into our everyday lives and leave it at that? He believes this emphasis on February 14th is a plot, maybe even a conspiracy, among women to get nice guys such as himself tangled up in our blues.

He may be right. Something like eighty-percent of all Valentine's cards are sold to women. There are, increasingly, whole lines of cards designed for women to send to other women--not female romantic partners, mind you, but just ordinary friends--as sort of compensatory items in recognition of the fact that girls just want to get cards on V-day.

There should also be, I think, a line of belated- Valentine's cards to be bought and sent on days like today-- in order to rectify any imbalances that might have occurred. More terrifying and heart-breaking than not getting a card yourself is getting a card from someone who wasn't on your list.

Remember this from grade school? Remember the kid who, like Charlie Brown, seemed to be perpetually forgotten? There should be casualty-lists; there should be Valentine's triage for such cases. I hear from friends with young children that in today's enlightened elementary schools, everybody gets cards--that the kids create and give their cards to every member of their class. I'm glad to hear it. This seems far more humane than our barbaric practice back in the '60s of buying press-out prefab slips and sneaking them into hands of only a few of our tiny cronies, thereby constructing an atmosphere of creepy self-congratulatory elitism which leads in adult life to such savage practices as grant applications and the possibility of post-tenure review.

Not that I'm bitter.

Actually, having said all this, I must admit to liking Valentine's day. Like Thanksgiving, it's a day I see mostly as an excuse to eat and indulge various appetites; chocolate and champagne are a nice combination, let's face it, even if you have to buy them for yourself. And, as part of the conspiracy team, I do usually get a lot of cards--yes, from my girl friends--because I send a lot of them. I'm thrilled to see more and more really funny cards out there, ones from the likes of cartoonist Nicole Hollander (whose "Sylvia" character is the best thing since chocolate and champagne) and Cathy Guisewite, whose irreverent but understanding perspectives on the holiday (and on life) are perfectly geared to those of us who know better but still hope to get a candy heart or two. Certainly laughter and Valentine's day make the perfect couple.

And if you didn't get what you wanted? Never mind. There's always next year, when you can start leaving those notes on the fridge in November if necessary. You can buy an armful of cards today to give out next year, you can eat half-price chocolate, and you can find for yourself what no one else could locate for you-- the discovery of what you're looking forward to so that next February 15th you'll wake up with a smile on your face, no matter what.

Knock on Wood

Knock on wood, I'm not superstitious. That doesn't mean, however, that there aren't just a few little rituals I take seriously. By "seriously" I mean that they take up several warehouses of emotional space in my life.

I make deals with myself all the time. For example, I have promised myself that when I finish this column I will go downstairs and eat, without guilt, all the remaining brownies in the Tupperware container (last count: three and a half). I can therefore make myself sit here at the screen because there is the little voice whispering "Just a couple of hundred words and then, wow!, three whole brownies and a small piece as a special delicacy"). Other writers have sexy or ethereal muses breathing life into their words; I have Julia Child.

If I make myself get the car washed, I can buy a lottery ticket. If I can bring myself to Armour-All the vehicle (a process adored by so many men they look forward to warm Saturday afternoons when this can be accomplished, whereas I see it as the equivalent of getting my ear-wax removed) I can treat myself to the purchase of a new lipstick.

If I grade all the papers from one entire class without swearing aloud, I get to use in my pen the annoying peacock blue ink that everyone in the nation despises, but which I for some reason adore, on the second batch of essays.

I used to do this sort of thing with unnerving regularity when I was in school. I'd make a bet with myself--if this station plays " Taxi" by Harry

Chapin before I leave this morning, then they won't give a pop-quiz in geometry--and I was certain I'd found the right way to predict (although not determine) the future. "If he doesn't call by eight this evening, then he's definitely seeing Fiona" was also the sort of equation I set up in my head. "If I don't pick up the phone by the time I count five hundred, then I don't really like him" went along the same lines. It was one way of making the chaos seem less terrifying.

Some folks do this for even more serious issues, making various pacts with the Cosmos (the great unknown in the universe, not the team or the diner, you cynics) in order to prophetize their destiny. They seem to shake hands with the Heavens, saying "If I do this, then You'll have to do that" as if God was offering a warranty. My grandmother, who interpreted religion very much her own way (she made it up) didn't go to Mass regularly, but insisted on having pictures of saints everywhere: in the bathroom, in the kitchen cupboards, in the linen closet (as if to pay homage to St. Springmaid, patron of fresh towels). If you dared to ask her about this eccentric practice, she'd whack you immediately on the back of the head, declare you a heretic, and shake her head with her eyes closed in sincere disapproval. Some of these religious pictures came out of old calendars or were clipped from magazines, but that didn't matter. As far as my grandmother was concerned, they watched out for all of us. The older I get, the more I congratulate her on her methodology; everybody did okay. Who's to say she wasn't right?

My friend Beth's mother called all of her children every evening to wish them a good night. This got a little old for Beth in college, but those calls are one of the things she misses most about her mother now that her mother's gone. Apparently the calls didn't keep her mom alive, just made her happier while she was. She once told Beth it was "like tucking you all in at night" and it helped her sleep. I hope it still helps.

Other rituals are less charming. I once knew a man who believed that if he spit on the tracks, the train would arrive sooner. I never wanted to be near him when he ordered food at a busy restaurant. I knew a young woman who thought that if she simply left the television on at all times she was protecting herself against thieves; she used to leave the back door unlocked, for example, but thought that even local robbers wouldn't be foolish enough to enter a home which was occupied. They would be tricked, by hearing voices, into thinking the family was home; that most families don't sound like either Ted Koppel or the cast of Seinfeld didn't occur to her. Thieves can be satiric, it seems: they stole her television. I heard about another young man whose ritual involved moving from apartment to apartment every time the refrigerator needed defrosting; he felt this would keep him footloose and fancy-free. Basically it kept him ice-free, nothing more, but he swore that his independence depended on moving from place to place.

Maybe that's what these pacts do: get us moving, somehow, into the future. Promising myself that I will shed a few pounds, for example, I find that I'm thinking about the new suit I'll buy for the spring. I picture something luxurious, diaphanous, and unmitigatedly feminine. I'm so taken by the idea of myself as a sort of Merchant-Ivory heroine that I go downstairs, have a cup of coffee and a few brownies. And I promise myself that after I finish these off, I'll really get back to work.

Division

I am twenty-two and have gone to England to be with a boy. We live in a small set of rooms across the street from the university. I could, and did, spend hours looking out the windows over the flower boxes filled with dusty plants, seeing whether I could spot him, coming or going to a class. It became a game for me, like being a hunter or fisherman, seeing whether I could catch him unawares. My attention was poised like a lasso; in months of this project, only five or six times did I actually see him, walking along oblivious to my sticking gaze, books under the arm, face averted from the winds that blew across the open quadrangle that stamped the center of campus.

Why was I sitting by a window all those hours? There were other places, after all, beckoning. A bookstore, marble and granite like a museum, was down the street. Sometimes I would go there to look at volumes whose authors ranged from A to Izzard. I rarely had a chance to get past the first half of the alphabet. Occasionally I had money in my pockets, made by infrequent bits of freelance work, "piece work" as he called it, which made it sound as if I were making paper flowers or stitching buttons. When I had money I would go to a cafe and get a cup of tea, put my hands over the cup to stop the steam from stealing all the heat. I would sit with a paperback spread open for protection, and I would manufacture tales of unhappy love affairs or clandestine meetings between the pairs of people neatly placed at other tables. These two, I would think, met on a train to Paris over a year ago and have still not slept together. That is why she moves her hands so gingerly away from his. These three are jealous of one another. Both those women like him. Both decide to make him choose in this public place to avoid a scene. The man is jealous that the women have planned so elaborately without him.

But usually I had no money so I stayed in the room, sitting at, or on top of, a big brown desk by the window. The boy's presence marked the days like punctuation. A phone call from him was like a comma, a visit was like a full stop. Although we lived only across the street, he did often telephone, almost as if he wished I were further away like other men's girlfriends, and had an existence apart from the window across the street, which was close enough to wave to, had he chosen to wave.

"You really don't have a life, do you?" He said this one day when he'd found me taking a nap, found me sullen from too much sleep in the middle of the afternoon. "Are you just going to sit up here in this room and wait for me like some pet, some little creature I have to take care of?" His voice remained mild and well modulated. "You're always watching for me like a witch out of the window."

"I do no such thing," I protested.

"Don't lie. I see you. My friends see you, for God's sake. You make me ashamed of you." He turned abruptly and left. The window, which had been open, slammed shut. Such actions are never accidental. Accident implies a lack of intention. Things without intention never do very much damage in the end.

Still I stayed.

A few days later I read a story in the paper about a woman who tried to smuggle herself across a border by stuffing herself in a suitcase. Her husband, privy to this plan, found her dead, of course, on her arrival. I could imagine the woman's face; she must have had other people help her. They must have told themselves that it would work. What was the husband thinking? Why was he safely across? What made him leave his wife behind? Did he really want to see her again? I kept reading the papers over the next few days, hungry for further information but the story was dropped. She was gone.

On the third, or maybe the fourth, afternoon after I'd read the story I began to pack my things. I packed away towels, clock, toothbrush, nightgowns, radio, iron. On second thought I left the iron. I had bought it to do his shirts. By virtue of this, it belonged to him.

He seemed strangely in love with me as I was telling him I had to go; he kept saying he loved me as I explained I had to leave. He hadn't said those words in months and months, and here he was, saying them now, in apparent gratitude at my departure. He did not ask me to stay, nor did he ask why I was leaving. Picking up my suitcase to carry it down the stairs he looked over his shoulder to give me a smile that would have broken my heart but that was no longer possible. I smiled back, serene as a nun, cool as cloth.

I moved ahead of him, walking like a judge's daughter. He wanted me because I was leaving and because, by leaving, I made him feel he didn't know me. It was all very simple and I worked it out in my head, like long division, while we waited for my train.

After The Fall

I grew up falling in love with every professor I ever had, including the ones who looked like extras from the bar scene in Star Wars. There was no common denominator between them except for the fact that they stood up in front of classrooms where I sat, patient among rows of similarly enthralled and ripely under-age students. There were women on the faculty where I went to college, but not many, and besides, I wasn't particularly interested in taking their classes. I'd had plenty of women teachers all the way through school. Nice enough, I figured they offered nothing exotic. A guy in a tweed jacket, complete with wry smile and a knowing look: now that was exotic.

If only I'd known that, at least up until 1985 or so, there was a fashion memo issued to all male would-be academics saying that they had to own at least one tweed jacket (preferably bought in England while they were doing a bit of research), one old, softly worn but brilliantly clean white shirt (washed by whose hands? I didn't allow myself to wonder), and one matching sardonic, wistful, perceptive hint of a smile to be brought out on infrequent but meaningful occasions, a smile that we looked for, longed for, and recorded in our notebooks.

And if only I'd known that the likes of me were cheaper by the dozen. Wiser men would have ducked when they saw us all getting off the train. We were every precocious, smart-mouthed, independent nineteen-year-olds in tight jeans and faded tee-shirts. There were an army of us and we eagerly (not to say hungrily) invaded campuses around the country every fall. In the fall we yipped and played like a litter of puppies, tossing each other around, pairing up and parting ways.

Things change, of course, after the fall.

After the fall we started looking towards the grown-ups. We discovered favorite professors. We took first one, then more, of their classes. We brought cups of coffee to student conferences, and we met them late in the afternoon in the offices that took on new shadings towards sunset. They were, quite effortlessly and naturally, brilliant. They were concerned about the fact that not all of our peers were as insightful and wise above our years as we ourselves seemed to be. They were slightly sad about the way their own work was going, and there was a hint that this pall of melancholy also fell on other parts of their lives they were too discreet to mention. They were disappointed in the lack of camaraderie among their colleagues, and puzzled that we, more than anyone, seemed to understand them.

We did independent studies. We found out more about their personal lives. We had a beer or two after the term was over to celebrate. There were longer silences, less talk, better papers, more research, higher achievements, and new goals. We wanted them to fall in love with us, or barring that, desire us. "See how extraordinary we are, dammit!" we wanted to shout. "See how different we are from everybody else! Recognize us! Know our names! Pick us!" What could they do, these poor souls? We had youth, urgency, vitality, and--make no mistake about it--firm flesh on our side (not to mention on our front and our back).

Why shouldn't they take us up on what was sometimes an almost explicit offer? After all, we'd been doing our reading. John Updike told us that "[G]entle and knowing defloration had been understood by some of the younger, less married faculty gallants as an extracurricular service they were being salaried to perform." One of Philip Roth's heroes imagines lecturing to the students about "the undisclosable--the story of the professor's desire, "where he makes clear that he finds "our classroom to be, in fact, the most suitable setting" for the "accounting of my erotic history." We knew it wasn't all fun and games. We'd read Villette, we'd read The Prime of Miss Jean

Brodie, we'd read Middlemarch; hell, we'd read Lolita. It wasn't like this was something new.

Not only had we been reading; we'd been observing. Lots of professors had married their former students; the faculty wives we'd meet were often once graduate students themselves. That they now seemed to be given to typing and child-rearing, making sandwiches for parties that were devoured without appreciation by hordes of other women's grown children didn't make us envy them any less. They'd married the teacher. They'd won the prize. They'd have for their very own those wonderful figures who wove magnificent patterns of understanding out of indecipherable texts, who could impart to them the mysteries and sad beauty of the ages. (Occasionally it was male students who'd married female professors, but that was as rare as being assigned a book written by a living woman author in a modern novel course). Most often young women married the older men who'd held in their eyes the promise of vast horizons of knowledge and pleasure.

Except that it doesn't work that way. Marry the teacher, you end up with the person. The teacher doesn't belch or fart; the person does. The teacher doesn't get cranky if dinner is late, the teacher doesn't want to watch a rerun of Weekend at Bernie's , the teacher doesn't mispronounce the name of a fine wine or embarrass you by not knowing that Bono is the lead singer for U-2 and not a guy married to Cher. Fay Weldon's comment in Down Among the Women, when one of her younger characters (kissing a man nearly forty years her senior), is tickled by the thought of how much of life he has seen, is appropriate here. The narrator cautions us: "It isn't her desire that is stirred, it is her imagination, but how is she to know this?" The point about the difference between desire and imagination mirrors the one about the confusion between loving the profession and loving the professor.

We were smart enough to know better, but we didn't. All right, all right, enough with the "we." I was smart enough to know better, but I didn't. I thought that the closest I could get to being the teacher was loving the teacher; I thought that the closest I could get to playing school was playing doctor with somebody who taught school. Following certain professors around for a couple of semesters at a time, I'm quite certain I made some of them feel as if they were the Clint Eastwood character in Play Misty For Me . They might well have signed up for witness protection programs just to get me out of their front rows.

I tried to make it hard to say "no." Granted, I wanted to be loved for myself alone and not my yellow hair (or whatever color it was that year), but I wasn't against perfuming said hair if it would help get me attention. And I wanted their attention and approval, not a better grade. I was pretty secure about being a good student; I wasn't secure about being pretty and a good student. I wanted a professor who would happily grade me on my life and recommend me for the highest award: himself. That these gentlemen were more or less interchangeable didn't strike me as odd at the time.

Thank God, for all concerned, that at one point I ended up taking a required class where there was a woman in the front of the room. The professor was brilliant. She was charming, magnetic, funny, wise, and astute. I leaned forward to hear her every word and wasn't conscious about whether or not my face was at a flattering angle. I sat in the front row without wondering whether I should cross my legs. I met her for coffee at eight o'clock in the morning with cornflakes in my hair, having run out of the dining hall to make our appointment on time. I looked at her with adoration, not thinking "Boy, would I like to go home with her" but instead thinking "Boy, would like to do what she does for a living." And so I have.

You'll accuse me of discrimination, of male-bashing, of sexual favoritism as egregious and damaging as that perpetrated by the worst of the bad old system. But it isn't so: I am grateful and eager to believe that few young women were as needy and flirtatious as I, and delighted to believe that things change for the better, that the men and women teaching in the classrooms are respectful in all ways of those who are there to learn. I believe--because I have seen it--that male professors can encourage, inspire, nurture, and support their women students without ever casting a shadow of inappropriate sexuality, and that the increasing number of women academics can do the same with the young men who pass through our offices. But it remains true that education, if it's done right, involves an intense and lasting link between two human beings. That link, however, doesn't have to be the first in a chain of mismatched sexual couplings we drag around through life. That moment of connection can instead lead to what happens when we translate our desire into a love of the subject, or the text, or the way the light hits a four o'clock window in a November classroom.

It's My Party. . . .

I'm writing this a long time before you're reading it, so that means I can say whatever I want. Tomorrow night we're having a party and that's just fine with me. I would have invited even more people but Michael said we had already exceeded our limits. He hinted darkly that the rural equivalent of the building superintendent, dorm representative, or Mother Superior would be coming over to say we had to send some guests away, explaining to us that (as Thomas Hardy would say--bonus points if you can name the novel--) We Are Too Many.

Instead we've invited a small circle by my calculations and a rather larger circle by his; whatever your own sense of geometry, imagine -- along with us --that this is a mid-sized group. We're expecting a lot, but by no means all, of the folks we know and like.

So I'm thrilled and Michael is, shall we say, a little bit nervous. This is how we work with parties: he worries about it and plans it, while I--in sharp contrast-- wing it. After all, I tell him, it's a party --organized frivolity, a home-made carnival. It's an occasion set aside deliberately for nothing else besides having a good time. This is not a trick: it's supposed to be a pleasurable experience. And he'll flash me his classic wry smile as soon as I start to make this argument.

This argument, of course, is almost exactly--to the syllable-- what he tells me whenever we embark on a vacation. These are --almost to the letter --the precise words he uses to reassure me as I'm saying my rosaries while we board the plane. As we prepare to enter what I think of as the tunnel of impending doom, and what others refer to as the airline terminal, I am stutteringly anxious that everything in the universe will unravel during our absence. Michael then proceeds to tell me in soothing and absolutely trustworthy language that I am wrong to fret, that everything will be fine, and that I'll have a good time once we're on our way. And so far he's been right.

But obviously I'm not doing as well in the reassuring-patter field. Although I try to tell him the same thing about parties, obviously I haven't mastered the "soothing and absolutely trustworthy language" part yet because he still torments himself about everything that could possibly wreck the party.

Maybe nobody will show up. Maybe we told people the wrong date, or the wrong time. Will we be left, sitting alone in the gloom, surrounded by bowls of uneaten treats? Maybe it'll rain and we won't be able to go outside; maybe it won't rain and people will be unwilling to come inside. Maybe our various groups of friends won't get along and will break into clumps, divided along political lines, or gender, or religious affiliation. (Like somebody's going to yell, "Okay, all the conservative female Methodists: meet over here by the Cheese Doodles.")

So how do we reassure ourselves? Some customs you can establish early and some things you can prepare in advance. In our case, we ritually stockpile approximately (let's give a rough guess) oh, about 278 times what we need of everything in the universe we could possibly (even in terms of remote cultures) be expected to provide our guests: chips, nuts, cookies, salsa, dip (both recognizable and unrecognizable flavors), napkins, candles, sweet wine, dry wine, seltzer, cake, baguettes, cheddar, double-glouchester with chives, brie, coffee (decaf and regular), crunchy vegetable bits, muffins, cheesecake, mints --as well as exotic delicacies (care of, naturally, the brilliant chefs from Husky Trail; trust me, I didn't make them) such as fabulous stuffed grape leaves and exquisite taramasalada. I only buy stuff we actually enjoy because usually we end up eating most of it, our guests being polite folk who have more than likely eaten at one or two points within the preceding weeks and therefore have no need to hoover up the tidbits as if they were a bunch of hyenas at a kill.

Let's put it this way: nobody leaves our house hungry. Some guests have needed to be rolled down the driveway because they're so full. Others have had to sit down and breathe deeply of the night air on the way to their vehicles. I particularly love when people take food home with them. Maybe they take it directly to the landfill (what do I know?) but it still makes me feel like I'm connected to the family parties back in Brooklyn. If you left my grandmother's house without a brown grocery bag full of food, you were either insulting her ("Whassa matter, you don't like my cooking anymore?") or you were sick ("He doesn't feel so good, I guess, because he ate nothing except those t-bones and the potatoes"). Our guests don't leave hungry, and I think I can say in all sincerity that they usually leave having had a good time.

Maybe the best part of the party, however, is in the cleaning up, when a couple of folks who have stayed late start helping bring the dishes to the sink, start making a second pot of coffee, and start talking about who said what, and "do you remember that story that she told? How did it end?" and "I had no idea that those two knew each other," and "wasn't a riot to see him dance," and "they seemed to be in good shape," and "wasn't it nice to see them again?"

And maybe the very, very best part of tomorrow evening will be when Michael will dry the final dish and say, "Now, you see? There was absolutely nothing to worry about," and I'll flick him with my tea towel, and we'll laugh.

Romance on the Rocks

On this first Valentine's Day of the new millennium, we should celebrate the fact that ROMANCE has branched out. You can fall head over heels for almost anything these days and deem it a passion.

There are guys who have a passion for golf, women who adore tennis, men who cherish their cars, and women who idolize books. There are people who sigh over antique glass and those who weaken in the presence of gourmet food. The hearts of some beat faster when foreign travel is mentioned; others bat their collective eyelashes at the very thought of the lottery, or the internet, or The Sopranos. There are couples so absorbed in perfecting the techniques of formal entertaining--getting the place settings exactly right, making flawless cocktails, choosing the ideal appetizers--you could write a sweepingly poignant novel about them titled "The Bridge Mix of Madison County."

This is not, however, what you hope will happen when you're dreaming of your future at age seventeen.

When you're very young, you fall in love with a god or goddess (if you're lucky, it'll be one of the cute gods, not one the one who rules over Hades or has three heads filled with snakes, etc.). In other words, as a youth, you fall for an unattainable ideal. When you're more mature, you fall in love with a person: "Sure, he has only one eye in the middle of his forehead," you'll rationalize, "But he never forgets my birthday." When you're Too Mature For Your Own Good, you fall in love with, well--almost anything that captures and can hold your attention for more than five or six minutes. "Goddess, schmoddess," you'll hear mature folks say, "Just so long as she can drive at night."

Since I just had a birthday, and since you're not getting any younger yourself, I'll just go ahead and assume that we're all in the Too Mature For Your Own Good category and proceed. Let's see how we can refigure the idea of romance on this holiday so that it slips out of its old, narrow, confining and confined compass and apply it to passions other than those falling under the heading of "kissy-kissy."

The very idea of romance has evolved, as it were, into a series of wide-ranging affections. We grow attached to different objects of desire as we get older--and I'm not just talking about switching partners à la Michael Douglas. "Tsk-tsking" in the manner of married women everywhere when I heard the news of Douglas's engagement to some dark-haired young lady, I asked my husband why the star would marry a girl not even half his age. Without looking up from his paper, my husband replied "Because he can."(I'm trying not to take it personally. I'm also considering the purchase of a small dog.)

Perhaps I've plucked Michael Douglas from amid the herds of older men falling for younger women because I remember him as the romantic hero in a movie I adored called ROMANCING THE STONE, where he played opposite Kathleen Turner. (The film was released, by the way, in 1984. That was 16 years ago. That means his current fiancee was somewhere between, oh, seventh and eighth grade. Not that I'm bitter.) He was a dashing, romantic (not to mention age-appropriate) hero for Turner's character and ROMANCING THE STONE was enormously popular.

So let's apply the title of that movie to our new picture of romance: instead of being focused on some elusive object of transitory affection or centered on a long-standing relationship with a partner of many years, what you long for, dream about, and desire takes on new shapes as you grow up and grow older. This means you become involved in Romancing--applying the principles of infatuation-- to anything that takes your fancy.

Some of the newer guises worn by Romance might be surprising.

ROMANCING THE CHROME--Cars

There is strikingly similar program devoted to automobiles (yes, it is true that we watch way too much t.v. at our house....). The fixation of the masculine mind on cars, however, is not a recent one. The songs of the early 1960s prove this: men were composing lyrically intricate ballads extolling the myriad glories of the "GTO," the "409" and the "little Deuce Coupe" while girls were whining high-self-esteem numbers such as"I Will Follow Him," and "Love Has No Pride" and "Rescue Me." These babes did not know that their boyfriends found sticky emotional life less engaging than, for example, stickshifts. Guys who couldn't remember your last name could, however, provide precise information on the year and color of the cars, in addition of course to stats on horsepower, driven by every male in his age group within a three-mile radius.

While we're at it, consider the parallels between car magazines and girlie magazines. Let's not even get into the idea of headlights and tailpipes. Ever notice that publications devoted to the exposure of intimate details concerning female anatomy often include sexy pictures of cars, mirroring the fact that publications devoted to the intimate details of automotive life often include sexy pictures of women? How about the fact that photographs of vehicles in car magazines resemble photographs of women in skin magazines--the doors of the cars opened slightly and at provocative angles, the hoods raised so you can just peek underneath, everything carefully lighted and surrounded by lushly furnished backdrops?

ROMANCING THE ZONE--Diets

Not that we women don't cherish our own romantic ideas concerning certain absurdities of contemporary life. A lot of otherwise sensible women carry a massive encyclopedia of statistics in their heads--not about cars, but about calories. They put all their hopes into a diet-scheme the way they might have once pinned all their hopes on Prince Charming: they will be transformed, rescued, revitalized, and they will live happily ever after. The Diet of the Day has replaced the Beau of the Month. Such gals will be swept off their feet by the hype and believe wholeheartedly that they will be transfigured into a new, almost unrecognizable version of their old dowdy self. The idea of the fairy godmother has been replaced by the idea of Suzanne Somers--or Richard Simmons.

I'm particularly fearful of the evangelical-type of dieter, the one so caught up by her obsession that she feels compelled to "share" her good fortune. Watching a woman who has found a regiment she believes will keep her at a size six is like watching your sister schmooch on the couch with her first boyfriend. You might be happy for her, you might even be envious, but you are in no serious hurry to have all the gory details explained to you. Especially if her tastes are radically different from yours.

The romantic glamor that people associate with love can be associated with weight loss--except that loyalty to the diet plan is often much fiercer and more fully developed than fidelity to the beloved. You can call somebody's husband a schlemiel and she'll laugh, but say her diet guru is a nut, she won't return your calls for weeks.

And guys are increasingly active acolytes in the religion of weight loss, which is not precisely what I had hoped for when I campaigned for equality. I had rather hoped it might mean that women could make as much money as men in the workplace, not that men as well as women would consume a whole lunch-hour telling me how to eat sprouts and astroturf--or cheese and bacon--in order to lose inches and live a better life through aggressively monitoring food intake. The dewy, glazed look of the One True Diet Believer resembles the innocent, uncritical, and ecstatic gaze of Juliet looking at Romeo, Victoria looking at Albert, or Barbra Streisand looking at James Brolin.

We need not stop here. Other examples include the following:

ROMANCING THE LOAN--Money

Certain types check their money every several minutes. I'm not talking about old guys who jiggle change in their trouser pockets or ladies who finger the dollar bills they're going to use to pay for the movie once the line gets moving--I'm talking about investors who log-on, speed-dial, or chain a personal broker to their wrist, simply in order to monitor their cash flow. They know whether the Dow is up, down, or running around in its pajamas. They eat, sleep, and drink risk management (mostly drink). The stimulating, perfumed scent of the potential Big Return is embedded in their hair and on their fingertips. They want to grab assets, lure credit into their arms, and invite capital upstairs to see their etchings.

ROMANCING THE TONE--Exercise

Then there are those who swoon over exercise regimes and fitness rituals, who spend their days dreaming of the moment they'll win the marathon-- or simply look like something other than a segmented insect while wearing Spandex. These people will fall in love with their own bodies. If you catch them looking at themselves in the mirror, you'll see that they give themselves a little smile and raise one eyebrow in a come-hither glance. You might even overhear a surreptitious chuckle or giggle at they check out their own backsides. They are coming on to themselves. (This might be filed next to or under another category--Romancing the Comb--of those who are obsessed with beauty-regimes and salon-based transformations).

Of course there are other possibilities as well: Romancing the Phone (for those whose entire lives center around fax machines, email cafes, cell phone conversations); Romancing the Loam (for those who put much of their vital energy in gardening and the cultivation of flowers, lawns, etc.); Romancing the Tomb (for those who spend their time threatening "If you don't listen to me this time, I'm changing the will and cutting you out of the plans for the funeral!"); and, of course, Romancing Alone (which we need not explain here but you catch the drift).

So here's a theory for the new century: possibly, just possibly, the important thing is not what you love, but that you love someone, some idea, even someTHING. Not that collecting Tupperware can surpass what Dante felt for Beatrice (Dante and Bea live in Bayridge and just celebrated their 50th wedding anniversary), or what Tristan felt for Isolde, or what Scarlett felt for

Rhett, and Ashley, and Frank Kennedy, and....well, you get the point. Good, or even bad, old-fashioned romance will always capture at least part of our imagination.

ROMANCING THE KNOWN --Old-Fashioned Romance

There is much to be said on behalf of the benefits of habit, even in romance. Couples love rehearsing early meetings, first dates, and the like. Not that this is always without stress. We have friends who have been married about thirty years-- to each other, no less--and naturally they remember the evening they met. This is no Cole-Porter-Experience, however, because they recently revealed what they both remember best about that magical first encounter. Both recall, in astonishingly vivid detail and with a great deal of relish, what LOSERS the other person's legitimate date for the evening happened to be. "The guy you came to the party with that night, remember, honey? Wasn't he the one wearing a shiny blue suit with an orange tie and pointed shoes? He was a real moron." "I don't remember that, sweetheart, but what I do remember was that the young lady you brought to the party--of course I'm using the word 'lady' loosely here, tee hee--was wearing a reddish-brown dress that was so tight it made her look like a Kielbasa on two legs. A rather short and stubby Kielbasa, but a Kielbasa nevertheless."

Asked what they themselves were wearing, they laugh. Each declares, with the blinking sincerity of participants in The Antique Roadshow when asked how much they think the object in their possession is worth, "I have NO idea." And they mean it. They are in the habit of teasing and flirting with each other and that, frankly, would be hard to match in terms of what romance has to offer.

But traditional romance is not the only thing that can fill our hearts or our happiest hours. When I lived in New York, one of my most elegant and elderly neighbors was inevitably accompanied by her small dog; he even accompanied her to the small private library where she volunteered three mornings a week. She adored the creature. She was forever buying him toys and warm little outfits. She served him only the finest foods and cleaned up after him without complaint. In casual conversation one day, she mentioned without irony that she'd been married and widowed twice and had three perfectly nice children, but she never really loved any of them more than she did her pet.

Perhaps in reaction to my rather shocked response, she calmly explained that she and Groucho (the aforementioned dog) lived in harmony, watched television together, ate at the same time, and that they would defend each other with their lives. She made up stories about Groucho's inner, albeit unspoken, emotions and worried what would happen if either of them died. She was neither lonely or pathetic, perhaps best illustrated by her parting line, said over her shoulder with an engaging smile, "I'm not this dog's master," she laughed gaily, "I'm his mistress."

I'm no longer surprised by the myriad forms that love pours itself into; the complex emotional and spiritual thirst it quenches is grateful whenever and wherever love is found, whatever object love's nourishing magic settles upon.

Just so long as it can drive at night.

The "C" Word: "Commitment"

Maybe we should have chosen a different word to describe what we want from those we adore.

Employing the term "commitment" when discussing relationships--not to mention pairing it with the "institution" when discussing marriage-- should give us pause. Dan Greenburg and Susan O'Malley, for example, consider the use of such language in their advice book, How to Avoid Love and Marriage. The authors wonder "What kind of word is 'commitment,' anyway? 'He was committed to an institution for the criminally insane.' 'She was committed to the federal penitentiary because she had committed manslaughter.' Right away you know that 'commitment' is not a fun word." They go on to offer an illuminating and edifying quiz, one asking the reader to choose the fun word from each of the following pairs:"Petting/Commitment;   French Kissing/Commitment;   One-night-stand/Commitment;   Cheap Thrills/Commitment."

Perhaps "commitment" is one of those gender-specific terms, one that gets itself all tangled up with individual definition even when those wielding it believe their meaning is clear. When a woman says she is in a "committed" relationship, for example, my guess would be that she believes the partnership is both honest and intimate, a monogamous coupling that will last a long time--maybe forever. Either that or she is dating an inmate. Or both.

When COUPLES use the word "commitment," however, I pay close attention. When married folks announce "we're committed to working it out" it means that one or both of them have already contacted lawyers. Did you ever hear two HAPPILY married people make such a statement? "We're committed to working it out" is right up there with the equally paradoxical declaration, "But we're just friends, right?" (When you're REALLY just friends with somebody, when there is no hint of romance, the declaration just doesn't come up. You don't have to emphasize this fact every time you meet. Most people don't walk into their office, say good morning to their co-workers, and then quickly add, "But we're just friends, right?" If they did, they would find themselves quickly "committed" to an "institution.")

But what about when the word "commitment" rolls off a man's tongue?

You can't blame men for being wary. Their use of the "C" word, however casual, will be scrutinized, taken out of context, and dragged through endless conversational vivisections until each of its ten letters is hopelessly frayed.

It is nevertheless interesting to locate the definition of the word when it IS used.

Here's the scene: we're at a large dinner party, seated next to folks we'd never met before, and enjoying everything thoroughly. The delightful couple on the other side of the table are mature, smart and charming. They are not married, despite their long romantic affiliation, and I have gleaned from her conversation that he, rather than she, is reluctant to make their courtship official by proposing marriage or offering any form of other public and lasting declaration.She has communicated this to me in the secret dinner-party code that women use during times of stress. Even though we have never met before, I have signaled to her my understanding, frustration, and sympathy for what she considers her unsatisfactory position.

The guys, meanwhile, are talking about the best rental car agencies to use when you travel in England and Ireland. They are happily and intensely discussing mileage and cost. So, in a less happy way, are we.

The conversation shifts as our host offers port to finish off the meal. The gentleman across from me declines; his ladyfriend accepts. I comment, all smiles, on this disparity. He explains, sighing, "I have to get up at five tomorrow morning to go fishing in Maine. I can't be late." I express surprise at the fact that he is cutting short a glorious evening only to get up before dawn, something he doesn't exactly sound enthused about, and he shrugs, "I can't back out now. I've made a COMMITMENT."

There it is, the "C" word. Ladyfriend and I lean forward, pupils dilated.

"Commitment?" I stutter, trying to draw him out from the protective shrubbery of polite conversation, "What do you mean? Can't you just back out if you don't want to go on this trip? Can't you telephone to say you simply can't make it?"

"No," he replied, all patient officiousness, "I cannot. As I said, I made a commitment."

"I'm sorry, I'm still not sure I understand," I pressed.

"You know," he explained as if to a child, "'Commitment.' As in PREPAID."

Ah, enlightenment.

Happy Valetine's Day.

Education

My C Minus

My French-Canadian mother didn't teach me any French. I'd learned to decipher the words she'd throw around when arguing with my Italian father (who, incidentally, didn't teach me any Italian) but these weren't exactly words you'd use in a classroom. If there was any discussion of "la plume de ma tante" it concerned an impolite reference to where you might place la plume. I did, however, take four years of high school French and found myself, at the start of my first semester in college, placed into a class designed for students of moderate ability who had studied the language for several years.

It was a great class. The teacher was absolutely brilliant--funny, savvy, smart, and secure--and I felt lucky. I felt so lucky, in fact, that I began to understand how much French I actually knew. Within the first couple of weeks, I started (for the first time in my life) to race ahead of some of my fellow students. The professor asked me to meet him for a conference whereupon he suggested, in all good faith and enthusiasm, that I'd be better off in a more advanced class. He thought it might be wise for me to transfer into the course he was offering, a class one level higher than the one I was already in. He thought I'd be more at home with more fluent students. I took his advice. Why not? I was enormously flattered and wanted to rise to the occasion. As if I were leaving to go to Paris itself, I bid adieu to my companions in the lower ranks and headed off into more demanding and tempting (if unfamiliar) territory.

I'm not saying it wasn't good advice overall; a gang of us in that advanced class got to know each other very well and have remained friends to this day. But I was way over my head in terms of the work; I could make myself understood when I spoke, but apparently this small talent deserted me completely when I tried to write. My essays came back full of green ink (the nice man avoided red, but the green was just as damning). I went to the language center tutors for advice. My boyfriend of the moment, a nice enough young man whose great virtue was patience, helped me straighten out the most basic of problems.

I got a C- for the course--the lowest grade I ever received during my twenty or so years of education--and even that was a gift. (For all the current sanctimonious rigmarole about grade inflation, I'd like to point out that, at least at private colleges, almost nobody--and I mean nobody--got below what was called a "Gentleman's C" because the institutions were too afraid to alienate the families of students who might give big bucks to the joint. Maybe things have changed. I'd be suspicious, however, of anyone who claims they have. Bucks is still Bucks, after all.) Anyway, mostly I was relieved to see that I didn't have to repeat the course. I knew I wouldn't do much better the next time around. I had simply skipped over what should have been an essential part of my education but unless I were willing to take months or even years to rectify the situation, I had to accept my failure. Even if the grade didn't quite declare it to the outside world as "failure," everyone around me knew the truth. And I knew the truth.

So I was disappointed in myself but grateful for the grade and for the professor's confidence (even if it was misplaced). Over the years I have grown increasingly appreciative of the experience of sitting in a class you love, working really hard, and still not being able to perform as well as you should. This hard-won perspective has made me into a better teacher, a more understanding adult (and, okay, into a traveler who mostly avoids Francophone countries).

We underestimate failure; we see it as "screwing up," or "messing around," or "not living up to potential." Sometimes, sure, it reflects all these.

But sometimes failure is simply the outcome of something we tried to do that we could not, even with real effort, accomplish. People fail even when they do their best, when they mean well, when they work hard, when they are eager to please others and themselves. Not everyone succeeds and no one succeeds all the time. Coping with failure is a crucial aspect of life, a course life offers for free. Many of us fail at failure, meaning that the very notion of it (not its consequences, but its very idea) is so devastating that one experience holds us back.

I loused up in French but did well in Failure. What was the lesson learned? So you failed; that's too bad. So now get on with the rest of what you're doing and do it as well as you can.

In Love With Libraries

I'm in love with libraries. Only during one phase of my life -- an unlikely one at that-- was I ever uncomfortable inside their walls.

You think it was when bricks were falling off the UConn library a couple of years back? No big deal. Bricks were popping off buildings on Madison Avenue like caps off beer bottles around the same time. Who noticed? Go back a few more years-- wasn't it the Hancock building in Boston that shed its windows the way a bird sheds feathers? Have you seen the Babbidge Library since they fixed it up? It's terrific: more welcoming, more comfortable, as well as easier on the eyes--and the spirit--than ever.

Sometimes things are bad; sometimes they get worse; sometimes they go on to get better.

Pretty much the same thing has happened in my relationships to libraries. In graduate school, when I was spending way too much time in basement rooms with fluorescent bulbs humming and crackling overhead (and that was just in my apartment....), I silently started resenting libraries, bitterly belittling them in my heart as tombs for useless thought, as mausoleums erected to preserve both the immaterial and the pointless. This was in marked contrast to my earliest memory: a summer afternoon, leaving a noisy house to walk to the local library.

Inside that building, quiet as a church or a hospital, I could relax and look around without fear of reprimand. Palpably different from the judgmental stillness of the cathedral or the anxious hush of a sick-room, a contagious sense of safety filled the library's rooms.This sense of safety is what I remember best. At the scaled-down children's desk, cherished because of its cartoonish size, I carefully arranged picture books across the pale wood table.

Once I started school, I spent even more time at the library. Unlike some kids, I didn't mind being assigned a research paper. I learned how to use the huge and intimidating microfilm reader which was sort of like learning how to operate heavy machinery designed by NASA. Eventually I decoded the processes whereby a regular person such as myself was permitted to have access to books usually reserved solely for use by Real Scholars. It was great: I felt like I was getting away with something.

Yes, the library at my undergraduate college was deservedly well-respected. What I remember best, however, is that at that pocket-size, imitation-Tudor style English Department library, tea and cookies could be bought for a chump change at four o'clock every weekday afternoon. This was wonderful. The idea of eating in a library was as illicit as reading a novel during a dinner party--it seemed eccentric and (in some unspoken-rule-breaking way) marvelous.

I continued to eat while studying and working at the library in New Hall, my college at Cambridge. That library was where I felt most at home during my years in England. I would sneak in a bag of crackers and small squares of sharp cheddar cheese, making absolutely sure that there were no crumbs left (my fear of library mice being strong and supported by powerful evidence). I was a devoted worker; my sin was, I believe, a venial one.

By the time I was working on my Ph.D., however, I was back living in New York, and tearing through bagel-and-fried-egg sandwiches before running up the steps of the NYPL. Maybe I'd simply had too much of it, but entrances into both large and small reading rooms became less inviting. There were days when I despaired; at certain low points, I harangued myself with the certainty that I was incapable of writing a laundry list, let alone a dissertation. Only after They Used to Call Me Snow White But I Drifted appeared in the card catalog (remember those?) did I start to feel at home again.

I have returned to being delighted by hours spent roving in the stacks. Mastering the internet has been amusing but I haven't fallen in love with it. In contrast, I have become desperately fond of interlibrary loan and regard it as my passport to libraries in, for example, other galaxies.

It's the weight of the book that calms me, the feel of the paper under my fingertips as I turn the page that grabs me. This pleasure is sharpened by the understanding that what I love at this moment has only been loaned to me. I can possess it fully but temporarily--sort of like life.

School Work

This one is for the folks who work in schools, especially for those students of mine who have headed out into the wild frontiers of classroom teaching:

--Here's to the teacher who understands that she can make or break the spirit of one of her students at any moment; who understands that each of her students projects the light or shadow of her legacy into the future.

--Here's to the teacher who can make his class smile--in recognition, in amusement, even despite themselves-- because they know his humor is a way of admitting them into the charmed circle of his knowledge. They'll remember his stories after they've forgotten his name.

--Here's to the teacher who pushes her students into better, stronger, and more original work by refusing to accept what is half-finished, half-right, or half-hearted. And here's to the teacher who understands that not everyone can be great at everything. (Specifically, here's to the math teacher I had in sixth grade who saw tears in my eyes and understood that even when I was doing my best I was going to do only adequate work. She helped me get to the point where "adequate" was just fine for both of us. Most importantly, she stopped me from torturing myself in an attempt to be something I could never be: perfect).

--Here's to the ones who stay after class when somebody needs to talk, or cry, or explain, or ask questions.

--Here's to the ones who show up for (at least some of) the school plays, concerts, games, and fairs--and who look like they're actually having a good time.

--Here's to the ones who read aloud: who breathe life into a passage, who mesmerize with language, who forever intertwine their voices with the words of a book.

--Here's to the coaches who get up on cold winter mornings and yell encouragement from the sidelines, who nurture and cheer, who advise and applaud, and who never bully, punish, or coerce. Here's to the ones who let everybody--everybody who shows up and who understands the game--play.

--Here's to the school nurse who hears more stories than she can ever tell, who mends what needs mending, whether obvious or buried, who soothes what needs soothing and who is trusted with the enormous task of deciding what to do when a child is hurt.

--Here's to the teacher who says "Go ahead, color outside the lines."

--Here's to the members of the custodial staff who come in during the empty times to tidy up the mess that life leaves; to the ones who make it easier to face the building every morning, who make it seem as if every day has a fresh start because the floors are clean and the window shades are opened.

--Here's to the teacher who fights for the right to teach a book others might try to erase from the list because it is too controversial, or too subversive, or too provocative; here's to the teacher who is willing to make the argument for art and ideas.

--Here's to the teacher who bothers to learn what his students are talking about: who occasionally watches television, who often reads the newspaper, and who has actually been known to listen to music recorded after 1975. (n.b.: he doesn't have to like it--he just has to have heard it).

--Here's to the teachers who learn their students' names.

--Here's to the teacher who makes it safe to be smart, who enjoys the challenge of a student who brings a new idea to the discussion and who rewards those who think rather than those who simply repeat what they've heard.

--Here's to the teacher who doesn't think kids are just dumber and lazier than they were in her day.

--Here's to the teacher who doesn't think sarcasm and contempt are appropriate methods of instruction.

--Here's to the teacher who could complete her own homework assignments and do well on her own tests.

--Here's to the teacher who knows what he's talking about and remembers why it's important.

--Here's to the ones who show up, day after day, and gladly teach.

wanted to keep them. I worried about being broke, about asking my father for cash, about the enormous number of loans I was taking out, about small debts to friends. In the middle of some anxious nights, I wondered how I became a foster-child of this affluent institution.

What remained entirely out of my reach was the polished look that comes from being a kid from a family with a solid financial and social foundation. We're not just talking good genes here, we're talking about something more complex, often referred to as breeding, a combination of inherited gifts and nurtured talents. As hard as it is to define, it is nevertheless essential to understand: people--not necessarily the irrefutably rich, but the socially and culturally privileged--have a distinct way of handling the world, as if they are simply overseeing what belongs to them. I didn't have this and I couldn't fake it.

I also couldn't name it until, in an independent study on the modern novel, I fell into a passage from John O'Hara's Butterfield 8: "all her life Emily had been looking at nice things, nice houses, cars, pictures, grounds, clothes, people. Things that were easy to look at, and people that were easy to look at; with healthy complexions and good teeth, people who had had pasteurized milk to drink and proper food all their lives from the time they were infants; people who lived in houses that were kept clean, and painted when paint was needed, who took care of their cars and their furniture and their bodies, and by doing so their minds were taken care of; and they got the look that Emily and girls--women--like her had."

I didn't have "the look," and so literally couldn't look at things from the same perspective. I had good grades and the stuff it took to get good grades. I had a bravado that often was mistaken for strength. I had a big mouth that was sometimes interpreted as self-confidence. And while I substituted swagger for poise and unashamedly used my sense of humor as a way to camouflage my almost perpetual discomfort, I couldn't fool myself or anyone else into thinking that Dartmouth was the kind of place that would have always let me in the front door.

Thirty years before my admission, half French-Canadian girls could never have been expected to do anything in Hanover but wash floors in the middle of the night and disappear, inaudible and imperceptible, before the owners of the place--the students--woke up. Half-Italian girls might have worked in kitchens or bars, or worked in the endlessly gray mill buildings leaning into New England's rivers. Girls like me, not so very long ago, would have lived in boarding houses, not dorms; they would have averted their eyes from college boys for fear of being thought too easy or too bold.

In retrospect, I think that I both exploited and evaded the confines of the role of working-class-kid on campus. True, I saw social and economic spikes everywhere and rushed to impale myself on them. But also, in time, I came to accept that the education and experience were mine--not just things that had been lent to me, like somebody's earrings or their car, to be returned undamaged and unsoiled at a later date. Finally, I know that only a good education could have prepared me to be a troublemaker. As a teacher at UConn, I see as one of my great obligations the need to pass this along.

A Dangerous Woman

Mrs. Luper was twenty-six, had gone to Holyoke, married her college boyfriend after a previous boyfriend had thrown himself out the window to die from his unrequited love of her, and had switched her major from medicine to English to accommodate the needs of her husband, Samuel, who was covetous of her time. She was going to be a great writer, maybe a poet, maybe a playwright, she hadn't decided which. We found this out on the first day of class in the tenth grade. It was 1973.

I remember looking at her from the bottom up: she was wearing bright yellow shoes, a short skirt and a striped top, enormous eye-glasses nearly eclipsing a small freckled face. Her hair was in a flip and she wore a headband the same lemon color as her shoes. This accessory secured for her the image of a life lived fully. I wanted to be liked by her immediately. I raised my hand at the first opportunity and while I do not recall the question, I know I meant it to be sophisticated yet disarming, meant to show her that I was a potential accomplice and ally. I was painfully and suddenly aware of my too-long skirt and too-fuzzy hair. I became aware of my bulk; she was tiny. I became aware of my loud voice; she spoke so softly it was difficult to hear every word and in this way she made the whole class lean forward. She was everything I wasn't and she became for me the image of everything I wanted to be.

To us, she represented to us everything that was charming and urbane and polished. She was dinner at ten and espresso and an apartment in

Lessons from School

Mrs. Pruitt was my first and second grade teacher. I loved her. She spoiled me by referring to me as "her sweetheart" and telling me that if she had a little girl she would have liked her to be like me. Pleasing the teacher was different at nineteen than at nine, but the dynamic was precisely the same. I wanted to be the teacher's pet.

I was a clever kid, one who had prepared rather carefully a series of bright and well-formed answers to the tepid questions handed to girls like myself. I was also bright enough to understand that, after puberty, it was simply not prudent to exclude the seductive dress--simply for good measure.

I kept adoring my teachers. In eighth grade I lingered after English class to talk to Mr. Tapp. He was all of 28 years old but let me tell you, that seems old when you're half his age, when you're fourteen. He asked me what I liked to do; as he spoke he was busy pulling down the afternoon shades, eclipsing all the natural light.

I said I liked "writing about love" even though I was still a child, still barely out of a play pen. I knew it would get a rise out of him; I wasn't sure, exactly, what would rise to meet me but I knew something would. In this case, God bless him wherever he is today, what rose to the occasion was his gentlemanly self. I sat cross-legged in my gypsy outfit, thriftshop skirt and hoop earrings, hair down my back like a woolly blanket, a poor man's junior Janis Joplin, willing if not eager.

But he was a gentleman and by today's standards, a hero. He didn't even make eye-contact with me, and of course his non-look left far more of an impression than his fingertips ever would have, or so I tell myself. I heard years later that he left teaching altogether, and was managing an electronics store. He only became a teacher to avoid the draft, anyway. That's the most intimate thing I found out about him that afternoon, the afternoon of the big shades.

This wasn't the first teacher I flirted with. I fell in love with every English teacher I had from sixth grade onwards. My seventh grade teacher, Mr. Trisco, had a handlebar mustache, wore pop-art ties the size of dinner plates, and looked like an illustration from a Peter Max poster. After the first day of classes, I wanted to be sure I learned his name right away, so I tried to figure out a way to remember it. Not knowing there was a word for mnemonic devices, I nevertheless convinced myself that I could remember his name by thinking that it was like a food shortening--Crisco -but with an "T."

When I next came into his class, I greeted him cheerfully, heart-pounding beneath my black Danskin leotard--and he asked me what I said. I replied, horrified, "I just said hi." "But what did you call me," he asked. "I called you Mr. Tazola, isn't that right?" I realized, of course, what I had done the moment I opened my mouth--substituted Mazola for Crisco, but I could hardly explain that to him--your name is like a cooking oil, but different-- I had sabotaged myself in my longing for his attention and approval--the best substitutes I could find for his true love--and so I pretty much shut up for the rest of the term.

But the most important thing I remember from school didn't come from a teacher. What is emblazoned across my memory, and which had actually been written across the top of my ninth grade black-and-white Composition notebook, is the phrase "Life is great, not easy." This was a phrase I heard everywhere because it was as close as we got to a "family saying."

My brother Hugo, six years older than I, had looked through my official science notebook, promptly crossed out "electron, neutron and proton" and substituted instead "fire, air and water," thereby exercising his prerogative of years to reconstruct my education. It was the beginning of something for me, my big brother's knowledge of crossing out, of permission to scribble across block letters, and print outside the lines.

I started writing across, but mostly, against the curriculum, the social script, and was often helped out of despair and away from anger by thinking "Hey, it's not supposed to be easy, remember?" I spent time wondering whether Einstein had a daughter. I spent time wondering how to change the world or at least make trouble. My weapons were a high wail of right answers, a tattoo of information. I was incandescent in my correctness.

It was crucial for me to come up with the right answer in those days. Not to be acknowledged as right, you understand : just to be heard.

Now I worry less about the rightness of answers and think more about how to ask an important question. One thing I do know: little has been easy. Much has been great.

Excess Baggage

I hadn't traveled much as a kid, and going to London at 20 was by far the biggest trip anybody in my family had taken since they all fled Sicily in 1909. Well, that's not strictly true; my older brother had bravely traveled much of the world by himself but you must remember that he was Older and a Boy so I could hardly use him as a role model. It's also true that my father got shipped off in a Liberator to bomb Germany in WWII, but he hardly enjoyed the trip. I left for London weighed down with amulets and various religious paraphernalia to guarantee a safe trip. I had one or two rosaries, assorted rabbits' feet, notes of support, a lucky necklace, and a hardcover copy of Gravity's Rainbow. Other wiser or more experienced students carried only sleeping bags, paperbacks, and backpacks. We choose our own baggage, I have since learned, but I wasn't aware of that in 1977. I took everything with me because I had no idea what to expect.

Along with the amulets, I carried the piece of paper from the Study Abroad office to reassure myself that this was all perfectly normal, but there were elements I found less than reassuring in this document. One of the items indicated that I might want a "rucksack". I figured that I wouldn't need this suggested and mysterious item because I didn't have a ruck on me. I was too embarrassed to ask what these words meant since they seemed self-explanatory to everyone but me.

My section of London looked about as quaint as Flatbush. It was also eighty degrees and all I had with me were fisherman knit sweaters and longjohns, along with other outfits I had packed in what was clearly a delirium: long skirts and glittering high heels. I heard people talking and laughing from the street below and it struck me as unbelievably odd that for everybody else it was simply Tuesday night. I left the light on when I finally slept. Why was I so unprepared for the differences I found?

I decided to do the only thing I could afford to do: walk. I walked to the law courts and admired the buildings. I walked to Kew Gardens. I walked down the Strand and went into bookstores, walked through the Regent's Park Zoo. I was thoroughly exhausted at night and could sleep without wondering every fifteen minutes what time it was "at home," and wondering what people were eating while I was eating Toad-in-the-Hole. During those first days I groped around as if I were exploring a dark cave, not realizing that I carried a light with me--even though I had packed badly.

One fine day I walked to the British Museum. I felt safe in museums, being a veteran of the Met, Museum of Natural History, and Brooklyn museums as a kid, so I immediately started searching for a place where I could buy a cup of coffee (usually my first stop). Then I walked past an illuminated manuscript of the medieval book, The Canterbury Tales.

Having studied this in one class or another, my attention was finally fully engaged by something outside myself. "Smalle birds Maken Melodye" I read, and my eyes filled with tears. This wasn't like anything I'd ever seen at home. This was Something Else, with a history longer than anything I could imagine. People had looked at this manuscript before it became required reading. These lusciously magnificent pages weren't hidden away in some small room for the exclusive and fetishistic gaze of serious scholars but were instead right there on the ground floor. Suddenly it felt as if there were enough of everything to go around. I knew, with smiling relief, that I wouldn't have to be too scared to be across the Atlantic anymore. I'd found a place of safety. If this manuscript could be safe here, then so could I.

Within a month I'd seen twelve plays, made good friends, and fallen in love with the city. But those first few days had as much learning as anything that followed, even if it wasn't part of the curriculum, even if what was necessary--a little courage, a little imagination, a little belief in the possibility of unforeseeable happiness--hadn't been listed as a suggested resource.

I left London with less baggage than I'd come with, and what I left behind was at least as important as what I took with me. I've heard the same stories from nearly every one who has ever lit out from home. You learn that you carry the ability to make a life for yourself wherever you are. It is a lesson that should never be underestimated; it is one of the few lessons on which we are all tested again and again.

What's A Nice Girl Like You Doing In a Place Like This?

My students and I were discussing the moment of the "irrevocable" in literature, that split-second when a character makes choices that define her role forever, those pivotal scenes when she chooses to act or think in a certain way thereby altering her destiny, moments which are especially powerful when the choice appears to be only of the smallest consequence at the time.

This morning's class got me thinking about the options and choices that have been thrown my way and I've come to the conclusion that the critical moment of my fate occurred when I was seven. In the second grade, I was cast in the role which would come irrevocably to define my function and position in the culture, which would come to establish my point of view in the academy, and which has, perhaps, provided the single most influential subtext underwriting my perceptions and actions for the thirty-four years since that momentous day.

In second grade I played The Cheshire Cat in our school's production of Alice in Wonderland.

Okay, so my pivotal moment isn't exactly up there with Scarlett O'Hara vowing "With my God as my witness, I shall never be hungry again" brought to us by Gone With the Wind or even with Lisa Simpson's crush on her substitute teacher brought to us by the Fox network. But don't assume it wasn't a big moment just because of that. For one thing, I had a great outfit, which, if I remember correctly, I insisted on wearing at all times throughout the run of the production--meaning that I wore it the night before the play and throughout the entire day, even after our half-hour of glory on the stage had passed-- and it is a credit both to my patient parents and the good citizens of my neighborhood that not once did anybody make a discourteous remark. To be perfectly honest, nobody noticed my costume, people dressed as animals being too familiar to provoke comment on the streets of major metropolitan areas.

To say I took my charge seriously is an understatement; I was determined to make the Cheshire Cat memorable. I wanted to live up to the costume. I wanted to please the teacher and I wanted to impress my peers. I hustled hard to get it right. Sometimes it's all too easy to forget or dismiss how hard little kids can hustle when they put their hearts into it.

To prepare for the role, I watched an animated adaptation which, as my good fortune would have it, was broadcast a few weeks before the play (this, you remember, was long before you could stick a tape in a VCR--you had to wait for things to come around on the t.v. and were dependent on a combination of luck and network schedules). I believe that the brilliantly cool Sammy Davis Jr. was the voice behind the cat's pink and purple cartoon image; I remember the character as wearing sunglasses and a beret, a very hep cat indeed. I learned the words to The Cheshire Cat's solo number instantly -- "What's a Nice Girl Like You Doing in a Place Like This?" --a tune which, as you might already feel confident in assuming, has remained my theme song to this day.

Not many photographs remain from my childhood but I do have one from the day of the second-grade's performance. The image imprints itself on the sepia inside of my eyelids even as I type this out: in it, I am smiling more broadly and am obviously happier than in any other single picture taken of me from infancy through high school. Forget the prom, the graduation, the first day of college; pictures from those times are washed-out watercolors compared to the vivid colors of the Cheshire Cat afternoon.

The teacher is holding my hand and she, too, is beaming. Only one other girl, a tall thin kid who played a flower, is visible in the background: she pouts and her eyebrows form one continuous dark line across her young forehead. She is evidence of the fact that even the best of days cannot be good days for everyone and, as a reminder, she is undeniably effective.

But on that day, even her palpable discontent couldn't touch me. Nothing could have undermined my sense of having found a role I could fit into, lines I could learn and shout, simple steps I could master which could bring me to the happiness of that moment in the photograph the way the right combination of numbers opens a safe. I grabbed at the Cheshire Cat's characteristics without deliberate intention--but also with undeniable alacrity. I embraced the whole package: the grin, the wisecracking, the cunning, the outsider's perspective, the disappearing act. "We're all mad here," declares the Cheshire Cat, unapologetic and categorical, purringly pleased to make a generalization--and then makes a quick exit.

Certain moments capture you, like safety nets or nooses, and there you stay.

Leaving Hanover

Not one for the grand gesture, what I remember best about my last days on campus was drinking cupfuls of Tia Maria at noon in a friend's room after I'd just slipped my last paper under a mean professor's door. Make no mistake: this is not a memory I cherish. It ranks right up there with other memories I don't cherish, such as slipping and falling right in front of Thayer on the first snowy day of my freshman year to the delight of the assembled congregation of suitably attired diners. (I was sporting ballet slippers, for God's sake, in what I can only recall as some wild desire to appear sweetly feminine. Needless to say the delicate effect was severely undermined when I ended up on my backside).

But there I was, stretched out on my kindly indulgent pal's floor, listening to Meat Loaf's Bat Out of Hell and thinking, hey, I'm almost outta here. This was in December of my senior year. If there were others in my class also leaving Hanover for good that cold bleak winter of what was still 1978, I didn't know them.There must have been others, it occurs to me now, but when I look back on that time it is so completely associated with isolation that it remains hard for me to think anyone could have passed through the same experience. Who else would have forfeited the fireworks and whistles signaling the end to a crucially important time of life? What other family would have allowed their kid to slip silently out of that world without any demarcation or distinction?

It was nobody else's business, believe me, that I left when I did. And it would be classier to say that I left because of a lofty issue, in protest over ideology, or because graduate schools just wouldn't hear of waiting another term of going on without me. But I chose to graduate early for reasons nearly unclear to me now, involving financial and emotional deprivation, involving a growing sense of uneasiness at life in a small town and the knowledge that I was no more "a man of Dartmouth" after three than I had been in 1975. In retrospect the time resembled nothing so much as the ending to an uncomfortable marriage made in one's first youth; an old joke involves one old friend saying to another "Harry, I hear you're getting a divorce. Why?" to which Harry answers smilingly "Because I can." Mostly I left because I could and there seemed to be few reasons to stay. For years it was something I didn't think about much. It has become something I now regret.

Leaving anywhere is tough. Maybe everybody knew but me; if there was a memo that went out to all of us at eighteen declaring this, I threw mine away without looking at it. I thought I was impervious to departure. I thought it would never matter that I hadn't gone to a college graduation. After all, I pretty much erased the high school version of this, which involved appearing on stage with the thousand other kids from my class for about three minutes. We looked like extras from an old Cecil B. DeMille movie right before the burning of Rome.

The one photograph my father took after the high school ceremony unfortunately positioned me directly in front of a sign blaring "No Parking Anytime." Maybe if the sign were in Latin it would have looked more like a graduation and less like Halloween, but with my standing in a white rayon rented gown, I looked like a cross between a very fallen angel on a bad hair day and a Klansman. So what could I be missing by not sticking around Hanover for two terms, paying what didn't need paying for? Friends, good friends who continue to be the best thing about my years at college, even then suggested I stay, that I find a job, or--at the very least--that I return from wherever I was to attend graduation in June. Faculty members who had been protective and generous and kind also said that maybe I shouldn't be so in love with final exits, shouldn't get so hooked on the smoke of burning bridges. They were right, but I couldn't see that, blinded as I was by my own shortsightedness.

The decision to leave made every difference in those last three months. One of the things I could never get used to in Hanover was hearing adults say in perfectly serious voices "Let's go to the Hop" because I always added, silently, the bass singer's follow-up on the 1950's 45: "Oh baby." But that last winter I remember sitting by a fire in The Hop while somebody played the piano. Struck by a sense of how inviting it was, I realized, for the first time, that I hadn't accepted the invitation. And, shrugging my shoulders, I thought it was too late to do anything about it.

Having tea and cookies at Sanborn House on a November afternoon after spending several dusty hours in the stacks also made me shiver with the idea that maybe I was leaving with my pockets emptied of what could have been mine. I thought about one of my cousins, who, when hearing that I was at college and working part-time at the writing center to earn my keep, commented that my days involved "no heavy lifting." I remembered his remark as I folded my hands around the warm cup of Constant Comment and watched the steam stealing all the heat. As lives went, this was pretty privileged. For my three years at Dartmouth I had been struck with a sense of being unwelcome, but how much more welcome I felt now that I was leaving. In December I took the bus back to New York for the last time, vowing like Scarlett O'Hara with her fist to the sky, that I would never take a long bus ride again.

By the time June came to Gower Street in London, Hanover seemed to be on another planet, not merely another continent. My friends sent letters describing their plans for the big weekend and I admit to feeling a deep, gut-level sense of envy. For many it was a big family event, with their becoming the most recent Dartmouth graduate in a long line of brothers, fathers, uncles and grandfathers. For others from neighborhoods more like mine, it was still a big day, maybe bigger: it was the world's acknowledgement that they had succeeded, that someone in the family had made good. My father wrote on lined paper to ask me if I wanted to come back for the event but I declined his too-generous invitation. I couldn't justify the expense, I explained, but I was giving myself too much credit. Now I realize that I must have been afraid to go back because I already suspected that I had cut my losses too soon, and that I had taken my vulnerabilities with me flying across the ocean clutching the stub of a one-way ticket.

Great things happened at graduation, I heard. Great laughter, great speeches, great good-byes and promises of future meetings. I could only half listen to the stories because otherwise I would have been caught up in longing; I had made my bed, I thought, and should lie in it, even when offered the possibility of more congenial lodging. I said I wasn't going back. Joyce's silence, exile, and cunning came to mind and I figured I could manage the last two even if the first seemed impossible. But Dartmouth, venerable institution it is, can hardly match leaving Ireland and the Catholic church; to ally myself with Joyce was disingenuous, a cover for my own fears and stubbornness. I was looking for excuses not to go back, and found many.

Until a few years ago. My husband and I were dating in 1990, and he suggested that we stop in Hanover on our way to Montreal. Resisting the idea, I came up with reasons he laughed aside, not out of disregard but because he heard them for the evasive and inconsistent alibis they were. I made him promise that we would leave if I had a sudden flashback and hit the ground at the sound of a fraternity song, but nothing like that happened. It was summer and it was beautiful. We were both English professors at another institution and he seemed more frankly interested in Frost's time at Dartmouth than mine, which allowed me to catch my breath and catch up with the last eleven years.

With his camera he took all the pictures I never had from my legitimate time there: in front of Baker Library, in front of my old dorm, in front of Thayer pointing to where I had fallen. It was a graduation of sorts, this return, because I saw that I had falsely denied the effect--positive and negative--that Dartmouth had on my life. I learned that it was after all only polite, as a southern friend once pointed out, "to dance with the one that brung ya." It felt good to dance with my past, but I felt the gentle rebuke of a place that didn't need but surely deserved more credit than I had allowed.

Fortunate enough to have been invited to speak to a number of college and school graduations over the last few years, I always make a point of telling the graduates that, for better or worse, this is a day they will inevitably recall, and suggest that as a service to their older selves they make the best of it, that a later draft of themselves will be eavesdropping on this day for the next forty or fifty years.

We had a bottle of champagne (not Tia Maria) that night of my first trip back to Hanover, and my husband and I toasted to a sense of return which, as all senses of return do, offered the comforting possibility of closure. We invented the ritual, improvised the steps and ad-libbed the lines, but that first night back was a celebration nonetheless. To the young woman I had been at the bus-stop in White River that December, and to the others who had left in the winter, or summer, or even the ones who left in June without breaking a visible ribbon, we raised our glasses to say the words that were not provided at the time: happy graduation.

Culture

Confessions of A Recovering Catholic

As what you might call a Recovering Catholic (I know that I am one, I have accepted that I can never be anything besides one, but I can't go out and practice it except at what I perceive to be my peril) I have a complex relationship to the idea of religion. But a number of folks have asked me to comment on the idea, and so here goes.

Drummed into me from an early age was the fact that God was the Father, which lead to my thinking of God as somebody home only at the weekends. Thinking about God as a Father also meant thinking of Him as a distant sort, One who wasn't to be disturbed because He was busy, One who was concerned with rules and punishments, and One having a short temper.

But Jesus was always presented as young, handsome, sometimes even smiling. God never seemed to smile, as far as I could tell. Maybe He'd nod once in a while if you nursed the sick or something, but Jesus seemed to be somebody you could sit next to at a party and have a good time. Jesus was like an older brother, someone who was still above you but not so distant that you couldn't approach with questions or tears or even anger. You could bother Jesus with requests for a good grade or new skates or a Barbie carry-all but you'd never ask God for that because he was busy doing stuff like Ending Hunger and Healing the Wounds of the Church. With God you had to line up and get a number, like at the bakery; with Jesus you could just walk over and see if he was busy at the moment. Not that he'd always look after you (I failed math, and never got new skates) but sometimes he's come through (I got the carry-all and I still have it, in partial talismanic hope that I am indeed one of Jesus's favorites. But I'm too embarrassed to have it blessed).

In J.D. Salinger's Franny and Zooey I met with an idea of Jesus I found enormously accessible. I have reminded myself, sometimes with great relief, of this one image of Jesus I can pocket and take along with me.

In the novel, twenty-ish Franny suffers from a "tenth-rate nervous breakdown" because of her inability to deal with the "phonies" around her at college and in her profession as an actress. She becomes obsessed with the Jesus prayer ("Lord Jesus Christ, have mercy on me"), a sort of Christian mantra, and wants nothing to do with what she has come to regard as the superficial, undignified, and ridiculous world of everyday routines. Her brother Zooey, a "verbal stunt pilot," is impatient with his younger sister's self-indulgent spiritual pride. Zooey is pretty fierce: he accuses Franny of falling in love with her blinkered idea of Jesus, wanting him to be more like St. Francis of Assisi and less like a rude guy getting mad at the money-changers ("[Y]ou're constitutionally unable to love or understand any son of God who says that a human being, any human being. . . is more valuable to God than any soft helpless Easter chick"). Zooey distrusts Franny's use of the prayer because she's using it to "set up some little, cozy, holier-than-thou trysting place with some sticky, adorable divine personage who'll take you into his arms and relieve you of all your duties and make all your nasty people go away."

Instead of seeing religion as something that will put her beyond the messy, ordinary world, Zooey insists that belief should put her right in the middle of it. He reminds her of their childhood appearances on a radio game show called "It's a Wise Child" and the fact that their brother Seymour, now dead, used to talk them into shining their shoes before every performance. When they protested, saying no one would see their shoes, Seymour insisted that they do it for the sake of "The Fat Lady,"the idea of the woman who listened and loved them and wanted them to do their best always. That Fat Lady, Zooey explains to Franny at the most crucial point in the novel, is Jesus

Christ himself. Franny's work as an actress--even in front of audiences who laugh and applaud in the wrong places--is nevertheless worship. When the curtain goes up, she's doing it for The Fat Lady. And although Salinger never uses the line, I draw comfort from the idea it all isn't over until The Fat Lady Sings, and so I think about the possibility of second chances, and unconditional love, and working in the world as we find it, with the hopes that we are not playing, finally, to an empty house.

Over Bored

Titanic was one heck of a disaster movie, at least from one perspective: the film itself was a real   disaster. I know I'll make deep enemies by saying this, but I totally hated Titanic. For one thing, why oh why   couldn't they say The Titanic, like a normal person? Did they think they'd have to pay extra for using the part of speech known as an "article"? Did the writers believe that, by omitting it, the dialogue sounded all English-y, that by saying "We're on Titanic" the way the Brits say "I'm off to hospital" we were meant to believe this was somehow (give me courage enough to say it) authentic?

This was one of the most unmistakably bad movies I've seen since Pretty Woman. (And, yeah, yeah, I know: these movies made more money in one-half hour than I'd make in ten lifetimes, but that doesn't mean they're good. You can make money stripping stolen cars, but that doesn't make the process good. You can make money burying bodies in the swamplands of New Jersey but that doesn't mean it's good).

Titanic makes Ace Ventura, Pet Detective seem Bergmanesque in its subtly, makes Volcano ("The Coast is Toast") look like Hamlet ("There's A Destiny That Shapes Our Ends"), makes The Poseidon Adventure seem as finely-crafted a work of art as Breaking The Waves.

I cannot believe I paid money, money I work for, money I could have used to buy Milano cookies or even kitty litter, to see this movie.

But more importantly--and let me stress the significance of the point I'm about to make-- Titanic ,(The) took over three and a half hours to watch.

Early on, I whispered to my husband, intending to make a joke, that they were filming the movie in real time. "No, no," he hissed (he hated it nearly as much as I did) and explained that in reality (and I'm not making this up; I checked his facts) the ship only took about two hours and forty minutes to sink . Let me say this again: it look longer to watch the movie than it took for the Titanic (the real ship, the big boat) to sink.

Now obviously I'm not in any danger of giving away the plot by saying that the boat sinks, right? Why else does anybody go see a disaster movie except to wait for the disaster? But the disaster here wasn't nearly disastrous enough to justify the fact that they dragged out, kicking and screaming, every sentimental cliche ever imagined since the beginning of time. Some of these cliches were first seen in primitive cave paintings. There's the spoiled rich girl and the sensitive, poor artist boy who wins her heart. He goes to a snotty dinner party and is smarter than all of them; she goes to a "oh-we're-poor-but-we-have-fun-don't-we-luv" bash below decks and out-drinks and out-dances all of them. Duh.

My favorite line between these two occurred when she was looking through his sketch book, which included drawings of (gasp) naked women, pointed to one page and said coyly "I think you must have had a love affair with this one, you've drawn her so often" (or something like that) and he replies--absolutely earnestly, you must understand, with no sense of irony--that no, he didn't sleep with her because "She was a one-legged prostitute." He pauses and goes on to say, as if in apology or explanation, "But she had a great sense of humor." I laughed out loud, thinking that at least here was a moment of self-parody that cut through all the treacle, but then I realized that I was the only one laughing. Most of the time when this happens in a theater, I feel sheepish or nuts, but this time I felt totally justified. Artist Boy remarks on the fact that the one-legged hooker has a terrific sense of humor, which is sort of like saying "That blind bus-driver had a good sense of smell" --and no one in the audience but me wants to yell out "Well, I guess she'd better have"?

I didn't like that the Italian spoke-a like-a this-a, or that all the big-eyed poverty-stricken, sacrificial children were astonishingly clean and quiet, or that the poor slobs who worked as waiters were seen as the same sort of traitorous slobs as The Rich, or that the two big moments of power for our young heroine--the two times she breaks free of her glossy shell to reveal her inner-most nature--involve, respectively, giving someone the finger and spitting in someone's eye. Subversive? Undermining of feminine stereotypes? Challenging the system? Give me a break. I knew Thelma and Louise, and let me tell you, she's no Thelma and Louise.

When the ship finally (thank you, thank you) sinks, the climactic scene contains all the beauty and grace of a garden hose spraying an ant farm. One simply doesn't know what to say. The final atrocity? That brilliant, fabulous Kathy Bates, one of the best actresses ever, has hardly any lines. I thought she'd be my life-saver, that her very presence would provide safe passage out of the suffocating melodrama.

But finally, there's no way out of Titanic (The). And it brings some of the best people down with it. One of my favorite students saw me a little while ago and said, breathless with enthusiasm, "Oh, Professor Barreca, you have to go see that movie!"

I wanted to weep, but I didn't want to be accused of going overboard.

It Even Smells Big

I'm waiting for the auditorium to fill up with the three hundred or so men and women who have come to celebrate the opening of a women's clinic at a county hospital in Maryland. Kind enough to invite me to give the keynote speech at this event, the organizers have led to me a small room near the stage where I can amuse myself by thumbing through some magazines.

And amused I am. There is a copy of Field and Stream, not a publication to which I have everyday access, and I am immediately struck by a huge ad, a two-page spread that runs from the front cover to the first page. There is a big, glossy picture of a Chevy SUV, wide-open landscape behind it, vehicle unoccupied but loaded with outdoorsy gear. The caption? "IT EVEN SMELLS BIG."

Wait a minute. "IT EVEN SMELLS BIG"?? Exactly who--and in what ad agency-- thought this one up? What kind of people, making the kinds of money most of us will never see, not even at a casino, sit around a polished mahogany table on Manhattan's East Side and decide that the way to move mega-numbers of Chevys off the lot is to claim that They Even Smell Big?

And dare I suggest that this is just a teensy-weensy bit gender-specific in terms of pitch? Quickly, there in Maryland, I flipped through the other magazines in the small room: Self, Good Housekeeping, Glamour. All high profile, high-profit, high circulation magazines, all with loyal, growing, and established readerships. Yet not one of these publications included any ads whatsoever suggesting that their reader purchase a product based on the fact that it might smell big. Nothing suggested that the woman scanning the ads be advised to buy a thing because it was massive, huge, gargantuan, prodigious, or mighty.

Indeed, the words "smell" and "big" are rarely used in magazines for women, as I discovered in my three-minute yet totally comprehensive survey. Even perfumes, which are supposed to make you smell a certain way after all, never seem to use the word "smell." Instead we hear of "fragrance," "bouquet," "a subtle hint of something-or-other," or "scent." Now, to tell you the truth, "scent" is a word I would have expected to find in Field and Stream, but never mind.

So I decided to open my talk with a discussion of gender-specific advertising. I held up the Chevy ad so they could see I wasn't inventing it. I compared it to an ad I saw in Elle magazine, also advertising a car; in this case the ad was promoting a Dodge-Plymouth Neon, something that smells, I presume, rather small. At any rate, the ad for the Neon said "How Do I Love Thee?," thereby invoking Elizabeth Barrett Browning's "Sonnets from the Portuguese," as every Elle reader knows. Okay, maybe it's my own nearsightedness, but I can't imagine an ad for any vehicle's advertisement in Field and Stream beginning with "How Do I Love Thee?" Not even ads for bait.

I then began to consider other products such as "Just For Men"hair coloring. This has always puzzled me. I keep seeing ads for this stuff emphasizing the fact that it only takes five minutes to apply, as if men wouldn't even think about spending more time on their appearance than it takes for them to polish off a Lifesaver. Which is maybe true, but still....

Why does it take thirty minutes at least for a woman to color her hair when it takes men only five? Don't give me the longer hair argument, either. You color the roots of your hair and then pull the color through (get the idea that I've had personal experience in this area?) and besides, lots of men have longer hair than women. The product isn't called "Just For Men With Really, Really Short Hair," after all, is it? Will I need to double my estrogen intake if I use "Just For Men"? Will I suddenly get a higher line of credit and be able, suddenly, to parallel park?

And how about "Secret" antiperspirant, which, as I remember it, has declared for years that it's "Strong Enough for a Man, but Made for a Woman"? Can we please apply this line of reasoning elsewhere? How about "A Job With A Salary High Enough For A Man, But Occupied By A Woman" or "Health Care Research Funded Munificently Enough For A Man's Disease But Directed At Diseases Associated With Women"?

Actually, those sound pretty good to me.

Maybe that's the real secret: to start applying the rhetoric of advertising to other areas of life. Stay Tuned For More Information On This Important Subject.

Just Don't Do It

Let's just say I'm not queen of the sporting life. Let's just say that my favorite athletic activities include Getting a Taxi (which involves an ability to run while pushing others out of the way, much like football, simultaneously coupled with the need for exceptional vision as well as the willingness to emit a loud whistle --not simply respond to one); the ever-daunting Shopping for Shoes (a very great challenge especially as one ages, involving much bending over in a highly -- perhaps we should say supremely--competitive atmosphere); and the always-popular Finding the Parking Space (drawing on quick reflexes, a finely attuned sense of timing, power steering, and the ability to fit a two-ton car into a space designed for skates). As for everything else falling under the aegis of "sport," I must turn to my mentor, Dorothy Parker, who summed it up for a number of us when she remarked "Skiing is difficult and none of my business."

Sport is difficult and none of my business.

This, as you probably know (and as a number of you are already shouting out loud), is no way to approach doing time at Dartmouth. It's sort of like heading into the desert muttering "But I'm very sun-sensitive" to which the only reply is "Why the hell didn't you think of that before you embarked on this journey?" The lame answer: I just didn't realize. Where I grew up, Lotto was considered a big sport; men did not run unless someone in a unmarked car was chasing them. Women didn't run, ever. You couldn't, wearing those tiny heels, which is probably why we were encouraged to wear them from adolescence onwards. I wore them in Hanover. I admit it: I was stupid.

But not stupid enough to be tricked by some upperclassman. There I am in 1975, my freshman year, hauling books to the library on this perfect autumn afternoon, ready to trade them in for the next batch, ready to make good on whatever efforts had sent me to this tiny town, ready to be the poster girl of a bona fide college student. I climb up the steps, get to the door of Baker, sacks full of weighty tomes across my shoulders like some medieval peddler. As I tug at the massive doors, even I can see (weak armed and weak shouldered as I am) that there is no movement. The doors are locked. How can this be? I am as puzzled as a character in the Twilight Zone. It's daylight; it's a weekend afternoon; there have been no reports of plague or riots; I am at an Ivy League school.

"Why the hell is the library closed?" I shout indignantly to some guys walking by.

"There's a football game," they shout back, apparently laughing at my question. I figure they are kidding. I sit on the steps, and a few minutes later ask the same question to an older couple walking by. The yell back the same answer.

At that moment I discover I am not in the Twilight Zone: I'm in the Outer Limits. I have gone to a college that closes its doors against the possibility of some student engaging in the highly subversive process of reading; I am the Rogue Reader, the Stealth Student. What have I done? Then I realize: I've gone to a world where They Shut Down the Library During Home Football Games.

Fifteen years later I am recounting this story to a wonderfully appreciative group over cocktails at a swanky New York party (the only town where the word "swanky" still applies) and this tall dark-haired guy at my left shoulder is listening. He hears me get to the punchline-- "And They Shut Down the Library During Home Football Games!" whereupon, as if on cue, everybody laughs out loud--except the tall man who says to me, with impeccable dignity, sophistication, timing, and a sly sense of James Bondian style, "And your point is?" and pauses. Then everybody laughs back at me.

Translation of his line: "Why on earth would anyone be at Baker library on the Saturday afternoon of a home game? Which planet are you from, exactly?"

The tall man and I are friends, but we still clash over the issue of athletics. He thinks sports are good and tends to repeat that phrase in an argument--and not only because it is comprised of words with only one syllable. No, this guy works with words for a living and although he claims to have been an athletic type in his day, I've never seen him in a sweatshirt or wearing a terry cloth wristband which makes me wonder if all those photographs of him on varsity teams are merely computer-generated.

But he loves this stuff, talks to me about scores and standing as if I had a clue what he meant, and expects me to support the college by cheering on its teams. My face still manages that grimace-like smile but, to tell the truth, I just don't get it. I still have trouble figuring out why playing outside in the dirt (or on the clay or carpet or whatever) is considered worthy of the attention and monies of grown people. If you want to play yourself, sure, have a good time, Godspeed and all that, but don't try to make me buy a ticket (or build a $12 billion stadium) to watch.

Since those folks who are deeply into sports are now so enraged that they have already started writing angry letters demanding my dismissal, I can now admit a sneaky little fact that quite possibly undermines the rest of my argument: I did cheer for a Dartmouth team recently. The women's basketball team played where I teach (in an arena, not actually in the room where I teach) and I was really engaged by the game. I rooted for one side and then the other--my loyalties deeply and obviously divided to the point where those listening to me cheer for both sides suggested medication. These young women were, I know, genuine scholar-athletes, and I like the fact that the hyphenated phrase works in the order it does: scholar comes first. They clearly enjoy the various and myriad parts of their lives, which makes it easy to commend them as role models. They seem to be able, as so few of us can manage, to live in the moment: their focus is this game, this evening, these comrades, these moments as a student. But I was shockingly happy when Dartmouth gathered up points (or tossed points in, or racked them up, or whatever it is one does with points). It was exciting and it was fun, even to watch, so it became clear, even to me, that it must be a blast to play. Not to worry: this did not make me purchase sneakers or anything drastic. But it did give me a sense of camaraderie with the tall guy that I hadn't felt before.

I think we're both in agreement on one point: that there are many students at Dartmouth who deserve our cheers. There are the ones who wait tables to pay for their tuition, the ones who fought through rough and unready high school educations to come to Hanover on scholarships, and the ones who spend their time tutoring other students instead of (or in addition to) playing a sport. But when the ones who are most visible achieve success and recognition, it can--at the best of moments--offer everyone a chance to yell and whoop and holler for them, and, by extension, for the rest of all of our endeavors.

Just do me a favor: don't tell the tall guy I even agree with him a little bit. I'll never hear the end of it.

No More Dead Heroines

Here's a new resolution, one that maybe shows my age better than anything else I could dictate for myself. This year I am making a serious promise: no more movies with dead women as the heroines. No more babes in self-sacrifice land. No more traipsing over the bodies of deceased ladies as I walk up the aisle in a theatre or rewind a tape on what is laughingly called my home entertainment system. Entertainment? Are you kidding? Maybe I could just poke myself in the eye with a stick for a while; that would be better and I'd save all that money on Kleenex. Nope: no more crying, no more schnooks, no more usher's dirty looks.

What prompts this declaration of independence? I just watched a lyrical, beautifully acted, and gorgeous foreign film called The Breaking Waves. While I don't want to give away the whole plot, let's just say the leading lady was lucky that she hadn't bought any green bananas, if you catch my drift. And because I'm preparing for a course on images of women in film adaptations of classic literature, I've also been having a jolly old holiday season watching Anna Karinina (Garbo), Madame Bovary (Ajani), Tess of the D'Urbervilles (Kinski), Wuthering Heights (O'Brien) and Butterfield 8 (Taylor). And it wasn't just Kinski's acting that made me cry. The whole wild bunch here includes broads with a wide range of talents and temperaments whose lives cross cultures and span eras. They have only one thing in common: they all wake up dead.

This doesn't make for what you'd call a really fun time over the popcorn.

Here's the scene: I'm sitting in the living room, cat on my lap, slippers on my feet, mesmerized, furious, and weeping. I'm trying to watch every gesture on the screen, eat every morsel from the bowl, and blow my nose all at the same time. It's not pretty. What do these film women do that's so incredibly bad that they need to be punished by death, which is in most cases a fairly final solution? They have adventures, they yell, they love passionately, they rebel, they talk back, maybe they drink and dance a little, they have breasts and hearts and thighs, and they escape the straightjacket of traditional femininity, however briefly.

So how do we reward them? We ship them off to a funeral--their own funeral--and that's if they're lucky. At least at a funeral they get to be the center of attention, wear a new dress, and receive flowers. Compared to their final moments on earth this event usually counts as a terrific alternative.

"Oh, come on," chides my friend Nancy, with whom I have wept in tandem over countless cinematic fatalities, "Not everybody dies." She pauses to consider and then gingerly offers a palliative: "Some only go crazy." Oh, goody. They get to gnash their teeth and rent their garments (but never get to raise the rent and keep the profits).

These crazy ladies of Hollywood are ever so slightly less appealing than the dead ones, given that madness is apparently easy to establish through the over use of make-up (particularly lipstick--misapplied lipstick is the single most common denominator among the female insane in cinema). Pathologically insane female characters are also famous for their ability to withstand bad hair days without comment. If there's a female character whose hair is frizzy or showing any signs of reverting to its natural color, and she doesn't complain actively about this, you know she's certifiable. You see roots and you should think: immediate institutionalization. Film logic insists that a woman who would let her grooming go is capable of any atrocity. Clearly it is only the matter of a few frames before she kills again or perhaps runs screaming through the streets scaring small children and trapping them for use in a curry.

So does my resolution mean that I will be watching only cartoons in

1998? Not if those cartoons are Bambi (dead mother) or Dumbo (insane and imprisoned mother). Can't go there, either, it seems, without jeopardizing my resolution. My nieces and nephews will have to watch by themselves while I stick my fingers in my ears and hum in another room. Too much of that, of course, and I'll soon be putting on my lipstick funny but it is a risk I'll have to take.

Okay, so how about this? How about we get to see a couple of flicks where strong women not only survive, but triumph? How about if they don't go over a cliff, under a train, or explode into space? How about if they get to stride into the sunrise, laughing, and do this while still remaining smart, attractive, compassionate, and witty? How about if they refuse to lie down and die just so that they can be revered in the memory of some guy or a couple of kids who will find a replacement for the missing character as soon as the final credits role?

How about the radical suggestion that the heroines get to endure long enough to hang out and have a good time (maybe even enjoy a guy and/or a couple of kids) without obvious injury to their bodies, psyches, without, perhaps, even sacrificing their sense of fashion awareness?

I know, I know: you'll accuse me of rejecting the pain of life, of refusing to accept that our existence on this earth is fraught with difficulties both insurmountable and overwhelming. Yes, life is very often very difficult. But it is also very often very ennobling, challenging, energizing, lively and very, very funny. And I think next year will be a good year for underwriting the female characters who dare to laugh--and live--out loud.

Les Temps Perdue. . .
Or, Confessions of a One-Chicken Woman

Let's talk about promiscuity, shall we? Let's talk about fidelity, loyalty, and the sort of unswerving commitment that doesn't admit impediments (even when they are as big as a house and you stand in their shadow). It must be obvious to everyone by now that I'm not talking about sexual fidelity and promiscuity; others can do a better job of that than I and still keep their day job. No, I'm interested in the blind, brain-numbing, often inherited loyalties that define who we are personally.

Personally, for example, I buy only one brand of chicken. I buy the one that used to be advertised by the company's owner, a man who bore an uncanny not to say unnerving resemblance to the former mayor of New York City, Ed Koch. I understand that there are no doubt equally fine purveyors for all my poultry needs (which are extensive) but I cannot shake (or bake) my commitment to this particular fowl family. Not only do I like the little magic button that pops up to say "I'm done, you fool! For God's sake, get me out of this oven or you'll end up serving Pop Tarts for Thanksgiving dinner!" I also like the really easy to read directions for cooking printed on the slimy vinyl bag which I inevitably throw away only to retrieve from the garbage to check on the timing a couple of hours into the procedure, just to make sure I know when to be there for the little button.

This explains, in part, why we eat out a lot.

I'm loyal to a fault when it comes to mascara (let others wear lavender and midnight blue; all my cousins--and probably all Italian-American women of a certain vintage--wear sooty black stuff that clumps charmingly and falls down one's cheek in a seductive, yet subtle, fashion). But when it comes to lipsticks, I admit to sluttish tendencies, trying on not only various shades but a variety of brands, including a bizarre kind that is green until you put it on your mouth whereupon it sort of turns your lips a garish but nevertheless interesting pink. I believe this was developed in Eastern Europe for the American market when Eastern Europe was still run by our enemies; it can't be good for you. I believe it makes your mouth glow in the dark thereby permitting a woman to be both a good companion and a nightlight simultaneously.

My father won't drink anything but a certain kind of supermarket-brand coffee. This means that he has to bring a bag of coffee with him when he comes up here from New York to visit. He says he doesn't mind because women will sit near him on Amtrak, attracted by the fresh-roasted scent. My grandmother would have impaled herself on a breadstick rather than change brands of pasta (no, she did not make her own. She left Sicily in order to get away from the expectation that she would have to make all her own staples, including water and air). My brother would fall on his own sword rather than switch shampoos but he has a roving eye when it comes to cereals, which I find on the surprising, even scandalous, side.

Bigger loyalties also divide and bring us together. I'm monogamous when it comes to cats; dogs and I don't really get along. I'm adverse to desserts which include citrus or "fruity bits" and must excuse myself when any form of coconut is present. I don't chew gum but I carry mints. I like country music and will not entertain those who denigrate its splendor. I want only to see movies that don't make me cry and involve some sort of huge but unlikely natural disaster. I don't like the songs of Whitney Houston, the humor of Tim Allen, or the novels of John Updike. While I know that this will not hurt them one little bit (it might, in fact, enhance their already spectacular reputations), I have come nearly to fisticuffs over my tastes when in a discussion with one of their admirers.

People used to be loyal to ideologies, political parties, religions, regions, car manufacturers, and teams but that sort of devotion seems to be wearing off. We are, I think, slightly the worse for that wear. Granted, I am happy to avoid the possible bloodshed that might occur were the World Wrestling Federation forced to face off against the forces of Martha Stewart, although it would certainly be fun to watch (The guys wouldn't stand a chance. Have you seen her hoist those four-ton terracotta pots?). But I think, too, that little loyalties might have displaced some of the bigger ones; obsessing about the details might prevent us from thinking about which issues, exactly, would force us to stand up and be counted. As long as the choices are thoughtfully made, with an understanding that there are competing viable options, then monogamy can indeed be a good thing--in chickens, in marriage, in music, and in life.

Family-Style Dining

When I drive past restaurants with signs boasting "Family Style Dining" I have a tendency (as they say in country music) to press the pedal to the metal, thereby leaving skid marks. (I used to start shaking and biting my lower lip but the medication has helped.)The words "family style" and "dining" should not be coupled since they cancel each other out in the same way that "jumbo shrimp" or "greater Cleveland" work against producing a coherent meaning when placed in immediate juxtaposition--or even close together. Let's face it: the entire concept of "family style dining" scares me.

What does "family style dining" (or FSD as we will call it) mean, exactly? People yell at you while you eat? Your older brother is allowed to grab the bigger piece because he's a boy? Your cousin will start kicking you under the table even though she is now thirty-eight years old and a successful journalist (two words that also arouse suspicion when placed together)? You have to finish everything on your plate or your car will be towed at your own expense? On certain nights you will be expected to clear and wash the dishes of others? If you ask for water you will be given a look so bitter and resentful that it is ordinarily reserved for the loyal girlfriends of serial killers? These are not business-attracting thoughts. These are not the sort of get-ahead ideas promoted in marketing classes at any reputable business school.

And I say all this as a kid coming from a family who liked to cook and loved to eat. What do people from other kinds of families think? I did a scientific survey of my closest friends and I'm happy to provide the results:

they don't like the idea either. To my husband (who initially thought FSD was an STD and was therefore suddenly concerned about how my column was catching on), "family style" means that cornflakes will somehow be involved in the meal, either as a main dish or as a key ingredient in preparation. To Christie, FSD means that no one will speak during the meal and that the whole affair will resemble a Swedish wake. To Liz it means that there will be conversation but it will be on assigned topics in order to prevent anyone from saying anything meaningful which might, after all, disrupt the digestive process. (Imagine the contrast to my family where it was announced, more or less ritually at every meal--including lunch on the weekends-- that someone's affair was destroying the family or that someone's child had been allocated the wrong paternity).To Stephanie it means that everyone will be watching what you eat, silently computing calories from fat and protein in order to tell you how much more you've consumed than any other woman at the table, suggesting helpfully that you should start ordering clothes from The Forgotten Woman .

At best, family-style dining means that you can relax when you walk into the place, that you get to know the servers by name, that you feel as if you are welcome when you show up asking to be looked after. My current favorite FSD isn't even a restaurant but a shiny luncheon cart with the name "Husky Trail" parked near my office; this where I get all the day's best food. The folks who run it work like they are offering salvation along with an egg salad sandwich (in my case, of course, that salvation literal but for others I understand that it is merely symbolic). The food is great but that's not the central feature drawing hungry throngs to their mobile kitchen: they represent the family we've all always wanted. Kind and attentive, they remember whether you like onions, or hate cucumbers, or always want a little extra sauce. They know what your secret heart longs for in order to feel as if you're cared for and they, in turn, want to provide to it. When I was in a bad mood one day, they gave me a huge piece of homemade custard pie and instructed that I share it with my husband. I did and felt better. It should have been covered by Blue Shield, that pie; that's how effective it was.

What they're like when they are eating alone at home, I don't know. Maybe they yell at each other or throw plates across the room. I doubt it, somehow. If they open a sit-down place, the sign should read "Family-Style Dining: From The Family You Always Wished You Had." Until then, I'll stick to Restaurant-Style Dining, where you can hear the words that no family member has ever said to any of their kin: "And what can I get for you this evening?"

Days of Whine and Roses

First it was the Cinderella Complex, then the Peter Pan Syndrome, and now I'd like to raise yet another motif: The Princess and the Pea Perplex. It could otherwise be titled Why Is It That Those Who Whimper Prettily Get All The Support?

You know the type: she's a delicate flower. (N.B.: Yes, I know: some men do it, too. But the culture congratulates women on helplessness while it punishes men--at least publicly. More about this in another column.) So what characterizes the delicate flower? She can't wear anything except eighteen-carat-gold jewelry without getting a rash; she can only have silk next to the skin (or pima cotton if she's really slumming it). She absolutely must have organically grown, hand-picked, hand-squeezed grapefruit juice and she would drop down dead if you applied anything but fresh tarragon to her chicken. She requires an office with a big window because she gets sad on long winter days but she pines for specially treated glass because she doesn't like to work in direct sunlight. She needs her own parking space because (coy giggle, little smile) she just never quite learned how to parallel park. She has never pumped her own gas.

Notice any impatience here? It's well earned; I claim a collective voice. I speak for all of us who purchase earrings where the fanciest metallic detail is wrought in aluminum, those of us who wear blouses made from E-Z Care rayon, who drink V-8, buy "Tubs O'Spice" from a warehouse club, work in the green cinderblock office where they put us, and park where we can a find a spot, arch or no arch. Does this make us good sports? Do people look at us with respect and say "You go, girl! You're a real trooper!" No, it makes us lumbering peasants, Cinderella's tacky sisters, pond scum far removed from the refined, exquisite, rare jewels who must be protected and cherished.

Okay, maybe I shouldn't complain about any woman getting attention any way she can, but it seems to me that the the weepy-whiney ones are letting us all down. These women were once the girls who broke movie dates with their best friends in order to wait at home in case a boy called; these are the ones who disassociate themselves from the causes around which other women rally because they want to be seen as unusual, as wonderfully different from the rest of their sex. In college they took over the entire bathroom. When we've all been fighting the good fight to be accepted as peers, they insist on being seen as sweet little things who can't stand the pressures of the big bad world. When I hear the high-pitched wail of the princess, I steam like a pot of overcooked pasta. What happened to the rewards of independence?

The typical case goes something like this: your co-worker never completes her projects on time but inevitably gets an extension because she weeps gently in a boss's office about the pressures of being the new member of the team (or the pressures of being a senior member of the team--take your pick). You, on the other hand, have often stayed in the office until dawn to complete your work but you get it in on time and have never missed a deadline. In order to do this, you promise the baby-sitter your new car if she'll stay until you get home. Your co-worker, in contrast, can't make her deadline because she's attending a fabulous screening. Are you congratulated for being competent? No. Is she penalized for being incompetent? No. If anything, she gets more attention and more support for her inability to do things well than you get credit for being successful.

Like the princess who couldn't sleep because she felt the tiny pea under all those mattresses, the helpless darling is more often regarded sympathetically as a dainty creature who needs all the help she can get just to survive in this cruel world. She makes others--especially men, but women too--feel necessary. When you complain about her, you're seen as insensitive and bullying, a workhorse of a woman who remains untouched by finer sensibilities. You lose.

My all-time favorite is this one: "I can't leave her. She'd fall apart without me. You, darling, will get over this quickly. You're a strong and brave woman and you'll be fine." This line is the real killer--or maybe it's just that I want to kill the folks who use it.

So should we all just learn to flutter our eyelashes?

No way. For once the answer usually offered as a palliative is true: while independence is occasionally complicating and often difficult, dependence is authentically and permanently crippling. Don't give in to whining. Those who seem to get away with something are paying a price higher, in the long run, than the world will be content to bear. Word will get out: The boss will need a job done on deadline and all the excuses in the world won't help it get done sooner. The lover will eventually tire of a woman who is no more self-animated or independent than a hand puppet. (If not, then they deserve each other. As the old Yiddish saying goes, "At least God didn't ruin two households.")

The woman who is secure in her abilities and strengths ultimately wins-- but it takes time. Cultivated incompetence is effective only in the short term. If you can't sleep with the pea under all those mattresses, you better not count on being rested--or rescued. Better to climb down carefully and find a better bed, one feathered with your own accomplishments, intelligence, and ability.

How Do You Solve a Problem Like Medea?

Do women trade recipes for revenge over the backyard fence the way they once traded recipes for pot roast? Has a generation of women grown up believing that Glenn Close is in fact the heroine of Fatal Attraction ? Should you take out extra insurance every time you make a copy of your house key for a new girlfriend?

Medea, queen of revenge, declared that "A woman's weak and timid in most matters; The noise of war, the look of steel make her a coward. But touch her right in marriage, and there's no bloodier spirit." And Medea had never even heard of Lorena Bobbit, Juvenal, the Rush Limbaugh of antiquity who was clearly not touched by issues of political correctness, made the provocative observation that "Indeed, it's always a paltry, feeble, tiny mind that takes pleasure in revenge. You can deduce it without further evidence than this, that no one delights more in vengeance than a woman."

Is this true? Are women prone to the paring knife and bemused by the burning bed? Do many women believe, as cartoonist Libby Reid suggested, that the quickest way to a cheating man's heart is a knife in his back? The Assistant Prosecutor in the Bobbitt trial, Mary Grace O'Brien, declared in a summation that "We don't live in a society governed by revenge." Her side lost. Does that mean we disagree with her?

Revenge fascinates all of us, but let's face it-- we have a particular appetite for stories about supposedly feminine young women getting mad and then getting even. Lorena Bobbitt, Amy Fisher and Tonya Harding may look like sorority girls but they act like the three witches from Macbeth. Lizzy Borden remains an icon in American culture in part because she is the poster child for the "good girl gets mad" school of thought--and because she got away with it. These figures have, for better or worse, captured our collective imagination.

In cases like Bobbitt's, Fisher's, and Harding's there are no winners, only losers. Yet we look to these tales for both confirmation and rebuttal of our basic instincts: we see that they confirm the maxim that the female of the species is deadlier than the male, and that, as Nietzsche suggested "In revenge and love, the woman is more barbarous than man." But we also comb revenge tales for a challenge to the other assumptions about women: that women are passive and powerless. We look to these mythologies not to excuse the villain but to explain and explore our own fears, rages, and sense of injustice. It seems that we care less for the real story than for the mythological one; discovering that the actual, flesh-and-blood women and men are tragic and tortured doesn't distract from our preoccupation with their actions. In other words, what actually happens is less significant than what we imagine it to be.

We become fixated particularly on the women who choose to act out their revenge far more often than we focus on their male counterparts. In October of 1992 The National Law Journal reported that in the first nine months of that year alone, seven disgruntled men killed a total of three ex-wives, two lawyers and two relatives in court (wounding over a dozen others). The statistic did not make headline news. (Some men not too high up the evolutionary chart might look at those 1992 statistics and cynically comment, as did one of my more bitter male acquaintances: "too bad about the relatives"). For the most part we tune out male violence. It's just guys, mad about unfair laws and alimony. Just guys with guns, and guys with guns don't make news.

But give a woman a knife, and then watch the cameras roll. After all, it's a standard plot for a drive-in movie, sort of like the forty-foot woman scaled down to apartment size. A woman who gets mad is still monstrous enough to make the front page and to guarantee a box-office hit.

And don't think that it's only women who are watching; this is not a Mary Tyler Moore rerun. Many guys seem completely enthralled. Guys without a professional interest in what lawyers call "the law" (in other words, guys who would applaud a shark feed if lawyers were used as bait) have been glued to court television for the last six months. Saloons that once showed only world-class wrestling suddenly started showing clips of figure skating. A woman who gets even with her man is the stuff of male fantasies about women. It ranks right up there with other unlikely events that populate the male imagination, like finding that the Doublemint Twins are looking for a date. Yet when Tom Hanks' character in Sleepless in Seattle yells at his preadolescent son that Fatal Attraction scared the sh-- out of every man in America," the audience burst into applause. The beautiful woman with the knife or the gun is a dangerous extension of an icon we recognize: the femme fatal.

Maybe if the women at the center of these revenge spectacles looked like prison matrons in grade-B movies we would not be as hooked on their stories as we are. If they were women of color, we might not grant them the same number of pay-per-session exclusive interviews or television movies. If they were very poor, or very fat, or very old, we would probably push them as far off the stage as possible. We don't like seeing the pain and anger of those who are genuinely and irrevocably pathetic. What we like seeing is Michelle Pfieffer as Cat Woman. We like a nice figure of a woman in our Medeas.

Indeed the cast of the most recent road show, including Mrs. Bobbitt, Tonya Harding, and Amy Fisher are considered conventionally attractive women. No doubt for those whose tastes run to big-hair and heavy eye-liner, they are a dream come true. To the rest of us, they are frankly terrifying--and fascinating. What we can't understand--and what therefore holds our attention--is that fact that these three appear to be "real girls" of the gum-chewing, hair-spray, high-heel wearing sort. They look as if they'd cry if you insulted them, not cut off your penis, shoot your wife, or try to break your knees. They didn't look tough, but obviously those around them learned to sit with their backs to the walls of restaurants and to sleep very, very lightly. Maybe with a nightlight.

The desire for revenge is a fundamental human emotion (and I'm not just saying that because my last name ends in a vowel). "Life being what it is," confessed Paul Gauguin, "One dreams of revenge." The Bible declares that man was created by God in His image, and we know that the god of both old and new testaments has a taste for revenge. Indeed, He has such an appetite for revenge that He wants exclusive rights. Are women (and men) coming too close to playing God when the idea of justice and revenge are removed from their institutionalized and ritualized forms and interpreted by ourselves? What informs the difference between the revenge fantasies of men and women?

Clearly John Wayne Bobbitt (and did you ever think you'd hear somebody's middle name being used this often after they let William Kennedy Smith go?) thought his wife was a good girl, one who might shrink a shirt on purpose but not shrink his anatomy. Guys just don't think about revenge the same way women do. For example, guys often think of destroying somebody's property when it comes to getting revenge, but it's my impression that Lorena Bobbitt probably didn't even think in terms of keying her husband's car. Guys sense, with itching-collar intuition, that many women don't buy the idea that living well is the best revenge. Women, especially the sweetie-pie, soft-spoken, real-girl sorts, often believe that revenge is the best revenge.

Lorena Bobbitt wanted to be called Mrs. Bobbitt, remember. None of this "Ms." stuff for Lorena, who apparently bought the white-wedding fantasy wholesale. This was not a woman who was campaigning for NOW but a woman whose wedding picture showed her being lifted high in the air as if she were a flag her husband was carrying into battle. She apparently liked being the little woman, at least initially. When she found out her husband didn't exactly have the integrity of a John Wayne character she dealt with him the way a woman once dealt with John the Baptist. Perhaps Lorena isn't Salome, after all, given that she wasn't acting on a whim and chose to wield the weapon herself instead of getting others to act out her fantasies for her.

That Mrs. Bobbitt acted out her revenge fantasy at all instead of sitting down for coffee with her girlfriends pretty much resembles the fact that her husband acted out his martial arts fantasies. Her revenge was evidence of powerlessness, not strength. Her act of vengeance was made not in order to control but because she was out of control. This was not cool Al Pacino in The Godfather. This was hysterical Kathy Bates in Misery.

My own most recent experience with plotting to get even took place a few months ago. A best pal from high school had been wronged, sort of in the way that Frankie was wronged in "Frankie and Johnny." " I told him that he could take me or leave me," she wailed, "But instead he did both--and in that order." Five of us had been sitting around a table for hours, drinking endless cups of coffee that by midnight had started to look like run-off from the Valdez oil slick. Five women, a grievance, and a sense of defiance makes for a heady, steamy atmosphere, believe me. "'Lipstick on his collar'" sang Rose with a touch of venom, "Should at least equal sugar in his gastank, don't you think?" "I heard a story about a Detroit woman who was dumped by her sales-rep boyfriend," offered Clara. "To get back at him she called the recorded-weather number in Cairo and left the phone off the hook for the ten days he was on the road. It cost him a fortune." Many of us giggled in an unseemly fashion for women our age. "You could always call the IRS and anonymously suggest that they look into his last three tax returns," offered a CPA who had recently emerged from a messy divorce and was only too happy to join in the fray.

I was originally invited to join this clan because I've been researching revenge in contemporary culture, looking at the everyday methods we use to get even with those we believe have caused us deliberate grief. To be honest, I'd once explained to Cindy that I personally translated the word "vendetta" as Italian for "What do you mean, 'you want to see other women'?" She understood my translation.

Our coven of cackling women posed no actual danger to the men under discussion and it certainly posed no problem for men at large. We are all nice women and it's just that we are not supposed to crave disaster, even when we experience pain, betrayal, humiliation, or ingratitude. It was fun, for those few hours, to be not so nice. The rampages remained reined in by reality and the evening ended in laughter at our imagined mercilessness. But it is also true that we left with a sense of exhilaration at having been able to give breath to these most secret wishes for quick, unrepentant personal justice. Dishing about dishing it out was enormously gratifying. Exciting, uncomfortable, delicious, and distasteful, we cannot exorcise revenge fantasies completely-- that is, if we can exorcise them at all.

Since the figure of the desiring or powerful woman remains threatening to the traditional definitions of femininity, there is a need to regard her as deviant. We need to regard her as freakish, as obsessed with anger and incapable of living rationally. Her revenge is initially dismissed with a slight contempt of the "isn't she cute when she's mad" variety--unless she can underscore the severity of her intentions with violence or with the threat of "real" (read: traditionally masculine) power. Women's revenge is characterized by the need for subterfuge and delay. If revenge is a dish best served cold, you have a lot of women learning to use the deep freeze.

Often excluded from the usual machinery of power, the female revenger must invent a method particular to her situation. It is perhaps the inverse of situational ethics; what we have is situational retribution. The woman in such a case will not be looking for restitution, since in all probability she will not want to be "restored" to any original position. "I don't want him back," said my betrayed friend from high school. "I just want him heartbroken." The woman in these cases is looking for vindication and affirmation of an elusive sense of entitlement. She may be driven by the motivations similar to the ones that drive a suitor to look for validation from the beloved. We usually want to get even to the same degree that we once loved. In this way, revenge becomes paradoxical since it insures that we maintain a continuing intimacy with the other person. For example, let's say you imagine the crestfallen expression on your old flame's face after catching a glimpse of you holding hands with an exotic and glamourous new lover. Let's say you also imagine, for good measure, that your ex stumbles across your name as a keynote speaker at a professional meeting and understands that this high-voltage new job is only a partial measure of your success without him. As fantasies go, these are fairly representative. The flaw lies with the fact that you're still filling your fantasy life with meetings, conversations, and emotions starring someone from your past. You're still hooked. You become as caught up with the idea of revenge as much as you were ever caught up with the idea of romance, in part because they uncannily resemble one another.

One classic American author, Nathaniel Hawthorne, has asked us to consider "Whether hatred and love be not the same thing at bottom. Each. . . supposes a high degree of intimacy and heart-knowledge. . . Each leaves the passionate lover, or the no less passionate hater, forlorn and desolate by the withdrawal of his object." Revenge and obsession are bedmates, and that is one reason why we so often and immediately associate revenge with personal betrayals of the heart. If we love deeply, it is not surprising that we grieve deeply if that love is taken away. It might also follow that we want to exact recompense and restitution. It feels like somebody stole our sense of self-esteem and self-worth and we want to get it back by stealing theirs. We might feel like we've been mugged, but the mugger doesn't actually know the scope of his crime. The trouble is, of course, that affection, respect and desire are not zero-sum games. If we lose a sense of self-respect, it isn't usually because somebody else stole it. It's usually because we gave it away. The person who we think has it is probably oblivious to the fact that he has walked off with all our invisible emotional baggage. We have been taught to forgive our enemies, but no where is it written that we have to forgive our loved ones.

"I've got a lot of patience, baby," sang Laura Nero on my favorite record during junior high, "And that's a lot of patience to lose." I remember singing that line like it was written for me despite the fact that the biggest betrayal I had faced up until that point was Tom asking Judy for a dance. (When he asked me out after they broke up I then happily reverted to the old Connie Francis tune "And Now It's Judy's Turn to Cry." I could barely suppress the "nyhh, nyhh" in my overheated heart). I also loved the chapters in Wuthering

Heights when Cathy defied everybody and the line in Gone With the Wind when Scarlett tells Rhett that she wants the most beautiful house in town so that the neighbors who once scorned her would be "pea green" with envy.

So you could say that I've been fascinated by revenge and recompense since childhood. But then childhood is filled with ideas about revenge. No one has as strong a sense of natural justice as a child. Any self-respecting kid will find a way to punish the bully, whether by bullying back, or "telling" or just by doing better than the bully in some other venue.

It seems that we learn to dampen down our wishes to get even as we get older, but they can remain a smoky, smoldering part of ourselves if we don't deal with what got us all fired up in the first place.

From childhood on, then, the desire for revenge is in place for many of us. We may be taught to turn the other cheek, but if in doing so we often get hit with the other fist, it's unlikely that we will assimilate the lesson. We devour articles about blood feuds and cat fights on the streets of L.A. and in Hollywood studios. We watch Phil Donahue interview ex-wives about their desires for revenge. We watch reruns of Alfred Hitchcock and Sherlock Holmes because the plots work deftly and because the good are rewarded with the punishment of the wicked. That the good end happily and the bad unhappily is, to borrow a line from Oscar Wilde, one of the primary definitions of fiction. No doubt part of our attraction to murder mysteries, Charles Bronson movies, Sylvester Stallone movies, and Animal House derives from our desire to see unofficial punishment fit the unrecognized crime. When we feel that society's machinery is too slow or too vague in terms of dealing with justice, we scan the hills for someone to rise above the law. And we want someone who will address the unwritten, everyday atrocities that hunt down our self-respect and leave us gasping for air. We whooped and hollered at the scene in Fried Green Tomatoes when our now familiar revenge heroine, Kathy Bates, rams the car of two snotty teenagers who not only stole her parking space but ridiculed her. When Thelma and Louise blew up the truck of the driver that had been harassing them, women high-fived one another in the theaters. For many people, the horizon of power remains out of focus and out of reach and the temptation therefore is to turn towards a more immediate and achievable revenge against the perceived cause of their failure. Can't get a promotion? It must be the fault of the boss in personnel, not the fault of the economy, poor training, or rotten odds. After all, it's hard to do something about the economy, and it's easier to get back at the poor soul in personnel.

Some methodologies for getting even are more acceptable than others. When a student at Pennsylvania's Geneva College decided to program his computer to telephone university administrators before dawn as a reprisal for their negligence in dealing with a faulty dorm fire-alarm system that had disturbed his sleep for months, one could hardly blame him. It was a case of red-eye for red-eye; sleeplessness for sleeplessness. It dealt with technology and seemed both clean and instructive. The alarm system was fixed with alacrity because, in part, the administrators no doubt had been "taught a lesson" and experienced what life was like from the student's perspective.

But what about when a Connecticut woman baked a cake for her final day at a job she hated and laced the chocolate icing with chocolate-flavored laxatives? What about the ex-wife who repeatedly stole the license plates from her husband's luxury car so that he had to spend more time at the DMV than in his BMW? What about the airport employee who, when faced with a viciously nasty customer, kept her smile throughout his tirade, got him onto his flight to Kansas City-- but sent his bags to Tokyo? What, in short, about the kinds of revenge--crafty, subtle, more emotional than mechanical--that women are likely to perpetrate? Women are less likely to stick the heads of vanquished enemies on stakes outside the city than men are, but that doesn't mean the aftermath of their anger is actually swept away. Just because women don't put heads on spikes, in other words, doesn't necessarily mean they wouldn't like to.

Early feminist, Elizabeth Cady Stanton, declared that "If women would indulge more freely in vituperation, they would enjoy ten times the health they do. It seems to me they are suffering from repression," and her words mirror the repression that women continue to feel today because we have not come such a very long way after all. We often tell ourselves that we seek revenge for higher reasons: to right some grievous wrong, to create balance where there had been dislocation and inequality.

And yet often these selfless actions are at least initiated by a moment of a personal desire to "get even" rather than to "make right," with justice as a by-product of the momentum of revenge. People have a genuine appetite for both hearing and telling their stories; revenge virtually cries out for the attention it has so long deserved. This is not about true confessions. It is about the way that people cut off from power learn to practice a kind of emotional terrorism in order to regain their self-esteem in a world that often seems bent on robbing them of even that. The administrative assistant who supports her family cannot afford to put her job in jeopardy no matter how much ritual humiliation is inflicted by her boss. She doesn't dare go over his head to a supervisor for fear of reprisal. So she broadcasts his conversation with his mistress over the speakerphone "by accident." She swears up and down that what he's been drinking all day is decaf, knowing full well that he'll now be awake for the next six weeks on all the caffeine flooding his system. She resorts to being sneaky, to being a pink-collar terrorist.

The possibilities for getting even are as endless as the possibilities for falling in love; the experience, while universal, will be different for each individual and will depend on a combination of circumstance, chance, need and expectations. The instinctive desire to punish someone who has injured us must surely be regarded as a common occurrence, and when revenge is cross-dressed as justice, then it becomes acceptable. The courts of law are to revenge what city halls and churches are to sexual passion. You pass through the imperious thresholds of these institutions and your personal expression is quickly translated into a socially acceptable vocabulary of statutes and scriptures. You learn to speak of recompense and restitution rather than revenge the way you might, for example learn to speak of romance rather than sexual need. "I'm not out to get anything for myself," says the voice denying revenge while playing it out. "I just don't want it to happen to someone else." If you are a victim of an assault, once in court your body becomes the body politic; if you are the victim of a swindler, your grievance is cast in terms of protecting others from your misfortune rather than seeking punishment for the injury to your sense of self-esteem. We walk around the notion of revenge, whistling in the dark to keep the very idea away, even as we draw closer and closer to it. Revenge exerts a formidable attraction because of its atavistic nature, and yet our culture keeps it hidden or translates it into only its most acceptable-- and by extension its most diluted--forms.

And sometimes, just sometimes, the desire for personal justice can actually lead to actual, objective, impersonal justice. There is such a thing as righteous anger, after all. What we call righteous anger usually means that somebody is playing by rules we can follow, even if the rules aren't written down. A classically elegant fifty-year-old female vice-president of a Fortune 500 company once told me such a story in dulcet tones, remaining throughout unapologetic and magnetic. "The best form of revenge is simply to make the truth known. You can virtually destroy someone by merely relating what he or she has said or done, without changing a word or a gesture." One could hardly disagree, I thought. In her own case, she had been working with a man who believed that whatever accomplishments a female employee garnered were worth far less than her male peers. Before leaving this man's employment, the woman photocopied private files that proved that virtually all the women in the company were paid twenty to twenty-five thousand dollars less per year than their male counterparts. Armed with their heretofore hidden knowledge, these female employees filed a grievance and won their case, all through this woman's act of revenge. "I did it for me," she smiled, "But I was happy for them." Obviously her own psychological need for retribution happily combined with an authentic need for the righting of a long-standing and hidden wrong.

The desire for revenge can be transformed into forgiveness--but only if there is a belief that justice will prevail. Swords can be turned into plowshares only if there is a belief in closure coupled with an assurance that the balance of power is guaranteed. Balance, however, can only be achieved if everyone has equal access to power; the powerless are fearless because they have nothing to lose. If the world were anything like what it should be, revenge would be as difficult for the ordinary person to understand as nuclear fission. The world being what it is, revenge flickers on our screen, fills up our pages, and lights bonfires in our imagination.

Fear and Feminism

I know that there are a few reasonable (if not downright charming) folks out there who believe that the words "fear" and "feminism" are either: 1). interchangeable or 2). redundant. Those who find the two words interchangeable are often given to remarks such as "She was one of those terrifying women" which, when translated, means "She ate the last piece of pie at lunch without even having the decency to ask me if I wanted it." Often it also means "Her car is bigger than mine."

The redundant group, in contrast, will be given to remarks such as "Of course she's a (pause, sneer, snort) feminist. She's afraid of being a real woman." This statement, when fully and accurately translated, means "The only reason she makes more money than I do is because her estrogen level is unnaturally low and they look for that when they do the Affirmative Action reports. The degree from M.I.T. has nothing to do with it and she probably only got a Ph.D. because she couldn't be an M.R.S.." Often it also means "Get out of the way and give me the pie."

Why is the "f" word-- "feminism"-- still so terrifying to men and women alike? Why should an article written by Catherine Stimpson titled "The 'F' Word: Why Can't We Say It in Public?" be as appropriate today as it was exactly ten years ago when it was first published?

Personally I have no problem using any "f" word in public, what with going to hockey games since the age of eleven, as well as having to fight my way through sales of drastically reduced merchandise at Filene's Basement.

But I am constantly surprised that the simple word "feminism" raises more eyebrows and initiates more sad-faced head-shaking than any elaborate stream of invective I have ever leveled at either the I.R.S. or the D.M.V. (and believe me, those are streams you wouldn't want to swim in).

Because I teach at a huge state university, I see literally hundreds of smart, ambitious, passionate, intellectually demanding 18 to 22 year-olds every year. Some of these kids are scholars, athletes, pre-med, pre-law, pre-masters-of-the-universe but they come up to me and say in the small surprised voices of whimsical but bewildered cartoon characters, "Professor Barreca, you don't look like a feminist."

What they mean, of course, is that I'm not actually wearing a Fedora, smoking a cigar, showing a cloven hoof, or toting a bludgeon--not even an ideological one. What they also mean is that they are confused by the idea that a card-carrying feminist can wear earrings, have long curly hair, be married to a guy who teaches down the hall, have pictures of kids in her office, eat steak, laugh out loud, and like the male students as much as the female ones. I sometimes tell them I was out of town when the "feminist fashion memo" was issued demanding that women wear only overalls and sandals with ankle-socks. The stereotype is as tight and unnatural as a girdle but far more difficult to shed.

But I still get all sad when they aren't sure whether to laugh. You see, the image they've been handed of feminism often implies (for "implies" here read "insists") that feminists are an unlaughing, unloving, unlovely, and uninspired group of hairy guy-wanna-bes.

And that's the most positive image they can conjure up.

Now, in contrast, I assume everyone I meet is a feminist. This is because I'm the type who likes to give people the benefit of the doubt.

I just assume that if you're walking upright, using cutlery, and not actually dragging your knuckles on the ground, that you'll naturally agree that every thinking, high-up-the-food-chain individual is, necessarily, a feminist. This is because you'll agree that feminism is best defined as the radical belief that women are human beings. You know, human beings: those creatures who spend part of each day actively differentiating themselves from doormats and appliances, those creatures who seek wisdom, strive for integrity, and refuse to yield their souls even when faced with the promise of jewelry, leisure, and uninterrupted television access.

So to the students who say "But you don't look like a feminist," I reply "This is what a feminist looks like."

To say that women are human beings is not a particularly complex definition of feminism but it is an effective one. When I am invited to talk to all-male corporate groups (who sometimes see posters advertising a discussion by Dr. Barreca and get all excited thinking "Hey, there's a workshop on sexual harassment!" because they think the session will be about how to do it better, as if we're going to sit in a circle and "share" stories about how to make Tailhook look like a N.O.W. meeting), even the most recalcitrant listener is reluctant to shout "Look, I walk upright but I'm no darn feminist!" because it sounds really stupid.

I consider this a good first step.

What else links fear and feminism? Is it only a matter of alliteration? (The power of which should not be underestimated, as the Shinola people found out). No, the larger issues linking fear and feminism are profound enough to make men and women cower.

Yep, women too: I don't want to be unfair. It certainly isn't just men who feel this way. I know one woman who is more adamantly anti-feminist than Rush Limbaugh. She usually defers to masculine judgment instead of using her own even when hers has proven unfailingly sound on those occasions when she's actually used it, and she wouldn't vote a woman into the White House if the opposition party elected as it's candidate, oh, Jabba the Hut. She considers women to be less able leaders than men, even though she has proven herself to be an admirable trail blazer in her own right. She believes women are cooks but that men are chefs, and that women are crafty but men are artists. She giggles instead of laughing. She continues to refer to herself as a "girl" even though she's over forty and she hesitates to go to a "woman doctor" (even after I quoted Carrie Snow's line to her, that going to a male gynecologist is like going to a mechanic who doesn't own his own car).

She will say things like "Oh, sure, I run the household and support the family by working at my own start-up business from my home-office but naturally I do this in addition to helping my husband promote his artwork and the kids with their music and of course I couldn't give up my dedication to the community group since if anything the need for our services has increased sharply over the last two years so it's essential that our involvement remain as firm as ever." She's a champ; everyone would agree.

So why won't she call herself a feminist? "Why, that would make me seem headstrong and unfeminine," she replies, while simultaneously mail-merging seven hundred letters to get the fundraising capital campaign in motion and using her right foot to open the door for her assistant.

This is who really drives me crazy--not the guy whose role model for emotional sensitivity is Al Bundy but the woman who is thoughtfully assertive, discriminatingly strong, and who nevertheless recoils at the term "feminist." She thinks the word "feminism" itself chains her to a flotilla of battleships (or battleaxes) who will sneeringly force her, against her will, to change her ways. She thinks that if she doesn't play the game of femininity correctly she'll end up alone, unliked, and looking like something out of "The Fall of the House of Usher."

To her I say: the best part of feminism is the idea of choice, the belief that everyone has a right to make and live a life based on informed decisions and authentic options. It isn't about legislating how things must be done, but about offering a menu of possible alternatives, each as nourishing and valuable as the other, not only for women but for men as well. Feminism is, at least in part, responsible for allowing those women who choose both to have children and a career, and to do so without feeling like they have to impale themselves on the sword of a culture demanding that every mother be superglued to her offspring until he or she gets a driver's license (the kid, that is, not the mom).

Feminism also paved the way for the growing number of men who take family-leave time (for the less enlightened out there: that's not when the company pays you to leave your family but instead to spend more time with them) in order to have a hand in raising their kid instead of just paying bills for eighteen years without ever learning their kid's birthday, favorite color, or middle name.

The collective voices of women have helped get us to places our mothers had difficulty entering, no matter how intelligent or eager they were. It's been pretty well established that institutions otherwise incredibly boring and unreflective often employ a remarkable degree of degenerate cunning in order to keep Certain Types of persons out. Women trying to get through the barriers were regarded as C.T.s with a vengeance. But somehow women prevailed (along with other Types, most of whom were not known to have prestige luggage or family names more than a few generations old). Now colleges, companies, political organizations, professions, not to mention certain after-hours clubs, must permit everyone fair entrance even if they don't wear plaid pants, own Pringle sweaters, or know the words to the Whiffenpoof song. It doesn't mean you actually have to frequent these places-- heaven forbid--but it's good to know they can't shut the door in your face or make you come in the service entrance.

Feminism is about the need to question the accepted wisdom of our culture. Politician Jill Ruckelshaus's observation--"It occurred to me when I was thirteen, wearing white gloves and Mary Janes and going to dancing school, that no one should have to move backwards all their lives"--can serve as Exhibit A. (Under this heading we can file a remark I heard recently: "Ginger Rogers did everything Fred Astaire did, and she did it backwards and in high heels").

Exhibit B might be comic Pam Stone's reflection on the problems of euphemisms surrounding and defining women's lives. A lot of women have trouble speaking about themselves and their intimate lives because to do so seems, somehow, unfeminine. "I had a girlfriend who told me she was in the hospital for female problems," Stone begins. "I said, 'Get real! What does that mean?' She says 'You know, female problems.' I said 'What? You can't parallel park? You can't get credit?'" When a grown person can't even name her own problems, organs, or body functions without resorting to cute evasions, let's all agree that there's a problem.

(Now, Erma Bombeck once told a story about women really naming their body parts. Listen to Aunt Erma: "I was so opposed to name tags at conferences that once when a woman slapped a gummed label over my left bosom that said, 'Hello! My name is Erma!' I leaned over and said, 'Now, what shall we name the other one?'" Even conference customs haven't been kind to the female participant. . . Ever had a sticky label take all the dye off one shoulder of a good suit? This doesn't happen to men because they are allowed to buy CLOTHES THAT LAST MORE THAN SEVEN HOURS BEFORE DISINTEGRATING AND/OR GOING OUT OF STYLE. Thank you. Whew. I feel better now).

Even though it's still pretty startling to some, the idea of treating women as human beings is not a new one, even if it wasn't called "feminism." Consider the letter from Abigail Adams to her husband John, written on March 31, 1776. She makes explicit her "desire [that] you would Remember the Ladies, and be more generous and favorable to them than your ancestors. Do not put such unlimited power into the hands of the Husbands. Remember all Men would be tyrants if they could. If particular care and attention is not paid to the Ladies we are determined to foment a Rebellion, and will not hold ourselves bound by any Laws in which we have no voice, or Representation. . .[that] your Sex are Naturally Tyrannical is a Truth so thoroughly established as to admit of no dispute, but such of you as wish to be happy willingly give up the harsh title of Master for the more tender and endearing one of Friend."

Abigail Adams' plea for the woman's "voice" to be heard by the government is one that echoes through over two hundred years of American history. The plea has called forth only the most perfunctory responses for the most part. (Her husband's reply, in a letter dated April 14, 1776, complains that her "Letter was the first Intimation that another Tribe more numerous and powerful than all the rest were grown discontented.--this is rather too coarse a Compliment but you are so saucy, I won't blot it out." In effect, his reply reduced her argument to a "saucy" bit of feminine nagging, a version of that nightmarish phrase, "ain't she cute when she's mad?").

Though Abigail Adams might have admitted there has been great progress made, this doesn't mean that there isn't still a great deal of work to be done. Comedian Roseanne (who learned, although rather late, that the idea of taking your husband's name in marriage can be tricky for any number of reasons. . .) perhaps put it best when she compared the past to the present: "The only options for girls [when we were growing up] were of course mother, secretary or teacher. At least that's what we all thought and were preparing ourselves for. Now, I must say how lucky we are, as women, to live in an age where 'Dental Hygienist' has been added to the list."

What needs to be done?

One area we need to target is (Okay, how many of you automatically inserted the words "hips," "abs," or "thighs"? This section is especially for you. . .) the Looks Police. Body image and feminism are inextricably linked by the notion that women's bodies are not public spaces, like lobbies, to be decorated, appraised, and found comfort in by folks who have no where else to be at the moment. Bodies are about strength, health, mobility, and pleasure--not nose jobs, chemical peels, cabbage-only diets (just imagine sitting next to someone on a plane who's on that diet and you'll understand how treacherous it is), and constant envy.

This, of course, is where we must pause for an ad from our sponsors. Let's divert our attention to the media, please. Look at television, at magazines, at beauty books, and movies. Do any of these folks look like people we've ever seen up close? You know how I can tell the guy out there who said "yes" is fibbing? Because these folks don't even look like themselves half the time: the images we see are touched up, recreated, remade into something even more unnatural than they started out.

Don't feel bad. Don't feel bad about having half-and-half in your morning coffee, or a couple of pancakes on the weekend, or even the occasional Devil Dog (which are not really manufactured by the Devil, no matter what you hear from the evangelist exercise-instructor; the Devil has larger fish--as well as the occasional diet guru--to fry). As long as you can walk up a flight of stairs without sounding like an old Chevy about to blow a gasket, as long as your fingers are not permanent strangers to your toes, you're probably okay.

In other words, to spend good worry time over whether or not you're retaining water is only useful if you are a boat. (If you are desperate to feel bad about food, try worrying about the fact that in some other places--not very far from where we are at this moment--somebody's hungry. Really hungry. And it's not their choice. And then choose do something about it yourself. That's also what defines feminism: accepting responsibility for change).

Perhaps most importantly, we need to pass onto the young women and young men coming up in the world the sense that there is room for excellence from anyone able to produce it. Girls, for the most part, are still not brought up to think of themselves as successes-in-the-making. They rarely admit their ambitions aloud not only for fear of failure, which they share with their male counterparts, but because wanting to succeed might make them seem less feminine. Listen to Flannery O'Connor when, in a letter to a young woman who also wants to be a writer, she insists on the importance of striving for success: "Success means being heard and don't stand there and tell me that you are indifferent to being heard. You may write for the joy of it, but the act of writing is not complete in itself. It has to end in its audience." Facing an audience who will judge them on their merit rather than their sincerity or their effort, girls are often encouraged to retreat. They bite their nails, they diet themselves into near invisibility, they cry behind closed doors. What a waste.

There are many reasons for this--many of my female students are reluctant to describe themselves as ambitious. When I ask why, they say softly that if they seem eager for success, they might not date. I suggest that perhaps they will simply avoid dates with guys who are so boring that they need to set the restaurant tablecloth on fire so that something interesting will happen. If they're graduate students or a little older, I suggest that possibly this will save them from a bad first marriage. I suggest that they can use those seven years or so more profitably by learning a foreign language, let's say, or taking up a sport.

There are shabby reasons given for what some perceive as women's lack of public success: "women are constitutionally unable to handle responsibility" (see any mother of five; see Queen Elizabeth I & II; see Joan of Arc; see Harriet Tubman; see Madeline Albright), "women were made exclusively for domesticity" (see above, plus Janet Reno, Jane Goodall, Oprah, Katherine Hepburn, Toni Morrison), and (my personal favorite) "women just aren't as talented as men" (see above, plus Edith Wharton, Mary Cassatt, Georgia O'Keeffe, Charlotte Brontë, Wendy Wasserstein, Emily Dickinson). Such reasons inevitably sound as if they came from a document penned by Archie Bunker with help from The Rules Girls (shudder, shudder, wince) and so should act as a catalyst to make every woman even more determined to achieve greatness in whatever role she chooses.

Let's face it: women have had restricted access, historically, to positions not only of privilege and power, but of possibility. One of my favorite passages by the essayist and novelist Virginia Woolf concerns the way she was barred from entering even the libraries at the great universities of England around the turn of the (last) century. As Woolf describes it in A Room of One's Own, she's walking along the paths at "Oxbridge" university when she's yelled at by the guard at the gate. Not surprisingly, she begins considering the nature of exclusion. Here is one of the century's greatest authors (not authoresses; if she's an authoress then I'm a professoress or a doctorella, and I can assure you that I find neither of those terms flattering) and she's not allowed to go into a university library because the male students and scholars cannot bear to be disturbed by a woman--and they find women essentially disturbing.

Woolf initially thinks "how unpleasant it is to be locked out." But it then occurs to her "how it is worse perhaps to be locked in."

Woolf wonders about the "safety and prosperity of the one sex and of the poverty and insecurity of the other and of the effect of tradition and of the lack of tradition" on the minds of the young who inherit the belief that one group is better than the other. To be denied access to a system is bad but it is nevertheless infinitely preferable to being immovably fixed and irrevocably locked into the system. Feminism is about choosing your own path and being able to walk in the front door. It's not about climbing a ladder to get above other people; in other words, feminism is not most accurately represented either by Sigourney Weaver in Working Girl or Kathy Bates in Dolores Claiborne. It's not about a bunch of wizened, chanting women gazing at every revered institution in the land and saying "Let us destroy the intellectual and cultural palaces of mankind, yes?"

Instead, feminism is about discovering that the scary wizards are just guys with levers controlling the smoke and mirrors. After the initial surprise wears off, you then discover that you have a few options: you can laugh about it, you can learn how to do it yourself, or you can change it. I'm trying to do at least a little bit of all three and it's pretty hectic, but damn, it's fun to make trouble. You clear away the dust and clouds and what you have is-- freedom. Freedom to reach a place where you can get the best, the widest, the least restricted--and least restrictive--view.

Confessions

This is just between us, okay?

I have a confession to make: I have become obsessed with the way that total strangers confide their inner-most secrets to other total strangers. I wake up nights wondering why we need to unzip our private stories and wave them in the faces of unsuspecting folk who just happen to be around when we have the urge to reveal ourselves. It turns out that people you hardly know will tell you not only about their dysfunctional family (this happens so often that the phrase "dysfunctional family" now seems redundant), but about their sexual history, their eating and drinking binges, their lies, their allergies, and their anxieties--everything except their salary. (That piece of information, apparently, they will take to the grave before discussing).

What is so seductive about confessing our secrets that we are willing to risk public shame, public scrutiny, and public disapproval? Do we just need to get up and testify, sing out our experience, however ignoble, so that we claim our turf in this world? Is it that we count on those who listen to grant us forgiveness and understanding? Or is it that we no longer believe truth has consequences, that absolution becomes obsolete when confession itself seems to be enough?

Do we, in other words, mistake superficial confidences for genuine intimacy?

Let's say you're minding your own business at a big office party, happily having secured a position right next to the shrimp and not far from the wine, and someone you've met maybe twice before in this lifetime decides that this is the right moment to tell you all about herself, her oral surgery, her sexual experiences, her miserable ex-lover (she should have never left her first husband but she called him once only to find that he's already remarried) and her sense of betrayal when, at age seven, her rotten parents flushed her goldfish down the bowl without even telling her that it was dead. She does this with all the ease, familiarity, and questionable sincerity of socialite Patsy on "Absolutely Fabulous" offering an air-kiss to an acquaintance at a fashion gala.

When this happens, do you gradually move away from the storyteller and the shrimp? (The goldfish story has made the seafood slightly less appetizing, after all). Or are you obliged not only to listen but to tell her that everything will work out for the best, thus performing a sort of secular "Go in Peace" (which might more accurately be translated as "Leave Me in Peace")? Have you come to know this woman any better than you did twenty minutes earlier, or is it just that you can recite details about the condition of her soft tissue and mauled heart?

Is this intimacy, or just information?

Playing out an emotional striptease, removing every layer of social formality or personal shame to reveal the "true" self buried underneath, has become a national pastime. It used to take us years to get to know one another; now we get into the juicy particulars on contact.

We applaud public figures who tell every sin they've committed and we show them that we accept their apologies by pouring more loot into their coffers. Politicians, celebrities, athletes--everybody, it seems--has turned the boasts of their youth ("I've had over two hundred lovers" ; "I can drink a six-pack and still drive") into the confessions of their adult lives.

This is the kind of stuff famous folks used to try to hide, but not any more. Now they hire publicists. (Remember Hugh Grant, whose confession ran something like: "Terribly sorry, chums, but I do have this rather nasty habit and now that I've apologized, can you all show your tender-hearted forgiveness by going to see the otherwise appalling film, 'Nine Months'?" He could be our poster-boy). What such figures once glorified, they now apparently choose to repent--all the while counting on the enthralled attention of their fans, on whose generosity they rely.

The rest of us non-famous folk often end up sounding like the old Yorkshire men from the sketch by Monty Python, retirees who compete with one another to tell the most appalling stories about the deprivations of childhood. ("You lived in a tenement? You were lucky. We dreamed of living in a tenement. We lived in a paper bag in the middle of the road"). One friend told me about a colleague who started every conversation by offering something dreadful that had happened to her recently by way of a greeting, as in "Hello? Is that really you? I can barely trust my senses considering the state of exhaustion I'm in after totally wrecking my life this weekend."

Judith Martin (a.k.a. Miss Manners) has an interesting perspective concerning the reasons why bad behavior no longer inspires indignation if the perpetrator admits to it. "This attitude started years ago," claims Martin, "When exercising judgment (good) turned into being judgmental (bad). Later, confession was seen as compensation for sin, as in, 'Sure, he rapes and pillages, but at least he has the courage to be honest about it.'"

My fixation with the motives for and results of confession was aroused by two distinct but not dissimilar experiences, one concerning my appearance on the daytime talk show circuit and one concerning my appearance in a church. With one, I found myself wondering what could possibly drive a troupe of poor souls to expose themselves and their families to the possibility of pity at best and ridicule at worst; with the other, I found myself wondering why I needed to whisper my sins to a stranger when I no longer counted myself a believer. One was very public, the other almost private, and both were unnerving. Not surprisingly, I intend to tell you details about both, in a rather confessional way, so here goes.

I'll start with church because it was more intimidating for me to appear nameless behind a screen in a confessional and speak for two minutes than it was for me to appear in front of thirty-two million viewers and talk for twenty-five.

host will make it impossible to hide whatever you've worked most hard to keep secret and there is inevitable relief in making a secret public.

Good confessions--meaning those where you not only tell the truth in order to accept responsibility for your wrongdoing, but those where you are also willing to understand that there will be some penalty for having stepped over the line--can offer the same sense of freedom as removing a sharp pebble from your shoe: nobody else could see it, but it was so incredibly annoying you could barely think about anything else. Confession and penitence lets you hurry on your way with less hidden aggravation.

A talk-show is a form of public confession where regular folks meet the familiar and trusted host, as well as one expert in a suit, to address issues usually deemed inappropriate for polite conversation. Similar to priests and therapists, the host and the expert are not expected to reciprocate in terms of storytelling, and rarely offer their privileged information in exchange for the confidential disclosure made by the guest. This is one of the most important differences between confession and ordinary conversation: one person speaks while the person nods (or soothes or applauds or offers understanding) so that the exchange flows one way only, without any expectation that the person in the position of power will offer up personal secrets. (This is one reason that a particularly memorable Oprah revolved around the host's admission that she had at one point in her life been addicted to the same drug that plagued her guest).

Confession in a talk-show setting is a process dependent upon the need of the guest to have others listen, and the desire of the audience to be assured (in the best way) that they are not alone, or, alternately, reassured (in the worst way) that however miserable they are, someone else's life is worse. ("Okay, my husband slept with the baby-sitter, but at least the baby-sitter wasn't a transvestite. And she was unrelated to our immediate family").

And there is something fascinating about watching the reactions of the studio audience, which is essentially a jury of one's peers, to the process of revelation. Like a Christmas pantomime performed in Victorian England, there is often a villain who will be hissed at and a sentimental favorite who will inspire tears. Unscripted, the shows are nevertheless predictable, and this is one way in which they part company with real life.

In real life, life outside the green room or the church, confession can be as dangerous as a loaded gun or a rusty knife. A confession may make you feel powerful for a moment, but its effects are often incalculable. "A man should be careful never to tell tales of himself to his own disadvantage," declared Samuel Johnson. "People may be amused at the time, but they will be remembered, and brought out against him upon some subsequent occasion." Words, as much as actions, have lives of their own. They are irrevocable. Confessions are like tattoos in that 1). You convince yourself that the immediate pain of going through the process means it won't bother you later on; 2) They are permanent.

What about the idea that the truth can set you free? Yes, it's true. But the truth can also lock the door behind you, preventing you from returning to the comforts housed in concealment and confidentiality. Sometimes life in the shade of kind dissimulation is better than life in the blinding sun of constant and relentless honesty.

Admit to your friend that you've deeply resented her inherited money for the last twelve years and she will think of you differently, and not only when she buys your birthday present. Tell your husband that you find his best friend sexier than him, and you risk being told that he's relieved to hear it because he's been sleeping with your college roommate since 1982. Confess your weakness, and run the risk of having that weakness become your signature character trait as it is reaffirmed for you by the expectations of others. Confess your strength, and run the risk of having that strength become the source of envy, conflict, and its own dissolution. Honesty might be best administered, like any powerful medicine, in judicious homeopathic doses.

I worry that confession has usurped the role of responsibility: if I admit to something sleazy, I have acquitted myself of the action. If I warn you that I'm a cad, then you are responsible for putting yourself in the sphere of my influence and I need not offer any apology for breaking your heart. If I announce that I am a needy, greedy, selfish creature, then you must forgive me for my foibles because I have been straightforward. It used to be that the penalty for wrongdoing was being forced to admit it publicly (remember Hawthorne's The Scarlet Letter--as opposed to Demi Moore's version?). Perhaps the penalty for wrongdoing these days should be having to live with it in silence. If you had an affair, for example, you would be punished by never being able to admit it, ever, to your loving spouse. If you had a substance abuse problem in the late sixties, you would no longer be able to weave vivid stories out of your experience to keep the young folks enthralled by your once-hip and dangerous life. Is it possible that we'd start behaving better if behaving badly was no longer considered the most fascinating topic of conversation? Casual confession, like casual sex, debases and trivializes intimacy. Choosing our confessional words, like choosing our partners, should be done carefully, rarely, and with the understanding that destiny can hang in the balance.

Have Yourself a Postmodern Little Christmas

"Postmodern" is not a word to toss out lightly, especially not during the busy holiday season when it might hit somebody and put out an eye-- or an "I" or an "AYE" or. . . . I'll stop now, but you get the point.

Yet there is something all postmoderny and terrifying (the two are, for your correspondent, virtually synonymous) about the fact that enormously large and tawdry stores are selling the characters who had once populated the Island of Misfit Toys as this year's adorable Christmas gifts.

Remember the Island of Misfit Toys from 1964's "Rudolph The Red Nose Reindeer" special?

(Personally it's been years since I've watched any television Christmas specials. They make me cry for such prolonged periods of time, that it has become necessary to swear off. I gave them up along with fast boys and handsome cars. I can't even be trusted with a whiff or taste: I recently caught a glimpse of Linus with the towel on his head reciting "And Lo..." and immediately burst into tears. The Coca-cola Bears make me cry when they give one another their winsome smiles. Mastercard ads, the ones ending with the word "priceless," where people spend small amounts of money in the company of those much older or much younger than themselves also make my cry. As does getting my bill from Mastercard. Let's see what happens when I scribble "priceless" in the area marked "write in amount paid. "I watched the repeat of the silly Ally McBeal episode where she sees a unicorn and I sniffled, ashamed. On this Monday's episode where Elaine tries to adopt a baby, even though it ripped off the storyline from an obscure early episode of The Honeymooners in which Alice and Ralph adopt a baby and then are asked to return it to the birth mother--I saw that Honeymooners clip only once and it left cleated-footprints on my heart-- I still cried. Like a fool, like a sap, like an extravagantly unpostmodern matron. And yes, this has all been one paragraph.)

But anyway, remember the Island of Misfit Toys? (Remember the beginning of this column?) The Misfit Toys have been exiled from Santa's workshop because they differ from conventional toys in crucial and substantive ways. 'Charlie'-in-the-Box is shunned because of his aberrant name; the tiny train sports square wheels; the rag doll didn't please her owner (don't even TRY to make a joke, okay? I'm serious here). This is where the wild things really are--the place where things go that don't fit in. They were like Beat Generation Beanie Babies. You could imagine a Sylvia Plath doll living there (without her own kitchen appliances) or a Henry David Thoreau doll (does not play well with others). Like Rudolph himself, The 1964 Misfit Toys embodied the possibility of finding pleasure in individuality. It was a celebration of non-conformity: a riff on the joys of being un-saleable and unwished-for. It worked because it posited a continent of ordinary toys passively waiting to sell out.

Now, however, The Misfit Toys are being sold as if they were just commonplace playthings. You find them next to Millennium Barbie. (And SHE does what, exactly? Does Millennium Barbie melt down at midnight? Does she turn into one of the Four Barbies of the Apocalypse? Now THOSE dolls would have GREAT OUTFITS. Talk about collectible). It bothers me to see the brave but nerdy elf who wants to be a dentist sitting right next to GI Joe whose job description is to kill other toys. I worry.

Mostly I worry about myself. Why should I care how imaginary characters are being marketed? If Snoopy has turned a profit all these years peddling life insurance, how can anything be absurd? If one of the My Little Pony characters ran for public office, would anyone be surprised? The pink and blue My Little Pony (with sparkles) is virtually guaranteed a spot on a ballot somewhere.   I bet she'd get a huge following. And not just in Minnesota.

What makes the issue go all nasty and postmoderny at the edges is this: The Misfit Toys now have an ordinary shelf-life. They dwindled from being rebels and become innocuous playthings, sort of like Roseanne, Woody Allen, or Marlon Brando. They are Carvel cakes being sold in supermarkets; they are Karl Marx being sold at Wal-Mart. Sort of funny and sad mixed together.

They have lost the shine of difference, a thing of irreplaceable importance--one that should NOT be confused with mere sparkles.

Just Like Home

The people I work with are like family. I don't mean this in a nice way. I spend a whole lot of time with the people in my workplace as well as with my family. In addition to the sheer number of hours I'm in their presence, I also think about them even when I'm in the privacy of my own automobile or bathtub, wondering whether I said the right thing before I hung up the phone and gleefully fantasizing about what would happen if I told them what I really thought. I write letters wherein I itemize, alphabetically, their shortcomings. I don't send these letters, of course, because I have not gone gothically, irrevocably insane. Besides, I want them to like me no matter how I feel about them. In other words, I exhibit unhealthy behavior towards both groups. This means that some of my most relaxing moments are spent on public transportation, a place very few of them can reach me unless they actually follow me onto the subway.

Families and offices are similar institutions. Naturally, I am committed to the idea of a strong family. It's just that I also think it's no coincidence that one is "committed" to strong families, as well as "committed to the institution" of the family. But when you think about the other context where the words "commitment" and "institution" are used, it isn't pretty. But this doesn't mean I don't like my family. After all, I'm stuck with them.

This leads me directly to my office. I genuinely like all (okay, most; okay, some) of my co-workers. They are an eclectic bunch, along the lines of those old war movies where you can divide up the characters neatly by stereotype:

The Kid, The Tough One, The Scared One, The Vaguely Psychotic One, and The One Who Never Thought of Heroism But Is A Hero. Every division gets allotted one of each type and if somebody new enters the fold it is imperative that they find their own unique designation, such as The One Who Whines Incessantly or The One Who Never Puts In Enough Money When You Go To Lunch And Split The Check. These are the business equivalents of familiar family members: The Nephew Who Drinks Too Much, The Aunt Who Criticizes Everything, The Cousin Who Gets In Trouble, The Smart Niece, The Pretty Niece, and the Uncle Who Never Puts In Enough Money When You Go To Dinner And Split The Check.

The biggest difference between literal families and office families, however, is the fact that your office family knows a great deal more about your life than anyone in your immediate family would ever dream of noticing. Every person in your office understands everything about you in molecular detail. Trust me. They have observed and discussed with others-- in the sort of minutia usually reserved for entomologists-- such issues as: your current and previous weight, whether you got what you wanted for your birthday, the name and price of your hair stylist, your method of birth control, the effectiveness of your method of birth control, whether or not you color your hair, wax your eyebrows, bite your cuticles, own your own home, and whether you would like to conduct medical experiments on your boss. They know when you secretly photocopy your updated c.v.. They know that you prefer TicTacs to Certs. They certainly know when you've been sleeping (and with whom); they know when you're awake. They're making a list and checking it twice. They're like Santa but without the presents.

And, let's face it, this is not one-sided. If I appeared on a game show where the prize was three years at the Ritz in Paris all expenses paid (including foot massages by a terribly sweet young man named Raoul), I could not provide one-sixteenth the intimate details about my first-cousin closest in age that I could give about the colleague with whom I regularly have lunch. Splitting a grilled-chicken Caesar salad and knowing who gets the croutons promotes the kind of bonding that rarely occurs over a family-style Thanksgiving dinner where one simply lunges for food while grunting monosyllabically. My assistant and I, for example, have long discussions about what color ink to use on our business cards. Try having that conversation with a cousin named Tony who makes his living by training guard dogs.

This is because, in reality, family members aren't the least bit interested in what you do for a living. They don't really want to hear whether you suspect that the entire marketing department actually mutated from a tribe of incestuous mountain-dwellers; they only want to know whether you're willing to drive Aunt Theresa home before she falls so deeply asleep she'll need to be moved by a winch. Your office family, in contrast, will be startlingly interested in your theory concerning the relationship between certain personnel and aberrant trends in evolution. In fact, they might be just a little too interested, if you catch my drift.

You have to watch how you frame your commentary at work because it just might happen that marketing will hear about your viewpoint and hold a meeting whereby they decide to rebut your argument by barricading you in the lounge area while holding your databases hostage. As in every extended community, there is suspicion as well as esprit de corps, creepiness as well as camaraderie. Just as you wouldn't want your Aunt Theresa to hear the winch remark, you wouldn't want certain of your colleagues to hear that you believe they eat their young.

Finally, workplace communities differ from the families you're born into insofar as you can't fire, or be fired by, your family. You can be laid off by your family, but you can't be made redundant; nor can you collect "unfamilied insurance" from the government. Most families also cannot offer 401K plans or provide the kind of quality health benefits we all expect in the 1990s (Grandma's chicken soup excepted).

Otherwise they are exactly the same.

Synopses

1. With the cheap iridescence of a pigeon's wing, the girl's blue eye shadow reflects light. Like a shark, she moves silently, eyes flat and shiny, among the store's tangled crowd. Her long legs move like scissors, and metal heels snip at the polished floor. The glass counters hang together like beads on a necklace; she trails fingernails over one, another, until her small, fine hand finds a loose catch, and with practiced skill, with a stroke deft, swift, unseen, she reaches inside, like a cat in a fish bowl, and pulls out something- a bauble, a trinket- she cannot even see, so quickly she drops it down her sleeve. Teeth tight together, but not in a smile, she breathes unevenly, as if too much air filled her lungs. She passes the guard who stands by the door; he watches her walk, approving the face, the legs, the quick flash of blue.

2. In an anonymous painting I see death and an angel braid the hair of a girl. One takes a handful, draws it carefully away from the straight whiteness of her neck. The girl waits patiently until they move together, weaving it so that a rope hangs down her back which will raise her up or pull her down. She, unknowing, bends her head over the pages of a book while they work behind her, one by each shoulder, gentle and willing to be fair.

3. In third grade I learned about discoveries and started wishing for hidden islands. Learning about fossils, I longed for ancient burial grounds. Hearing of the Milky Way, I dreamed of silver galaxies. My mouth fills with

chalk dust in the remembering. But for the colored globe that sat like a piece of fruit in the center of the bookcase, my classroom might have been mistaken for a seedy lobby, or the waiting room at a bus station. The patterns of damp on the ceiling became frontier trails; a web of fine cracks grew splendidly, like crystals on the ocean floor. In thirty-five years I have not heard of Brazil, or atriums, or Vasco de Gama without longing for the time when my own territories were unmapped, when morning held imagination, like an apple, in its hand.

4. His words had a hard edge: knives sharpened on a strap. He sliced the air as he spoke. Everything about him had a cutting angle. She was too easy. Like paper into ribbons she went, like confetti she was scattered everywhere when he was finished. He went through her like steel blades go through new grass, like new nails go through new wood. They built nothing. She was too easy. He longed for the crack of metal against stone, the sparks and fires of iron and heat.

5. He looks at himself in the shiny surface of the elevator wall. The navy blue coat, left over from his college days, makes him look like a character from a French film. He always says "film" and never says "movie." His fiancee always says "movie" and he wonders now, for the first time in all their years of knowing each other, whether she deliberately chooses to say the word "movie" in reaction to his use of the word "film" or whether it is just a left over habit from her days at nursing school before they began a serious romantic relationship. The doors of the elevator open, and he turns down the collar of his overcoat because he is walking into the office building where he works. He will raise the collar, like a flag, when he leaves in the late afternoon.

6. I read the journals of the nineteenth-century artist Marie Baskirtseff who died too young. I read about how the canvases, big as doors, absorbed the Paris morning light. How pencil sketches, made in the rain, were

overturned. White paints rub into her hair, red oils stain her fingers; she moves in sudden gestures and broad strokes, murmuring, mad, scared, insisting: "Paint more quickly." As a child writing in the night she recorded premonitions: three candles lit in a room and a sparrow caught in the greenhouse, flying against the glass. She feared her early death as shopkeepers fear thieves. Yet darker words written by an older hand say that magic and signs have little power. Tragedies do not happen, Marie, because mirrors break; mirrors break because tragedies will happen. You were thankful, you wrote, for the warning.

7. The way old ladies board the bus without change I sit by paper and try to write without words. At this hour I could say anything: call a friend in a foreign country, wake her up with a noisy American jolt, call the information operator in Iowa and ask what the weather is like, this evening, out there. I can, tonight, say anything. Words may orbit the earth as sound, but soon they are gone. Typeface is a recrimination: bad phrases like hangovers inspire at best regret, at worst abstinence. What I liked earlier now appears a cheat, a fake: like a hologram, it has no real dimension. Gritty details of the day's conversation intrude but do not inspire. I leave the typewriter as I will, no doubt, someday disembark from the bus, jangling the wrong coins, avoiding the driver's eye, embarrassed.

Faking It

I grow weary of the stance of moral superiority assumed by those who wear natural fibers, purchase unsalted nuts, and who cover their floors with rugs made from rustic materials such as hemp or--as we used to call it in the old country-- "rope." I want to cast my vote for artifice: I write in sincere celebration of the Phony, the Fabulous, the Fake.

I love artificial stuff. When I was in my twenties I had wonderful nails, all mine, of which I was rather vain. Somehow the trauma of the last twenty years or so reduced my nails to self-destructive and cranky objects. Against my better judgment (I thought), I was talked into getting synthetic nails a couple of months ago. It's sad to admit how much I love them. I look at my hands all the time now and delight in painting this high-grade plastic product from Germany a wide variety of different colors. I also spend a lot more time at Headliners, getting to know Michelle and Debbie, because part of the deal with these nails is that I tend to break them. Michelle and Debbie fix them with the expertise and patience of practiced mechanics working on a vintage Jaguar brought in by an eccentric owner.

It's not only fake nails that I enjoy. Like Kramer from Seinfeld, I positively crave MSG and have no problem with restaurants that choose to jazz up their food with this additive--that is, as long as I'm not having dinner with my husband. MSG makes Michael act like one of those cartoon characters who eats the too-hot chili: his eyes pop and his ears get red and his scalp sort of flies off his head like a frisbee. It's not pretty. But dining on my own, MSG is just fine.

I also have no problem with eating highly processed foods, the kinds that have no expiration date. Breads that are so packed with health you could use them as building materials are too healthy for me; square tomatoes, genetically engineered to fit into the shipping boxes, taste almost as good as the round ones to my jaded palate even though I am aware of their bastardized origins. That they were not "of other tomatoes" born doesn't bug me.

And speaking of bugs (you could see that one coming, right?), I don't want them in my food even though they are part of Nature. Ecology stops where my plate starts. While I do not believe the earth loaned to us by our ancestors should be plagued by chemical horrors and thereby corrupted for future generations, neither do I believe I should have to face anything that has more eyes than I have during dinner. It was my rule when I was dating and, heck, it's still my rule now.

For too long we've been swindled into believing that if it ain't au naturel, it ain't nothin'. Even Foxwoods toots its own money-filled horn by claiming to provide "gaming in its natural state," as if shooting craps was Thoreau's favorite pastime, or as if Lewis and Clark walked through vast, unspoiled vistas only to be offered--by the delighted original inhabitants-- a chance to put a few bucks on "Let It Ride."

I don't see gambling as necessarily attached in any manner whatsoever to something "natural." Casinos are riotous monuments to the artificial: adult theme-parks based on the idea that whether it's night or day, you can stay up late, make noise, and play games. The best you can say is they make you feel like you did when you were a kid and stayed up on the week-ends or holidays to watch television.

Television is, of course, the very cornerstone of artificiality. The situations it frames in order to encourage our envy, our edification, and our aspirations, are by definition, fake. Even the "real" people are cossetted by camera crews, producers, and editors; even the word "fact" needs quotation marks around it because factual material is also engineered to fit neatly into prefabricated boxes for easy handling. Television keeps encouraging us to believe that families can solve problems in thirty-minute segments, that news is reported dispassionately, and that grown men talk to each other about how much younger they'll look if they get rid of the grey in their hair, but nobody believes it. You'd no more believe what you see on t.v. than what you'd, well, read in the Sunday papers, right?

But believing and enjoying remain, thank goodness, two different categories of experience. I can enjoy a movie even knowing it's all made up; I can enjoy getting ready for an evening out even knowing I am all made up. I wouldn't want to swap the Courant for The News of The World when I need to get my details straight, but that doesn't mean I can't enjoy the stories about alien babies with long fake fingernails eating genetically engineered tomatoes. (n.b.: those stories appear in That Other Paper).

Just don't show me any pictures of bugs.

Gender Quiz

I have the great privilege of giving talks to groups of men and women about a variety of issues revolving around gender-difference and communication. Sometimes the two groups are actually in the same room at the same time, but this happens rarely (most companies aren't insured for that sort of thing). As a result, I have been permitted rare insight into how the two tribes function independently of one another. I hear, for example, legendary tales of how incredibly, morbidly, fantastically wrong the other group can be in their perceptions of and responses to a number of situations. I have, in the interests of science, decided to compile a series of questions which will enable the reader to detect any lapses in his or her own menu of reactions. Since everyone cheats on these sorts of quizzes (that being one of the few impulses we all have in common) I have made it easy even for the most impatient respondent: the correct answers are all placed last.

For Men:
When you hear the following comment made by a woman, how are you most likely to reply?

1. Do you think I'll look as good as Tina Turner when I'm her age?
a) You didn't look as good as Tina Turner when you were nineteen. I'd love to hear how you expect to catch up at fifty.
b) It's unreasonable to compare yourself to a goddess.
c) I wouldn't trade you for a thousand women like Tina.

2. Does this outfit make me look heavy?

a) Heavier than what?

b) What do you expect to look like if you continue to buy clothes two sizes too small?

c) You look fabulous. Come give me a hug.

3. Should I put in for that promotion?

a) Why? Are they trying to raise the estrogen level of that division?

b) Sure, if you want to learn to deal more effectively with rejection.

c) The sky's the limit. Tell me what I can do to help.

4. I'm feeling insecure about my future. I can't believe this is really my life.

a) Trust me, it's your life. Your name is on all the bills that arrived this morning.

b) You're feeling insecure? At least you don't have to worry about actuarial tables predicting that you'll drop dead approximately two weeks after you retire.

c) You have people who love you, a wonderful community of friends and co-workers, and someone who believes the stars revolve around you. Doesn't that help give you a sense of well-being? You look fabulous. Come give me a hug. Tell me what I can do to help. I wouldn't trade you for a thousand women like Tina.

For Women:

When you hear the following comment made by a man, how are you most likely to reply?

1). Why do you want to go to the movies to see "Two Men Argue Over Who Loves A Woman More" when we could instead see "Large Fast Cars Driven By Maniac Terrorists Who Then Blow Up Public Buildings," which, by the way, got surprisingly excellent reviews ?

a) I live with loud sudden noises, an unfortunate sense of futile destruction, and a random sense of panic everyday, and therefore don't feel a need to pay $7.00 to have my daily anxiety recreated on a large screen.

b) Because if I don't hear a man being nice to a woman pretty soon I'm going to forget what it sounds like.

c) Sure, let's go see "Maniac Terrorists." I hear it's actually a wonderfully ironic statement on violence in twentieth-century. I'll treat.

2). Am I losing my hair?

a) It's not lost. It's just moved to your ears.

b) At least you'll be told you look distinguished. If a woman loses her hair, she is made to feel like she's from the Galaxy Milgroob.

c) I love that little pink spot on the top. You know Sean Connery is my favorite actor. Also Mitch Pileggi from "The X-Files."

3). Should I buy a convertible?

a) If you want to announce your mid-life crisis, why not just have a banner made?

b) Do you think that's wise, given the fact that you're losing your hair?

c) I can't imagine anything sexier. I'll treat.

4). How do I compare to the other men in your life?

a) You're here.

b) First you tell me how I compare to the other women in yours-- then we'll talk.

c) What other men?

Give yourself 6.765 points for every correct answer while deducting 2.557 for every incorrect answer. Then crumple up the piece of paper and throw it away: there can be no scientifically proven, absolutely correct answers to such sticky questions. For example, I would immediately suggest incarceration for any person whose instinct is to reply (c) to all of the questions on the grounds

in Brooklyn, New York I at one time flirted with the marvelous illusion that I was native to this country, but having driven slightly westward last month I saw a sign welcoming me to Pennsylvania. The sign read: "America Starts Here." Oh, I thought, my travel agent didn't warn me about this. "I forgot the passport and foolishly have only the currency from my native land, "I remarked to Michael. Then I thought "I should talk to my accountant about getting back all those federal taxes I've been paying for twenty years." Finally I realized, "Oh, they must be kidding: it's that rollicking Amish sense of humor for which Pennsylvania is so famous."

It wasn't that I felt bad for myself, it's just that I didn't like to think of America as disowning the whole of the east coast. What about nice little Rhode Island that never hurt anybody. Or western New Jersey, even, which is spitting distance (and honestly, I'm speaking only metaphorically) from Pennsylvania? Can't they sneak into America, at least on weekends?

I decided to take Pennsylvania's sign seriously. (I take most signs seriously. You should see how seriously I've taken signs such as "Falling Rock Zone" or "Bridge Freezes Before Road;" I've started life anew on several occasions simply to avoid having to travel through those treacherous places). I decided to see America with a new vision, and I headed happily towards the midwest.

I passed places along the way calling attention to themselves with the names (I'm not kidding now) "Grampa's Cheesetown" and "Suzy's Antiques: New and Used." I saw a lot of white people, not that there's anything wrong with that, but it did look as if the melting pot had mostly melted together potatoes, butter, and products from Grandpa's cheesetown without too much salsa or paprika or oregano thrown in. Me, I'd have sprinkled in some fresh basil and a little sweet pepper, at the very least, just to increase appetites. Lots of people looked the same; it was as if a whole bunch of towns were populated by folks whose family trees hadn't forked. But who I am to say anything?

This difference between the east coast and America became most apparent to me, when I was shopping at a flea market in the country of PA.

Filled with fabulously gaudy, useless, and tantalizing objects, I walked down row after row and delightedly looted the shelves in this foreign land where 1962 Barbie dolls could still be bought in their original packaging for three bucks. I bought bags of stuff for a couple of dollars and felt like a queen. Like the queen of another land, true, but I didn't much mind. I'll get back to America sometime soon, but for now I'll hang up my (very comfortable) walking shoes and stay in the lovely country of Connecticut.

Happiness

Ask a person if he or she is happy and a person will look at you like you're trying to sell them something. It's not a look you would call "welcoming."

When faced with that simple question, people are instantly transformed from forthright individuals into sardonic philosophers. "Am I happy?" they'll repeat, in order to emphasize the ludicrous nature of the expression. "What exactly do you mean by 'happy'? I could probably be more unhappy than I am, but whether or not I'm actually 'happy,' I don't know if I could say." They'll squint and regard you with deep suspicion, demanding "Why do you want to know?" as if you are trying to get their emotional PIN numbers or find out the available balance in their spiritual checking accounts. Soon after they'll get cranky and find excuses to leave.

Could it be that we're wary of the question because we secretly suspect that other people are happier than we are ourselves?

Let's start with what is incontrovertible: a whole lot of people are a whole lot less happy than we are. Daily and genuine disaster is demonstrated every time we watch the news or read the paper, only to see desperate faces peering out of tragic wastelands in worlds less fortunate than our own. Big-time, irrevocable, and unalterable misery is the stuff of many lives where poverty, deprivation, and disease are as familiar as sundown.

And some of these worlds are just down the street.

Juxtaposed with these images are the more comfortable--bordering on

at an interview. However hard I try not to compare myself to these Alien Creatures, occasionally it is inevitable. These occasions often occur after we've gone to a dinner party with a bunch of other couples.

I would bet a winning lottery ticket on the fact that every couple leaving a dinner party pretty much believes every other couple (or at least two out of three) does a better job making their relationship blissful. Picture it: four pairs of long-term partners leave a nice evening's entertainment. They climb into their respective Volvos, Subarus, and Dodges; they are quiet for the first ten or fifteen minutes of the chilly ride home. Then one of them says "Did you see the way Bob held the chair for Susan? Just like they were still dating," to which the other replies after a pause, "Yeah, well, did you see the way Brenda told us all how well Dick is doing at work? I didn't hear you telling everybody how proud you are of me," to which there is inevitably a swift and glacial reply along the lines of "Why should I be proud of someone who doesn't even bother to hold a chair out for me?" This is when you start to hope there's a good tune on the radio.

So much for comparisons.

The only way comparisons do not become invidious and might actually become helpful are those moments when they help us realize and define the limits of what we can expect from life-- a process that can make the acquisition of happiness a little easier. This might mean resetting the margins of personal expectations. Margaret Atwood offers a particularly good example of this in her novel, The Robber Bride, when she has one character make a realistic life choice based on the perimeters delineated for herself: "Roz can see that she will never be prettier, daintier, thinner, sexier, or harder to impress than these girls are. She decides instead to be smarter, funnier, and richer, and once she has managed that they can all kiss her fanny." You can't but wish Roz luck.

But if sizing up someone else's happiness or unhappiness doesn't help us clarify our terms, then what does?

Wholesale definitions are problematic because while the idea of happiness is universal, definitions of happiness are not. The brilliant short-story writer and critic, Dorothy Parker, unquestionably found this to be true in 1927 when she reviewed a contemporary best-seller titled Happiness. Describing the small volume as "second only to a rubber duck as the ideal bathtub companion," Parker nevertheless makes it clear that the Yale professor who penned this book was not bent on constructing a watertight argument.

When confronting Phelps' definitions of happiness-- "'The happiest person is the person who thinks the most interesting thoughts'"-- Parker is, to put it mildly, troubled. "Promptly one starts recalling such Happiness Boys as Nietzsche, Socrates, deMaupassant, Jean-Jacques Rousseau, William Blake, and Poe," Parker writes. "One wonders, with hungry curiosity, what were some of the other definitions that Professor Phelps chucked aside in order to give preference to this one."

Happiness, like honor, a good reputation, or skill at poker, is something that must be won; it is not just given like a gift or thrust upon us while our backs are turned. Explanations that underrate the complexity and challenge of happiness are not only reductive: they are misleading.

True, we can say that some of us are predisposed to take, with alacrity, the opportunity for happiness when we first recognize it as such. But too many of us think that happiness will somehow occur, like the weather, while we're busy doing other things; indeed, our culture encourages us to confuse "busy" with "happy" almost as much as it encourages us to confuse "busy" with "successful."

These pairings might be coincidental, but they are not causal. The guy with the cell phone might be lazy and unhappy, no matter how he looks; the woman with the corner office and six assistants may have a full calendar but an empty heart. Even if you are successful in terms of achieving wealth, for example, or having access to pleasure, getting what you want does not necessarily result in happiness. We would hardly deem a wolf about to sink its teeth into the neck of a lamb "happy" even though he might be satisfied with the result of his pursuit.

Happiness isn't like dandruff: it doesn't just happen to some people, or, for that matter, only to Other People. Most cooks would not, for example, prepare an important, elaborate, and difficult dish on the back-burner. Neither should we relegate the cultivation and preparation of happiness to a position where it is both hard to reach and difficult to infuse with new ingredients.

Most traditional views of happiness argue that the cultivation of humor and play is significant because it helps us "let off steam" so that things can continue as they are. For many of us, however, recognizing the genuine absurdities of a situation, or even those of a particular plight, gives us the power to change the situation--not merely to accept it. Turning the steam into energy, after all, allows you to move on. This is not to suggest that experience should in any way be covered up or denied; paradoxically, what was most difficult to get through in life is often transformed into the funniest, most gratifying stories. As the old equation goes: what's truly funny= pain + time.

The greatest comics, for example, have always complained about their lives, and the best ones still do. Carol Leifer's complaint about her ex-husband--"It was a mixed marriage," she confides, "I'm human, he was Klingon"-- is very different from the tedious repetition of wrongs so familiar from those daytime television programs. Learning to frame our disappointments and unhappiness by using the perspective that humor offers can give us a sense of control over our own lives as well as letting other people express their concern without having to manipulate them into sympathy.

And happiness is more than a tool for survival--at it's best moments, it becomes an act of redemption. It allows us to redeem moments that might otherwise have been lost to pain or despair--being able to laugh is sometimes more about working through an issue than it is about avoiding or treating it lightly. Laughter is, after all, the most human of activities--it's one of the few things people do that animals do not (the other activities that animals do not perform involve applying artificial fingernails and singing out loud to Aretha Franklin's "Respect" on the car radio).

And, life being what is it, we really need to find and cultivate moments of happiness. We might choose laughter over despair at moments of crisis because the other alternatives are, as one woman put it, crying or throwing up. Neither of those makes you look good.

Poet Muriel Rukeyser said that "The universe is made up of stories, not atoms," and it's clear to me that she's right. The stories we tell ourselves and the ones we tell each other give us a way to survive those long days and longer nights when survival itself seems nearly impossible. The idea that you might just be able to laugh--however mixed that laughter is with tears--is sometimes enough to keep you going. If the tragedy of life is not so much what we suffer but what we miss, then missing an opportunity for happiness, laughter, or joy is indeed tragic.

We should remind ourselves that laughing together is as close as you can get to another person without touching, and sometimes it represents a closer tie than touching ever could. The freedom that laughter echoes and hints at is the freedom to welcome pleasure, perspective, and finally, love. And sometimes we try so hard to be happy that we can't possibly have a good time. This makes it especially necessary to be in touch with the irony of the everyday. Embracing a sense of humor about troubled times is like having a sense of humor about sex or death--humor allows you to have perspective on an otherwise potentially overwhelming prospect.

The power and effects of misery, of unhappiness, and of fear are so obvious in everyday life that they can too easily eclipse the great possibilities and powers of happiness. Perhaps British author Fay Weldon comes closest to defining the power happiness can wield in our lives when she explains in The Hearts and Lives of Men that "To the happy all things come: happiness can even bring the dead back to life. It is our resentments, our dreariness, our hate and envy, unrecognized by us, which keeps us miserable. Yet these things are in our heads, not out of our hands; we own them. We can throw them out if we choose."

Happiness is an act of will, a challenge, a complex mechanism depending on circumstance and perspective. Not only does happiness allow for the elevation and exploration rather than denigration of feelings and ideas; at its best it encourages us to make trouble and to take risks. Making trouble and taking risks--changing things for the better--isn't that why we're here? Even at those moments when happiness seems as elusive as daylight before dawn, life depends on seeing the small, nascent possibilities for joy.

What Makes You Mad?

It's tough to type with a clenched fist, but I'm trying. I wanted to write about anger while I was actually mad at something, which means I couldn't start working on this essay for a good, oh, ten or fifteen minutes. If anger were mileage I'd be a very frequent flyer, right up there in First Class; if it were food I'd have to be hauled around by a winch. If anger were sex I'd have my own 900 number.

But anger is like none of these things. It's an itch, an allergic reaction to some little piece of life's pollen blown your way. Anger is personal. Somebody else might not even notice what's bothering you, but the grievance sets your heart racing and your eyes watering and your face blushing. Anger is more particular than sexual attraction or greed. Anger is the quintessential individual-signature emotion: I am what makes me mad.

In my case, this makes me a trucker whose vehicle is making love to the rear end of my Volvo or an automatic teller machine that summarily eats my bankcard without telling me what exactly I've done to offend it.

What else am I mad at? Do you want the list in alphabetical or chronological order, or would it be better to organize the list by height or perhaps geographical location? Today I am furious at everyone and everything around me. I started off the day by getting mad at myself. I forgot to put gas in the car yesterday which means that I need to go to the service station before heading into the office, which means I'll be late for my first meeting. I'm mad at the foolish woman I was yesterday who didn't plan for the efficient and considerate woman that I woke up as today. I'd like to go back and yell at me. (When this wish to tell myself off in different voices becomes too frequent, I'm going to book into the Sybil School of Behavioral and Chemical Therapy).

I'm mad at my husband. I come home after getting a thirty dollar haircut which, I was assured, makes me look glamorous, thin, sophisticated, and adorable (none of which I looked when I went in to get the haircut). My husband greets me not with adoration, but with the less than glamorous and delightful news that the cat threw up on the good rug. I am not thrilled with the cat, whom I resent only slightly less than my husband at this point. My haircut and I clean up after my indifferent pet, who sits grooming herself in disdain and contempt, as if to say "I never need a hair cut. So much for being higher up the food chain." (No doubt she is mad because her bowl contained only cat food and not Mouse du Jour).

Now, I return to the living room and dare to use the terrifying phrase "Notice anything different?"on my spouse. My husband, wildly scanning his imagination for possible answers as if he were being asked a tough question on the marital S.A.T.s, suggests that perhaps I've changed my make-up. I mention that I'm not wearing make-up. He says that counts as a change and so he has answered correctly and has to get full marks for the response. I tell him I got my hair cut. He asks me what he should say about it.

I leave the room and count to 5, 987, return to where he is reading the paper, and proceed to tell him that he might say something like "Your hair looks nice." He says "Your hair looks nice. You should see how it looks if you put on make-up" at which point he returns to reading the paper. I leave the room and count to 9 x 5,987 which is a very high number, and contemplate a life of celibacy.

I'm mad at a colleague who has sneered "Well, if I wanted to stay home and write popular books, I'd consider myself a traitor to the academy," and equally angry at the student who has somehow calculated that by getting a C+, a C, and a C- on last term's exams, she deserves at least a B "because I showed up to almost every class and took a lot of notes."

I'm not feeling all warm and fuzzy about the old friend who has told me that he's getting divorced because "After she turned forty, she just couldn't make me feel the same as she did when we were first together." I grip the phone until my knuckles are white and give in to the temptation to tell him that he hasn't exactly become Mel Gibson in the passing years. I can hear him smile when he says, "Oh, but it's different for a man." I am mostly angry that he is right, and angry that in the space of five years Sally Field went from playing Tom Hanks' object of desire in Punchline to playing his mom in Forrest Gump because she hit the age wall in the film business. And all the while I'm thinking that it's a really good thing that gun control laws exist and apply to me personally.

It's Gross Generalization time: men and women have different ways of expressing anger. Women eat too much, cry, throw up, and ruin their lover's garments. (One woman I know accomplished this by washing all of her husband's underwear with his red socks so that his skivvies were a perfect shade of pink, which just tickled the guys at the firehouse where he worked; they made several comments about his taste in Fruit of the Loom).

When men get mad, they could steam vegetables with the heat of their rage. They drink too much, drive too fast (when there's a car screeching out of a driveway at sixty miles an hour, you know there's a husband who isn't finding wedded bliss), get sarcastic and mock their wives' voices to torture them.

Men act out their anger, and women absorb theirs. For many women I know, anger takes over when they're feeling out of control in their lives (when the kids are screaming or the doctor won't return a phone call or they can't get a line of credit because they lack a Y chromosome). For many men I know, anger is what they use to try to control the world around them (the very threat of their wrath keeps the kids silent in the back seat for at least fifteen minutes. They stare the car mechanic in the eye and demand a loaner by lowering their voices to a growl. They punch each other when words no longer articulate their needs).

Neither gender is particularly cute when mad. And the responses of neither particularly helps to foster an atmosphere of trust. A friend of mine who lives in a small suburban town plagued by armed robberies grew fearful enough to suggest to her husband that they buy a handgun to protect themselves. The husband thought for a while but then decided it would be a bad idea. "You can't keep ice-cream in the house for more than two hours without eating it," he pointed out to her. "You think it would be a good idea for you to own a gun?"

Because anger depends on a lack of perspective, it distorts reality. In this way, Anger resembles its sexier sister, Lust. They both involve tension, irritation, obsession, intellectual blindness, and lots of late-night phone calls. When we're lusting after someone we see only their desirable qualities; when we're angry, we see only the negative ones. Both assessments are unrealistic.

Interestingly, anger and lust are also elusive states once they have passed. Trying to recall why you were angry about something when you've calmed down is like trying to remember why you were in love with someone who no longer attracts you: the initial impulse triggering the emotion is impossible to recapture.

So what can be done with--and about--anger? It's like nuclear waste; if you bury it, it only reemerges at a later date in a more obscure and destructive form. The ghosts of undead resentment haunt the best of us: we're driven to bad dreams and indigestion from all the words we've bitten back and all the bile we've swallowed.

Anger is like a magnifying glass: depending on your perspective, it either distorts everything or makes everything clearer. Anger is one of the last remaining emotions that can, when looked at honestly, make us feel ashamed of ourselves. It's embarrassing to be angry, and so many of us have learned how to hide anger so effectively that we sometimes manage to hide it even from ourselves. But anger doesn't disappear just because it's not seen; every closed eye doesn't mean a peaceful sleep.

Paradoxically, anger is also an emotion that can make us feel unashamed, can make us feel stronger after we have felt defeated and humiliated. It can help to restore a sense of self worth--anger is an indication that you merit judicious treatment. It's also an indication that you believe the world is not chaotic, not unreasonable, and not random in its distribution of goodies and whacks. Anger indicates that you think life should be fair.

When life isn't fair, we get angry. Perhaps I should narrow this down a bit: when life isn't fair to us or to those we love, we get angry. When life is unfair to others we get philosophical. It's pretty easy to deal with the gross inequities of the world when you're dealing with them from a distance. Anger is a response that draws on the immediacy of experience, although it must be emphasized that historically the best and most productive anger does move beyond the personal into the political and the social. When, for example, individuals are angry enough at an injustice perpetrated by the society of which they are a part to take it personally, they can effect great and lasting change.

Anger, like smoke, curls around the edges of many civil rights demonstrations; anger informs and always has informed some of the most important debates and movements in this country. To believe in a cause with passion is to risk encountering anger--in one's self, in one's opponent--but the risk is sometimes worth it.

To say we are willing to fight for a cause might not be literal but the figure of speech is telling: when we put ourselves on the line for an idea there is at least an implied threat that the overthrow or defeat of our position will raise a response--that we will become angry, and perhaps angry enough to literalize the metaphor. We might actually have to fight in order to win. When it comes to matters of belief, we might find that we would rather fight than switch. Anger is inflexible. Perhaps its inflexibility is what makes it a sin.

It's undeniable that inflexibility can be a weakness; after all, anger makes us lash out at our loved ones, makes us bitter and self-destructive, makes us miserable company. But righteous anger's unwillingness to compromise can also be a strength. And the same can be said of anger: it can mark a blind and foolish refusal to negotiate with life's realities and disappointments, but it can also mark a triumphant turning point. "Anger stirs and wakes in her," writes Toni Morrison in The Bluest Eye, a novel about an abused child's coming of age, "It opens its mouth, and like a hot-mouthed puppy, laps up the dredges of her shame. Anger is better. There is a sense of being in anger. A reality and presence. An awareness of worth."

This last point is perhaps the most important one: if you allow yourself to get angry at an injustice committed against you, you underwrite your emotion with a sense of self-worth. If you get angry at an injustice committed against others, you underwrite their value with a sense of shared worth. Call it Quality Anger, perhaps, because it isn't petulant or selfish but rather driven by a sense of community and humanity. Anger can offer a sense of indignity to replace a sense of shame, and offer a voice--raised above others--which can finally be heard. Those voices are most effective when they are raised in unison, when they have mercy as well as anger behind them, and when, instead of roaring at the anger of old pain, they sing about the glorious possibilities of a future where anger has a smaller house than hope.

Growing Up

Childhood is Not Kid Stuff

As a kid, I kept watch. I learned to decipher moods, gauge states of mind, and I grew adept at the exercise of emotional caution. My goal was to make my mother happy, to cheer her on--or at least cheer her up. My mother was, after all, not a happy woman and she didn't disguise that fact, so much of my childhood was spent in the pursuit of my mother's happiness. I longed to be and dreaded being her confidante and her friend. I tried to be everything and failed; of course I failed. I was not a sister who knew her as an adventurous young woman, nor was I a grown-up who could share her sense of missed opportunity. I was a little girl, a bit-player in the drama dominated by a woman who was stuck with the biggest and most tragic roles.

When I came home in the afternoons my mother would be drinking Metrical with an expression of twinned despair and abandon, sort of like Hamlet's mother drinking from the poisoned chalice. I thought she was old because, to me, she was. Now I understand that she wasn't; she was probably in her late thirties at that point, a suburban mother of two who was smarter than most of the people she knew and who was frustrated by the petty, ordinary, tedious routine of her days. My mother would blow smoke out the side of her mouth and lift her head slightly as if hearing interesting conversation from another room. This is how I best remember her.

Adult life, with all the pains and pleasures of choosing your destiny, is a foreign land to children. As someone who visited that land too early, I want to testify that it should stay that way: adult life should be unfamiliar to a child. I was damaged by being treated as if I were my mother's contemporary instead of her daughter. That I was never really a little girl, but instead an adult in disguise, was a family joke in many ways, and of course I was proud of the fact that I could pass for older than my years. It was the equivalent of wearing high heels or smearing on lipstick--absurd, probably endearing, and comic. It became my role and my routine, this acting adult. But I would not have chosen to be what she would, laughingly, (and yes, affectionately) call me: "ten years old going on forty."

I needed a parent, not a friend, not someone who would make me into an accomplice. What I needed, like any kid, was neatly fenced-in emotional security, the psychological equivalent of a closed yard. What she provided was a mapless guide into the wilderness of shattered dreams and broken promises. My mother played out her life to a virtually empty house, so it is not shocking that, as the occupant of the seat right in front of her, I received the most florid of her performances. Having said this, however, it is nevertheless true that she was the one who needed the support and the audience and who could blame her? But I also suspect that, however strong the seduction of treating children as adults, it is always a seduction to resist.

When she would tell me details about my father's affair, or explain why she and her sisters were not on speaking terms, I looked her in the eye and nodded, listening. To be what I thought she wanted me to be, I mimicked adult intelligence and parroted-back overheard, second-hand wisdom. Apparently it made no difference that I didn't actually understand half of what I was saying. All that mattered was whether what I said calmed her, reassured her, or made her smile. Sometimes I could make her laugh at herself and those were the best moments for both of us. It isn't that she wanted to be sad, it was simply a fact that she was; when she laughed, I felt safe and needed--felt, in other words, exactly as everyone wants to feel.

There is much for which I am grateful from those days, make no mistake about it. Perpetual eavesdropper on the world, the ability to listen in and make sense of emotion is something I've turned into intellectual and social capital. Making people laugh is the single trinket in my pack of tricks I would not trade. Yet I imagine that, were my mother here now, I'd have the guts to cite her on what might be termed, in all our fancy and clinical language, "inappropriate behavior." Or maybe I wouldn't have the courage for raw questions. Maybe I am still too fearful of the sharp intake of breath heralding her tears or of her sorrow. Maybe what I am is forty-two going on ten, which not a good thing to be.

The Passive Voice

Today is one of those days when laboriously clicking out one word after the other is the most I can accomplish. Most days I Get Things Done; I keep up a pretty steady pace--most days.

This is not one of those days.

This is more like the days of my youth. My early twenties were spent in a state of suspended animation, in an emotional version of the physical slowing down you see in movies about space travel. The only thing missing was the glass pod, the neat outfit, and the fact that time did indeed speed along at its usual pace in terms of my aging. I really was Snow White, not the happy one dancing with all those little guys, but instead the one in the glass case who held in her breath, her life, waiting for the clocks in the kingdom to start telling time again.

But I wasn't counting the months and years then; I had, I thought, all the time in the world. I would throw away whole days the way you throw stale bread to ducks--casually, easily, without paying much attention to the gesture. I'd sulk when I didn't get my way and pretend cool indifference even when something really mattered. I'd watch myself in the mirror when I cried just to see how sad I looked: I waited for those I loved to ask me what was wrong. When they did ask, I'd turn their question against them, asking what they thought might be wrong. These were not good times.

Not knowing what I wanted or where I was going, I spent lots of days waiting for things to happen: waiting for signals from destiny, waiting for the right moment to emerge from my cocoon, or stupor, or hibernation--whatever the correct name--and embrace life with the same appetite I had in my teens.

It wasn't prince charming I was waiting for--him I thought I already had. It was myself I was missing. I could remember what it was like to do fifty things at once, but somehow I could no longer manage any of it. Taking a shower was an accomplishment; writing a letter or making a phone call was a triumph.

To give myself credit, I always showed up for work on time. And I always made my bed as soon as I got up; this perfunctory act was, on more than one morning, the only thing that stopped me from crawling right back under the covers-- the only place I wanted to be. I still have no idea what the bed-making meant; did I remember hearing my grandmother claim that "you make your bed and then you lie in it"? Did I believe that by keeping control over at least one part of my life, the chaos outside the room could also be muffled or covered over? Why did some part of me insist on this small show of strength?

I wish I knew and might therefore harness that sense of determination right now. Wishing for myself a day full of practical achievement, I have instead managed only a few hours of forced labor. There's a list right here at my left elbow with phrases underlined to indicate the enormous significance of the tasks to be completed by tomorrow at the latest, and the most I have been able to accomplish is pushing the list a little further out of my field of vision. I wrote it out; I know I'm not kidding myself. This stuff needs to get done, but even as I slip into the passive voice ("This needs to get done" vs. "I need to do this") I fear the day is lost.

But not irretrievably lost, not thrown away, not like bread to ducks, thrown out onto the water not as a gift but as an indication of its worthlessness. There are moments I will not give up, even from today. I have mushrooms and onions in a vermouth and butter sauce cooking on the stove; one cat is at the window and the other is at my feet. I called an aged uncle who was happy to hear from me, I spoke to two friends, and Michael is outside working on the lawn.

Like steel pegs holding down a tent in a high wind, these things keep me anchored, keep me making the bed every morning, keep me putting one word after another, even when it's tough, in the belief that time never stands still--never even goes slowly--and that getting out of the passive voice is the only way to get anywhere you'll ever need to be.

Child's Play

I think of myself in 1963, when I was six years old. I picture myself cutting the hair off my newest doll; at six, this is my absolute favorite playtime activity. My poor mother frantically searches for yet another hiding place to stash her sewing box; she can only hide the scissors with so much dexterity because she wants to be able to find them herself when necessary. I, however, am never fooled for long. When I find the scissors, as I inevitably eventually do, I lift them with the finely honed skill of an expert thief. I then proceed to snip away curl after glossy curl of perfect blond doll hair.

This, remember, is a thousand years ago and when no dark-haired dolls walk the earth. I possess an obscene number of dolls, and I love them, yet they are--sooner rather than later--completely bald and totally naked. Some of these dolls are so new they still smell that special brand-new doll smell, straight from the box, but as quickly as I have thanked their gullible giver and hugged them, I go hunting for the shears. Soon afterwards my long-suffering mother will find an eerie little pile of hair near the television set or on the bathroom floor, as if there is an extremely small mass murderer in the family.

Their hair is usually much lighter, much straighter, and much prettier than my own and we're on a more equal footing when it's gone.

I still don't know precisely why I made my beloved dolls look like tiny victims from cheap late-night movies or, worse, like a cross between Brigitte Nielsen, (a.k.a. "Stallone Babe"), and Suzanne Powers, (a.k.a. "Diet Guru"). I was genuinely fond of them (the dolls) and much of my play revolved around the complexities of their vinyl lives (still talking about the dolls). These toys were my companions, my pets, my extended family, my entrance into the elaborate neighborhood doll games where you brought your favorite (usually a Barbie because they traveled well) to a playmate's house and made them trade stories.

These stories were, as I remember them, inevitably tragic in nature. Often one of the dolls had contracted a fatal disease or had just lost her dream home in a fire (nobody actually owned one of the fancy pink plastic dream homes so this plot offered a plausible excuse for the home's palpable absence). The dolls would break up with boyfriends, get arrested (sometimes for murder, other times for minor crimes, such as stealing scissors), argue with the other dolls, go spectacularly insane and so tear at their garments (we avoided simple depression or a quiet sense of weltzschmerz because we quite liked tearing at the garments. We had never heard of menopause).

If someone could provide a Ken doll, the toys would have shockingly close encounters, all of which remain far too embarrassing to describe now that I'm an adult. Let's just say our dolls didn't just hold hands; the fact that they were not anatomically correct in no way seemed to infringe on their imaginary trysts. When they were tired out, the dolls might be involved in a traffic accident because one girl had a plastic dream convertible and there is nothing interesting to do with a toy car except make it crash, as all little boys already know.

As well as hacking up their hair, I also used to bite the feet of my Barbies. It wasn't a pretty habit. It was, however, better than my neighbor Vicki's habit of coloring in the legs with permanent markers so that the dolls looked as if they had skid marks on them (although, as you can imagine, her dolls were strikingly effective for those accident scenarios). Mild foot-biting was also preferable to my friend Katy's routine. To summarize: Katy rather violently removed the heads of her dolls, painstakingly placed the heads on the tops of pencils, and then lost them. Her headless toys looked like the specters out of gothic horror films, mannequins from a British wax museum, or members of the French aristocracy after a seriously tough afternoon. True, my dolls had bad hair days, but that clearly paled in comparison to the fact that her dolls had bad head days.

The atrocities committed by small girls on their prized dolls are extreme, legion, and reassuringly familiar. Toys are the only things in the world less powerful than little girls, so it is perhaps not surprising that we fiddle with them, torment them, and irrevocably alter them according to our whims. Bite their feet, cut their hair, draw on their limbs, and they remain mute and continue to smile.

Too often big girls do the same things when faced with real dangers.

Too often we try to smile through the damage.

Highway 40 (Revisited)

A year ago I turned forty. It wasn't bad: big party, lots of friends, bushels of cards, hugs and kisses and reassurances that everything would be fine. It has been--a few ups and downs, a few better and worse days--but so far so good. I'm knocking on wood as I say that.

Now, however, as happens if you're lucky to get from one birthday to another, I'm facing forty-one. It's within spitting distance and attached to it is all the charm inherent in that phrase. Forty was child's play because it was, as one friend would say, "a goof." It was like buying your first drink at 21 and feeling sophisticated because you could sit at a bar legally (as if sitting at a bar was a huge accomplishment).

Forty was like realizing in your early thirties that you should no longer under any circumstances shop in the "Juniors" section even if you can fit into the sizes because dressed in "Juniors" clothing women over a certain ago look like hookers or cross-dressers. It isn't pretty. So forty had a lock on all the rite-of-passage, big-time, big-deal rituals and realizations. People shook my hand and patted me on the back when I said "I just turned forty" in a way that made it seem like an accomplishment.

Forty-one? Say that out loud and the same people avert their eyes. They don't want to know; I guess telling someone how old you are, even if they ask, is as unacceptable as telling them your weight or how much you saved by using coupons this week at Highland Market. They simply aren't interested. Even if they feign a pleasant sense of curiosity, they are longing to get away. The magnetic pull of any other conversation (even the one about the comparable merits of brown and white rice in terms of roughage) becomes increasingly strong when faced with someone who, at an advanced age, clings to the childish notion that people want to hear about your precocity even when, frankly, it no longer matters.

It's as if you were faced with an adult who kept telling you that they are tall for their age or that they have truly excellent eyesight. The only response is to leave as quickly as possible and move to the other side of the room while avoiding eye contact.

Trust me on this one: it took a full year to learn. Little kids can be cute and precocious; grown people cannot. It's like watching Benny Hill dress as a five year old or seeing the old cat try to play with the little cat's rubber mouse. It's amusing but for all the wrong reasons.

Heaven knows I tried to make this schtick work. For a while there, I would try smiling coyly (useless gesture) and admit, "Well, having only just turned forty, I guess I think I've done all right. . . ." This routine stopped abruptly when my brother (six years my senior) suddenly got fed up. "WHAT DO YOU EXPECT? BALLOONS FOR HOLDING DOWN A FULL-TIME JOB? TRUMPETS TO SIGNAL EVERY TIME YOU MEET A DEADLINE? ROSES FOR STILL HAVING MOST OF YOUR MAJOR ORGANS INTACT AS YOU APPROACH MENOPAUSE? WHAT, EXACTLY, ARE YOU BRAGGING ABOUT? YOU'RE OVER FORTY--YOU NO LONGER GET A GOLD STAR FOR THE PRIVILEGE OF LIVING YOUR LIFE. GET OVER IT. BE THANKFUL AND SHUT UP." At least, I think that's what he said; if he didn't say it, he should have.

And while I have failed miserably at shutting up, I am certainly making a habit of being thankful. God knows I was never an ingenue, but I need to remind myself that this getting older business is indeed a privilege and not a chore. Not everybody gets to do it, for one thing: that in itself should make us greet the dawn with appreciation if not genuine relief at having at least made it to another day, even if that day is a Monday.

But part of what's difficult, I've decided, is that when you've been rewarded for relative youth (I'll skip the obvious joke about relatives--you can say it silently to yourselves) it's tough to let go. Those gold stars in school were nice; so was being told "My, I thought you'd be older" when you show up for an interview, or talk, or conference.

Okay, so nobody says that anymore. I'll trade that pleasure in on one condition (and since it's my birthday I get to make wishes out loud). The condition is that I get to hang around long enough to hear that other golden phrase: "We had no idea you'd still be able to write/talk/listen/eat while sitting up at your age." I figure there's a while to go until I can claim that one for my own, but I hope that--lots of birthdays down this long highway--I'll get there.

Stuff I Didn't Think Would Still Bother Me At My Age (But Does)

Whether too much soda will make me break out

Whether or not my father approves of what I do

Whether the person who hung up the phone without
leaving a message was the person I had really hoped would call

Wondering how highly a not-well-liked peer scored
on his or her SATS

How high was the verbal vs. the math

Whether I'll ever dance in high heels to "Because the Night"
(as sung by Patti Smith) on a hot July evening again

How I look from the back

Whether my teeth are their whitest

The relationship of salaries to verbal SAT scores;
also the relationship of SAT scores to how people look from the back

If my tan lines show

If the fake tanning product I have administered with less than professional results makes me look as if I haven't washed my ankles since 1972

If anybody's looking

If I'll ever be able to spell "verisimilitude"
without checking on the number of "s"s

Ditto for "buses" (it always looks incorrect)

My height

Whether I have to finish a book I don't like because I started it
(n.b.: this applies both to reading and writing)

The height of Others

Whether my small and few but sincere virtues outweigh
my ample and various but (insert fluttering of eyelashes here)
inconsequential vices

Whether I'm carrying around a chip on my shoulder
the size of Paramus, New Jersey

Whether I'm too loud

Who it is who will decide if I am too loud

Whether I should buy new clothes for the first day of school

How my desperate, if not downright maniacal,
avoidance of all team sports will affect my personal life

Whether my friends like me as much as I like them

Whether I make a decent cup of coffee

Wondering if my face is round, pear-shaped, square, or
oval and feeling a deep need to make a decision concerning this

Whether I tip too little (and seem cheap) or tip too much
(and seem clumsily extravagant)

Noises in the middle of the night

Whether someone taller than I am will sit in front of me
at the movies after the feature film has already started so
that it will be impossible to move and I will see all the action
as if it were being emitted from a large ear

Whether I'm wearing too much perfume

If I'm wearing the right shoes for my outfit

When I'm giving a party, spending the entire hour before its
commencement wondering whether anyone will actually show up

Wondering whether anyone else in the universe will ever comment
on what I consider to be my virtually unique and unquestionably
charming ability to sing the first line of every song recorded
between 1962 and 1983

Suspecting that when the phone rings in the middle of the night,
I will hear a friend's voice announcing the break-up of a long-term
relationship

Whether I will ever luxuriate in cooking a truly tasty eggplant

Whether I will ever enjoy cooking any vegetable, except those
which I throw (in what must be called a rather "cavalier"--French
for "haphazard"-- fashion) into a stew

Whether anything good will appear on the fall television line-up

Whether anything good will appear in the fall fashion line-up

What I'll wear while watching t.v. in the fall

Whether I'll ever dance--or even rock back and forth rhythmically
on my heels while sitting down-- in any kind of footwear whatsoever
to "Sweet Jane" (as sung by Lou Reed) on a hot July evening again

Whether I should send a birthday card to a friend who always forgets
to send me one

Whether the friend actually forgets or just doesn't bother

My bony elbows and the little bits of skin that bunch up around them
which, I was recently informed, are called "noops"

Whether I'm the only one to spend time worrying about this stuff
at this age when, after all, there are more important things
to worry about

Whether that means I've been worrying in all the wrong ways
all these years. . . .

Reading Secrets

We are maybe fourteen, maybe just fifteen. We are all babysitting by this point, not being popular enough to date like Lynn, the beige-colored girl whose mother knew the mothers of all the cute boys (we said) which is why she got dates (we said) despite the fact that she had no personality to speak of (we said). The last part made us mad. "Personality is what you develop when you ain't got looks," summed up my Aunt Rose and damned if she wasn't right. With frizzy hair and flat feet, I was a girl working hard on her personality.

Oh, we had dated all right, but not steadily. Our dance cards were not exactly full. I had an appetite for sophisticated men of sixteen or seventeen and a couple of my older brother's friends had tried, very successfully I must add, to kiss me when they weren't in jeopardy of being seen by anyone remotely their own age. I was promiscuous in my fantasies, going from tall long-haired boy to tall long-haired boy. My friend Gale was monogamous in her dream, secretly liking since grade school an icily handsome boy named Brett. He never asked her out on a date or anything but he remained her dream boyfriend. Lisa never had specific tastes in guys. She dodged questions about who she liked. She evaded our prying words, but played the game generally. She liked the idea of romance but never came up with a target.

So there we were on Saturday nights with our variously developing personalities, babysitting the kids of impossibly old parents of thirty, maybe thirty-three, thinking that we were merely going through a dress rehearsal for our real lives which would begin any time now, probably on the day we got asked out by a boy who could have (had he lacked the taste for personality) gone out with Lynn.

So we babysat. And we snooped. It took us a while to admit how we found them, but eventually we did. We dug them out of night table drawers, lingerie cabinets, under mattresses, behind books in bookcases, inside paper bags in the pantry. Once we started looking they were absolutely everywhere.

Pornographic books. Magazines. Sometimes photographs of the couples themselves--which were hysterical, of course, and counted as the least erotic stuff we could imagine. (It was too early for videos, but we would have found those had they been in existence). Too trustworthy to dare being found out, we were expert at our activity. We learned to replace everything as we found it. We never felt guilty.

We didn't see anything harmful in investigating every drawer, closet, box, attic and basement in the house once the kiddies were fast asleep. It didn't seem to bother anybody. What our employers didn't know wouldn't hurt them. They had fun looking at the stuff, so why shouldn't we? We were starving for sexual attention, but who knew it? We thought we were now playing in the big leagues, at least by proxy.

It was an afternoon, not an evening, that changed everything. None of us got caught; we caught, without hunting, someone else. Lisa invited us to her house and, stealthily, showed us her father's stack of pornographic magazines. At first the four of us who were brave enough to follow her upstairs on what we knew was a dangerous mission were sizzlingly delighted to have at our collective fingertips a real treasure of trash. Her parents were out for the whole day and the afternoon stretched ahead of us like an open highway into forbidden territory.

But as we passed the slick and finger-worn pages around, one by one we started to feel bad. It was easy to see that this wasn't funny anymore. It was Lisa's dad that came up here to read these. She said that she was sure her mother didn't even know about them. It worried me that Lisa knew about them. I asked her how she found them. She said her father showed them to her.

Nobody asked anything further, but one by one we found excuses to leave. Lisa tried to keep us kidding around about everything, but the mood had changed. I remember saying good-bye at her doorstep as if I were seeing her in a snapshot of herself, stuck in that moment while the rest us of could leave. I felt as if I were leaving for another country instead of just down the block.

I wondered what it would be like to live in that house knowing those pictures were up there in the attic, but I didn't dare allow myself to think about that for very long. This wasn't something shared by a cute young couple. If this was shared, it was shared in some unholy alliance that I didn't have a name for and that I didn't want to know about.

We were young and we scampered as far away from it as we could, even at the expense of abandoning the one of our own who had dared show us a wound. Looking back on it now, I picture a circle of girls scattering, leaving one lone figure behind who cannot decide in which direction to move and so remains motionless. No one retrieves her. No one goes back.

The Big, Really Big Book of Memories

My mind is cluttered with totally useless pieces of information and I can't figure out why; no doubt I could figure out why if my mind wasn't so cluttered with useless pieces of information.

I remember the telephone number of my high-school boyfriend. I remember my student i.d. number from college. I remember, to my genuine dismay, all the words to the following television theme songs: Gilligan's Island ("The millionaire--and his wife"); The Patty Duke Show ("a hot dog makes her lose control."); Green Acres ("You're my wife--Good-bye city life!"); and 60 Minutes ("Tick, tick, tick, tick. . . ."). I can even duplicate the exact moment when the breathless but enthusiastic girls stage-whispered Petticoat Junction and when somebody, also breathy, said It's Burke's Law -- despite the fact that I have no recoverable memory of the program wherein this final breathiness appeared. Yet that one line is irrevocably lodged in some tiny (very tiny) brain cell to the exclusion of some other morsel of more valuable data, such as where I put the book of stamps I bought only two hours ago.

I can produce the words to every song I've ever heard--okay, almost every song--but I don't. I have a basically generous nature and therefore do not make this pack of memories public because it would involve singing. Singing the words is the only way I can remember the words, which is perhaps not a shock since singing the little song is also the only way I can remember the alphabet. I cannot carry a tune for love, money, or even fine real estate. So if you're ever desperate to know all the words to "Rescue Me," "Nowhere to

Run," "Mustang Sally," "See You in September," "Leader of the Pack" (including those parts where she shouts "Lookoutlookoutlookout!"), or any number of any Beatles recording, I'm your girl--as long as you can put up with my melodic voice.

If you want to know the words to the songs from the Mary Martin production of Peter Pan ("I Gotta Crow" included) or the Tim Curry version of The Rocky Horror Picture Show ("Don't get strung out by the way I look, don't judge a book by its cover. . ."), just give me a call. So what if Mary dresses as a boy and Tim dresses as a girl? It's the lyrics that make a lasting impression.

Having drastically misspent my early youth (see above), I am nevertheless able to toss out --when the occasion demands--some nifty stuff, such as great lines from various plays and novels. You read a work often enough, it dives straight down into your unconscious and becomes as familiar as your home address; it's interesting, therefore, to find out precisely what bits and pieces folks remember from the books they read, write about, and teach. I can recite the opening speech from Richard III, where the misshapen, bitter hero ends up invoking heaven's support for bastards (which is sort of unnerving since I rarely teach Shakespeare). But I also carry around in my heart the sweet speeches from the end of A Midsummer Night's Dream and so can reassure myself that life has some balance.

Every once in a while, there's a pleasant surprise in what you can dredge up. I am convinced that my husband Michael first took notice of me when, in some silly conversation, I quoted the first lines from Edgar Allen Poe's short story "The Cask of Amontillado" ("The thousand injuries of Fortunado I had borne as best I could, but when he ventured upon insult, I vowed revenge. You, who so well know the nature of my soul, will not suppose, however, that I gave utterance to a threat. At length I would be avenged. . . .").

As a professor of literature, he wasn't amazed I knew a couple of lines from a couple of books, but it was the fact that I could quote from an American author that impressed him--American and British writers being segregated, typically, into different areas of study. Or maybe--and, on second thought this sounds more plausible--he was merely concerned that such a line as uttered by an Italian girl might include several shades of meaning. (And I did after all go on to write a book called Sweet Revenge where Poe pops up yet again.)

So, like some puzzled traveler with a bag full of random and not particularly sensibly-chosen objects, I carry around the flotsam and jetsam of memory--phrases, rhymes, bits of dialogue from episodes of I Love Lucy ("It's so tasty, too, just like candy!"), unsung songs, and even the exact way morning light brushed across the ceiling of my childhood home. When the journey gets too tiring, I hope I'll be able to sit down and figure out why I've carried what I've carried for so long.

Ask Me How Old I Am

I had a seriously mid-life moment the other day: I forgot my age. Just plain old forgot how old I am. A friend in Florida asked me how old I turned on my last birthday and I cheerfully answered "forty-one." My husband was, as luck would have it, right there in the room and so he was able to correct me. "Forty-three," he announced, practically hollering out the number in the manner of an auctioneer, "Forty-three as of last Friday."

It wasn't like I was trying to dissemble; a little thing like dissembling I could understand and forgive myself. (One of the lovely parts of growing older is how much easier it is to forgive myself. It has become quite an absorbing hobby.) Lots of women, as well as some men, of my acquaintance regularly lie about their age and consider the sin wholly inconsequential, sort of like smudging the truth about how often you exercise or how much you weigh. You can say anything you want, they reason, because you shouldn't have been asked the question in the first place.

So lying about one's age is considered socially acceptable, as is declaring the fact that your age is nobody's business. This is interesting, given that perfidy and telling people to "butt out" are usually regarded as graceless gestures when applied to other situations. Imagine a scene: at lunch, a co-worker casually asks, "How long have you and your husband been married?" and is gently and coyly rebuked with "Oh, a lady never reveals that sort of information!" This is said wholly without irony and as if the friendly question itself was as an exercise in bad taste.

The co-worker, after a baffled pause, decides to eat at the OTHER table from now on.

It's not like asking somebody's age is the same as asking how many sexual partners they've had (now THAT is an interesting question to toss out around a lunch table at work). But lying about or concealing your age is practically mandatory.

When I was a teenager I wanted to be thought of as older. Older girls seemed sophisticated, hip, and independent. Now that I am ACTUALLY older, it's younger women who seem sophisticated, hip, and independent. Go figure.

But don't get me wrong-- I would not be any other age for love or money, not even on a dare. I work with people in their late teens and early twenties. I respect and have great affection for my students but in NO way do I envy them. Yes, they are healthy creatures with boundless energy, a species who can stay up all night to write a paper and still go for a run in the morning. True, they have all their teeth, do not undergo gastric reflux--nor do they require Viagra or Vivelle.

But they suffer from the incurable maladies of youth: the gripping fear of the unveiled future, the pernicious panic of inexperience, the constant crises of love wanted and love lost. I see long, shadowed hallways in their eyes when they come to explain why a book made them cry, or when they come to argue that I have been too critical of work they know is not their best. They argue and weep for irrepressible reasons. Yet the reasons are familiar to me because I have traveled through the place they are coming from. And I have no wish to revisit the landscape that produces such storms.

Do you remember Oscar Wilde's wonderful injunction, "One should never trust a woman who tells her real age. A woman who would tell one that would tell one anything"? That's going to become my motto. I'm going to have tee-shirts emblazoned with Wilde's maxim.

I'll invest the words with a meaning, however, that Wilde probably did not intend.

One of my goals is to become somebody who will "tell one anything" without shame, hesitation, or befuddlement. I want to embrace being old enough to say "I'm a big girl now and too old to act cute, shut up, or be demure," the way, as a child, I wanted to say "I'm old enough to play outside after sundown." If growing up doesn't guarantee increased access to places that had once been roped off, what good is it?

I may have forgotten my age for a moment and, in so doing, illustrated the very fact of my aging. I can live with the passage of years. After all, growing older still seems better than the alternative.

A Womb With A View

Part 1 Hearing the News Nobody Wants to Hear

I'll answer your most important question first: yes, I did get a second opinion. And a third, and a fourth, and they all said the same thing: for goodness' sake, have the operation, there's nothing else to be done. So please don't tell me there are other ways to do this, even if you believe that through meditation, osmosis, feminism, exercise, herbal teas, or the systematic collection of certain retired Beanie Babies, I can be cured without surgery. I'm having the surgery very soon and I need you to wish me well, okay?

The operation I'm having is a hysterectomy. They are removing what I refer to as my "bits," those decidedly female organs wherein are lodged fibroid tumors the size of Delaware, items that are small for a state but on the largish side for carrying around under your belt. I'm losing my uterus and my ovaries, which is sort of like losing your house keys: something pretty essential and familiar will disappear--poof--while I'm not looking. Unlike house keys, I'm not about to have another set made. These were factory-issued parts and they are irreplaceable. The best I can do is deal with the loss and get on with my life.

Which poses an interesting question: what, if anything, am I losing? It's tricky. Michael, my husband, got into Serious Trouble when he compared my hysterectomy to an appendectomy: "They're taking out a part of you that you've never seen, and since it is a part that isn't working right, isn't that an easy option?" The answer is no, although I've been trying to decide precisely why the answer is "no" for a couple of months now. No, I'm not planning to have babies--sad, but true--nor do I have principles preventing me from removing what ails me. So why should it be troublesome? A no-womber should be a no-brainer, right?

I'm scared, that's the problem. I'm scared of surgery--as I always say, "elective surgery" has always been an oxymoron in my family, sort of like "jumbo shrimp"--and I'm particularly wary of anything that will touch what I've regarded as the sort of mainspring of my life. I guess, to put it in architectural terms, my uterus and ovaries have always seemed like a load-bearing beam, crucial to the integrity of the infrastructure. I've come to think of them as inside information; I've come to regard them as buried treasure. Not that I've celebrated every period--I have not gone out and bought red balloons on the fourth week of every month or anything--but in 41 years I've come to view cycles as vital and viable measurements of time, as small flags in the book of my life, as small markers which I can trace all the way back to the end of childhood.

But don't let me romanticize too much: there's a lot I won't miss. I won't miss concealing tampons on my person at all times as if they were unlicensed weapons (giving a whole new meaning to the idea of feminine protection) and I can cancel my subscription to "Menopause Today," a monthly magazine published irregularly. No, the loss of my "bits" isn't what worries me as much as the idea of the loss of myself.

To clarify: a whole bunch of women in my family have died before they turned fifty. When I go for check-ups and have to fill in those forms asking you to list your family history, I feel embarrassed to hand them to the nice office personnel, all of whom glance at them and then look at me as if they'll never see me again, as if to say "If I were you, honey, I wouldn't buy any green bananas." I have no interest in becoming yet another female family member to cash in her chips before the game is over; I'm having too good a time and I intend to cling fiercely to life, given half a chance. Like the Springsteen song says, some may want to die young, but I want all the time that heaven will allow.

So having cleared that up, this is what I need to say: that with everything else--the emotional, the superstitious, the political, the historical, the pharmacological-- surrounding this event for me, the absolutely last thing I need is to be embarrassed about naming it for what is it. When I wrote a note to my (male) boss requesting a medical leave, I thought more about his reaction to the news of this operation than my own: I feared that he would wince and shudder at the very idea. I felt badly for him; hello . . .is something wrong with this picture? If I were having a by-pass performed or a gall-bladder removed, I believe I would have felt differently. I would have announced it as a challenge: confront and overcome: I could see it as a battle I could win with courage and fortitude. I find myself--twenty years of feminist theory aside-- needing to overcome the temptation to regard this hysterectomy as a kind of punishment, or penalty, or fine, or tax, for being female. You know when they put a "boot" on your car's tire when you haven't paid your parking tickets? Something metal, with teeth, not letting you move, but nothing--they tell you-- to be scared of? That's what this feels like.

Which is unreasonable, which is illogical, which is silly, and which is sad--all of which I'm feeling right now. The best I can come up with is this old piece of woman's wisdom: whatever you lose in your life will inevitably make room for something new. I hope that's true.

Part 2 The Night Before

I can't believe I have to go into the hospital tomorrow. This sounds really stupid and self-indulgent, but I have no idea what to expect. It's late at night now and I'm suddenly thinking of the myriad questions I should have thought of earlier. Do I bring my own nightgown? Toothpaste? Seltzer? Am I allowed to bring my own pillow or blanket? How soon will I be able to speak on the phone and drink diet beverages, the two central activities of my day? Will I want to read? Can I read stuff that will make me laugh, or will laughter be the last thing I want to experience--I suspect that, after a hysterectomy, being in stitches and "being in stitches" might have contradictory effects.

Will the nurses be nice to me? Should I bring boxes of chocolates to appease them? Will I appear weak and foolish to them, this community of strong people who deal with real illness every day? Will they consider me impertinent if I ask them too many questions; will they consider me aloof if I don't? Am I allowed to go to the bathroom by myself, or do I need to raise my hand and ask for help like in first grade? What time will I have to go to bed? Can I watch television late at night if I promise to keep the sound down? Can I read in bed if I use a flashlight?

Will I be lonely? Will I be scared? Will this remind me of the time I had my tonsils out when I was four, one of my earliest memories and not a happy one, when I felt like I would never go home again, even though I was only gone overnight?

I know I'm making a big deal out of this. I know that this is nothing special. This operation is not a big deal for anyone else -- "routine surgery," nothing fancy, nothing new, nothing extraordinary. But some people face this day-before-the-procedure not knowing that wonderful Dr. DiLeo has performed this particular surgery a whole bunch of times when nothing else would do the trick. They deal with their fears without the absolute confidence that their doc could handle the procedure (if he needed to) in his sleep, in the back of a Chevy Blazer, while doing pirouettes in The Ice Capades, whatever. He's a pro, he's a nice guy, he knows what he's doing (and, to be fair, he kept asking me if I had any questions--I just didn't know until this evening that I did indeed have some). I'd let this guy cut my hair, fix my car, edit my books, take care of my cats, perform surgery on my family if they needed it, and I'd let him prepare Christmas Eve dinner; in an Italian family, that's the very definition of confidence.

Having said that, how do other people face tougher times? The ones who are sitting there the night before an uncommon occurrence, before an experimental procedure, before something not out of a standard-issue medical journal, but out of an old science fiction movie? This happens every day, but how do the patients get through it? Because there is no alternative?

Because their strength and faith and courage is beyond what I can even fathom? Some people are facing the truly unknown, not just the new-to-them, not just the ordinary tasks of medicine's most ordinary days. I honestly don't know if I'd have it in me, if --even at life's borderland--I could wrangle up enough courage and imagination to get through it, or if I'd just head out for the territories, passport in hand. What I'm dealing with is merely difficult; what some other braver, more exceptional people must face is not merely difficult, but virtually unimaginable.

Facing fear is rarely as bad as worrying about its approach; acknowledging fear is inevitably better than desperately pretending what frightens us doesn't exist. Emily Dickinson wrote a poem about facing her worst fear: a snake obliterating her sense of calm when out for an afternoon's walk. She describes her sense of sudden terror as feeling "zero at the bone," and the hollow, empty, intense, and deeply felt sensation is invoked by that phrase. What is feared scratches at the glass behind a dark window in every woman's and man's soul. The darkness is the same, the metallic taste of fear is the same for everyone but the individual causes for fear-- the shape of the windows framing the darkness-- are wildly different in their detail and essentially the same at their core. There is no such thing as absolute safety; there is no place to rest in the certainty that you'll wake up better than you set down. Having said that, there is nevertheless hope (the thing with feathers, etc.--see E.D.'s other poems) and a sense of possibility with each day.

Tomorrow will be tough, but no tougher than the tomorrows of a lot of other folks. You face your fear, you go through it, you come out the other side (one way or another) and it's gone, a skin you've shed, a badge you've earned, a ladder you've walked under, a dream from which you have--finally, gratefully -- awakened.

Part 3 "If You Can Read This, You're Too Close"

I was far less nervous the morning of the surgery than I had been the night before. This odd decline in my levels of anxiety also happens when I fly;

the anticipation is almost always worse than facing the experience. I even slept several hours, surprising myself. Since I had packed everything up the previous evening I was pretty much ready to get in the car and go around sunrise. Michael had coffee and piece of toast--I couldn't eat anything and so of course desperately coveted his meal, watching every sip as if it were meant for me--and we headed out into a beautiful, clear morning.

Packing for the hospital was curious. I was clueless, but my instincts took over and actually led me in the right direction. I decided to take lots of stuff that would comfort me. I brought toys friends had given me, everything from the teddy-bear a young friend brought to silly pens and a brand new cheap notebook. I brought my own pillow with a very brightly colored pillow case so that it would not be mistaken for the hospital's own. I brought good face washes and my own fuzzy slippers, even though I knew versions of these would probably be provided for me; I wanted to have some familiar textures and smells around me in this unfamiliar place.

Unfamiliar, yes, but certainly not unfriendly. I was greeted by cheerful people at the desk who discreetly looked away as I said good-bye to Michael and then I went on to be reassured by what seemed like an astonishing number of people who were coming by to introduce themselves as I sat in the preparation area. I had asked if I could get an epidural and was told that my wishes were perfectly fine, so long as everything went according to plan. Again, the very presence of my own doctor had a strengthening effect on me- I knew he knew what was about to happen even if I didn't. I trusted him and therefore trusted the people he chose to work with; such confidence made, I'm sure, all the difference.

I can honestly say that I felt no pain in preparation for or during the surgery--not from the injection for the epidural, not from anything at all--and so I'm glad I was able to forgo the general anesthetic. Not only does the idea spook me because of my control-freak ways, but I wanted to be as conscious as soon as possible so that I could actually face the experience of what I was going through.

Facing the experience happened sooner than I expected, and I'm grateful-

-although some people might be shocked by what I'm going to say. I was asleep for much of the operation but woke up just about when they had managed to separate (to be as delicate as possible, which believe me isn't easy right now) what had not been working in me from what--by all accounts--was working just fine. I asked to see what they'd removed. It wasn't pretty but it was fascinating and I'm glad I had the chance to observe.

Now, I never thought I was having a phantom hysterectomy or anything, but somehow my being awake enough to talk about it, ask what they were doing, and look at what they'd done, made the whole process seem more real to me. We even kidded around a little bit; I suggested when they sewed me up they should embroider "If You Can Read This, You're Too Close" wherever they thought it was appropriate. I remember them laughing, but that could have just been my drugs speaking.

Wheeled into the curtained-off cubicle of the recovery area, I was happy to see that Michael was permitted to come in right away. He looked remarkably relieved which is when it fully hit me how difficult all of this had been for him; he'd been scared, too, but didn't let himself (or me) understand that until now, seeing me after it was all over (so to speak), he could let his emotions rip. He did, I did, and, that accomplished, we set about the business of feeling better.

Part 4 A Womb With A Better View

I was scheduled to be in the hospital for three nights and four days. I couldn't figure out whether this sounded like a long time or a short time to recover from major surgery. Turns out, however, that such questions are moot: time loses all meaning in the hospital. It's sort of like being on a different, albeit friendly and efficient, planet. Even the outfits inhabitants wear look like they're cast offs from old (really old) episodes of "Star Trek," only the colors and cut are not as flattering. And that's saying something.

But, fashion statements aside, the hospital experience was still decidedly other-worldly. This is not a complaint, merely an observation. Granted, I was orbiting around the twin-planets of pain and medication, so this wasn't exactly a dispassionate fact finding mission. (I'm going to stop all references to outer space pretty soon, I promise.) But my overall impression of my time in the hospital is of an extended period of suspended animation, which, perhaps, is precisely how it is designed.

Okay, so there I am, getting wheeled into the room after leaving the recovery area. I've already been cared for by wonderful nurses, Dr. DiLeo has checked in, and Michael has been sufficiently reassured to go get himself some lunch at the cafeteria. I'm wheeled up to a double room, although for the moment I have the place to myself. This means I get the window view and even in my stupor I can see that the view is fabulous, a view you'd have to pay extra for if this were a fancy hotel. I'm encouraged by the lapidary blue of the sky and cheered by the riotous colors of the trees. I am happy, in short, to be alive. Keeping this thought in mind helps me put the pain in perspective.

For a while. The epidural helps me get through the first hours of post-op and then they administer some other drug that also erases the pain-- magically, beautifully--and then it all starts to unravel as I have a ridiculous but nevertheless unbelievably powerful itching response to the meds. No rash, nothing terrible, just the worst, skin-crawling, nerve-seering itching in the universe. It's late evening now and I can't believe I'm actually asking the poor nurse to scratch my back for me because otherwise I will start to howl like a coyote in frustration and bother the other, more normal patients. She does it and I'm embarrassed but thankful. I ask the staff to call for help, but everybody--the docs who deal with this sort of thing--is temporarily tied up. I tell them that "tied up" is how they'll be carting me out of the place if this itching doesn't calm down soon.

They get a young doctor (maybe a resident? I don't remember) to come up and take a look. I'm sure she's had a long day, and I've watched enough episodes of "E.R." to understand she needs her sugar to stay awake, but she is chomping on a wad of gum or toffee so large that all possible communication between us is rendered impossible. To her credit, she explains "I have a big piece of candy"(which comes out, muffled and apologetic, as "Mihave a whig wheece of khandee" but I can decipher what she means). It is clear, however, that she is not going to remove it. I believe, to my discredit, that at this point I started to cry. Long story short: they changed the medication and everything was fine. New point of fact in my life: I prefer pain to itching. Pain you can understand, put inside some known category of received stimuli; itching is physical chaos, the entrance to the abyss. Hell, as designed for me, won't be full of spikes: it'll be full of mosquitoes.

After that evening, the rest of the stay was a piece of cake (no candy). The nurses and doctors were perfect--cheerful, sensitive, smart, and careful--and I once again offered thanks to the universe that people choose to spend their lives working with the sick and the injured, the scared and the damaged. I knew that the simple procedure I went through was nothing compared to what others around me in that building had to face, but those who cared for me made me feel as if I were under their wing and therefore guaranteed of their kindness and protection. Each day was easier, but the humbling lesson of being aware of even the smallest physical action is one I will try to remember. I was thrilled when I could eat solid foods and blissful when I could walk around.

And I was never as happy to come home in my life.

Shades of Grey

I have to stop listening to people. They mix me up. There I was, thinking that I'd been as intimidated as I could ever be by fashion, by magazines, by the images of women on television and in the movies. And then I listened to a few women--all wonderful, all genuinely good friends--and now I'm all bothered again. I'm back to spending all sorts of stupid time looking at clothes in my closet as if any minute now my shirts are going to break into song.

This is what happened: one day Maggie was describing a cafe where she'd gone to listen to music the night before. She described the place as vaguely depressing and so I asked her for details. What were the people like, I asked, what were they wearing? "Well," she replied, happy to have come up with an example that would clarify her position, "All these women were dressed in black, but it was like they were wearing three or four kinds of black, none of which matched or complimented each other, you know what I mean?" I guess I must have been staring at her like she was from a parallel universe because she asked me if I were okay. "I'm fine," I responded, "But please explain what you mean about wearing different shades of black."

Suddenly, even as she spoke, I was reviewing twenty-five years of fashion choices; they were spinning before my eyes the way stars speed by when movie spaceships enter a time warp. I was in my personal little time warp, trying to remember if anybody had ever mentioned this patently obvious point before this moment. I came up with a blank. I also came up with a new tiny cause for stress: even as Maggie's innocent words sunk in, I realized my black leggings clashed with my black socks which were as different a color from the black in my shoes as fushia is from fire-engine red. Fashion casualty that I am, even I wouldn't wear a pinky-red with an orange-y red, so how could I have not seen the differences in my dark clothes, the clothes I wear pretty much as a uniform every day?

I could, once again, place all blame conveniently on my early history and genetic coding. Back in Brooklyn all the women who weren't wearing floral print house dresses were wearing black, at least in my immediate family (of 118). After a certain age, a woman automatically started wearing black-- enough people die, your wardrobe changes. But I don't remember my Aunt Clara trying to discern whether her black orthopedic shoes matched her black support hose, and she never held them up to discover whether they matched the shiny black cotton of her short-sleeved black dress. They fit, they were washable, they didn't bind, they were on sale, that was good enough.

But, having learned to accept responsibility for my own choices in life (particularly those involving fabric), I couldn't believe the errors of my way were all due to my early upbringing. No, I had to admit that before Maggie named it, I hadn't seen it.

But this experience paled in comparison to one brought on by a brief comment made by another friend, Viv, who, when trying on a great pair of trousers, declared "But I'll never wear them. See how they look on me when I sit down?" whereupon she promptly and without warning or explanation plopped herself down on the floor of the store's dressing room. If she'd suddenly burst into an aria from Wagner I could not have been more surprised. "What on earth are you doing?!" I shrieked, trying to pull her up to her adult height. "I'm seeing how they'll look when I sit. See how everything bunches up above the waist? See how they emphasize my hips? Forget it," she shrugged, and left the pants hanging beautifully on their hanger, having brushed off any debris they might have picked up on the floor.

Terrific. For the rest of my life I'll have to go through a full range of possible positions in which I can be viewed before making a twenty-dollar purchase. Now I pretend to sit down or bend over in a dressing room: it must be fun to watch on the closed-circuit security monitor. I end up going through so many motions I look like a mime. Now I am aware of just how a jacket will look when I'm actually wearing it, not just how it looks while I'm standing as straight as a Marine and holding my breath in order to suck in my stomach.

Once you hear these things, you can't forget them. Sure, you can choose to ignore them or discard them, but even then you don't forget them. For example, Genny said that her mother said (and mothers are often the sources of these pieces of grave information) a lady should not wear more than three colors at the same time. Okay, this is where I drew the line: I can't wear black for fear of messing that up, that much I now understand--but is it also true that I'm not supposed to wear more than three colors?

That's it. Enough is enough. I'm going to find where Aunt Clara bought her clothes and set up an account. They can send me a new dress every year. It'll be my job to make sure the stockings match.

billboards and ads imply that she does. Frankly I don't want to know any facts whatsoever. I don't want anything to interfere with this glorious sense of righteous indignation. Just save the stamp.)

Here's the strange part: I think Michael looks exactly the same age he looked eight years ago, whereas I seem increasingly to resemble those women you see in photographs from Tibet. You know, those women who live to be a hundred-and-twenty-years-old by existing only on a strict diet of yogurt and wool? That's me, only without the tan.

But what really makes me crazy is that I thought, eight years ago, that I didn't look good in those pictures. I thought they made me look dumpy or cranky. I thought my upper arms looked lousy and so I wore long sleeves even in the summer. What was I thinking? Was I thinking, "Hey, I'll cover myself up now because as I leave my thirties and enter my forties I will no doubt miraculously turn into a more finely-flexing creature of beauty?"

Ah, um, yeah.

With God as my witness, I did think something like that. Every year since I turned thirteen, I've promised myself that I would look better next year: once I gained height, lost weight, cleared up my skin, got great high-heels, got a better haircut, exercised daily, waxed my eyebrows, waxed my legs, waxed my upper-lip (I was starting to think of myself as an extra in "Teen Wolf"), exercised regularly, bought better clothes, got a great tan, exercised more effectively, bought better foundation garments, rid myself of the effects of over-tanning, started taking estrogen, got my bunion removed, exercised at all, then I would look terrific and resemble hardly at all the fuzzy, round girl in the photograph.

Only now what has happened is this: I can't believe I didn't think I looked good in those earlier pictures. I looked absolutely fine--no great beauty, because I wasn't born to be a great beauty and that's how these things go--but never once did I believe I even looked okay. You couldn't have paid me money to believe it. I would have showed you why my chin looked flabby at twenty (it didn't) or why my legs looked heavy at thirty (they didn't).

I want to go back to and shake myself by my (always covered-up) shoulders and say "Yo, smarty-pants, you think all this will improve? You think somehow you'll be happier with how you look from the back at forty-two than at thirty-two? What planet are you from?" Why didn't I permit myself to enjoy those photographic moments then, always worried about how I would look?

The only way to compensate for earlier stupidities is to wise up. I'm taking pictures of myself in a bathing suit this summer without draping assorted pieces of fabric across my person as if attempting to disguise myself as an Algerian market stall. I will show my arms and display my neck, as if appearing on the Discovery Channel in a documentary on mating rituals. I will smile for the camera and trust that some older version of myself, or even somebody else, might say "No so bad."And I will stand next to my Distinguished husband, we'll both be laughing, and later on that's all anyone will notice because it is the only thing that matters.

Will My Seat Become a Flotation Device?

I had blueberry pancakes for breakfast this morning. I had them absolutely covered with a substance I still refer to in hushed tones, with a sort of religious awe-- I had them covered with Real Maple Syrup.

And I had a lot of them.

I just turned forty-one and so I should be having whole grain Astroturf with seaweed for breakfast in order to keep my girlish figure. By "girlish" I mean the kind of figure that still allows me to climb out a bedroom window if there's a fire.

Who, exactly, is saying I "should" eat Astroturf? It's that whiny voice that comes along and nags you to conform to someone else's idea of what you ought to be doing, insisting that you ignore your own needs, desires, and appetites. I don't know about you, but I'm shutting that voice down. I'm seeing the truth behind some of what I've always known was right, not because I understand the wisdom being offered by those who have said "You are not your thighs."

I used to agree, secretly, with Helen Rowland, the turn-of-the-century writer who quipped that "from the day on which she weighs 140, the chief excitement of a woman's life consists in spotting women who are fatter than she is." I'd look at other women and try to guess their weight as if I were at a State Fair trying to win a prize. I knew better than to confess publicly a fear of fat because that would undercut, I thought, my feminist credentials. Of all people, I was meant to know better than to believe that women should take up as little space as possible. I was supposed to know that you can be much too thin and far too rich, and that a woman's body is her own to take care of as well as she'd take care of one belonging to someone she loved.

You know what? Now, past forty -- and better late than never-- I do know these things. For real.

I have come to the conclusion that you really are loved, or respected, or admired, for yourself alone and not your finely-honed thighs, or firm buttocks, or steel bust, or sinewy upper arms. If somebody likes your style, they like your style. They'll take you fifteen pounds over, ten pounds under, whatever, because it's incidental, not essential. If somebody likes only bits of your anatomy--breasts or thighs, for example--let them go see what Frank Perdue can do for them.

You'll think that I'm encouraging women to eat until we look like floats from Macy's Thanksgiving Day Parade, but that's not so. What I'm saying is that after thirty years of trying to look like somebody from a magazine (we start young, remember; something like almost half of all preteen girls think they're overweight) I've decided to enjoy how I look now. And that, my dears, is very much a feminist act because it, too, is about making choices that permit you to make your life (and therefore the lives of others) better. This doesn't mean I'm giving up the earrings or the lipstick: it is not about abandoning the girl-stuff I get pleasure from playing with. It's not about gorging or gluttony. And it's not about buying tent dresses made from real tents.

So, back to the original question: Why do so many of us forgo the pancakes because we think we look too fat--even though we're active and healthy by all accounts? Even though a reality check would clear us of any real problems--except vanity?

This, of course, is where we must pause for an ad from our sponsors. Look at television, at magazines, and movies. Do any of these folks look like people we've ever seen up close? You know how I can tell the guy out there who said "yes" is fibbing? Because these folks don't even look like themselves half the time: the images we see are touched up, recreated, remade. Do you realize that Cindy Crawford, for heaven's sake, isn't perfect enough for the cover of Cosmo? Some computer techie fiddles with the photographic image so she'll look presentable. This should make us feel okay about putting mayonnaise on a sandwich.

As long as you can walk up a flight of stairs without sounding like an old Chevy about to blow a gasket, as long as your fingers are not permanent strangers to your toes, you're probably okay.

An old joke I heard in Florida serves as a surprisingly good summary of the central issues: Two socialite Palm Beach ladies are walking past Tiffany's on Worth Avenue. A shabby man comes over to them and humbly confesses "Ladies, I haven't eaten in three days. . ." They look at him with sympathy. One takes his hand in hers and says, "Poor dear, you must force yourself."

In other words, if you are desperate to feel bad, there's a whole lot of other stuff to worry about apart from your waistline: try worrying about homelessness, or date rape, or the rising cost of education. Or worry about the idea that in some other places--not very far from where we are at this moment--somebody's hungry. Really hungry. And it's not their choice.

But to spend good worry time over whether or not you're retaining water is only useful if you are a boat.

The first thing we should do is get rid of envy as a motivating force. When those commercials come on television saying that summer is approaching and we should get ready to look as good as the "competition," I suggest that we turn to our friends, offer them another helping of pasta, and agree that we won't wreck this summer by starving ourselves.

We'll just get bigger tans.

Skin Deep

It is a little tough for me to write about this, but since I've never seen anything in print about it I figured it might be something other people scanned pages for, even if they might not admit it. It's nothing fancy, but here goes.

For most of my life I absolutely believed that if I had better skin, the whole world would be a wonderful place to be. Everything would be easier; this is what I figured at sixteen, then nineteen, then twenty-two. I would automatically become more desirable and charming. I could be cute; I could even try being "girlish" and sweet just for the heck of it. I could look straight into any camera. I could cut my hair short; I could wear a pony-tail in public. I could use cheap make-up without worrying that I'd break out or look lurid and tough. I could lighten up. I could be less angry, less defensive, less miserable.

I figured I'd be less ashamed of facing the day without a scarred face. And I was ashamed--constantly and profoundly ashamed. As a teenager, I totally blamed myself for the poor condition of my skin and would make serious, often written, vows to give up soda, pizza, and chocolate--too bad, since now most dermatologists agree that diet doesn't have much to do with acne. Almost every diary from those years begins with a new year's resolution to forgo oily foods, as if that was going to begin my Cinderella-like transformation into a girl who could appear on the page of Seventeen or Mademoiselle.

I especially identified with Cinderella out of all the fairy-tale possibilities because it seemed to me that bad skin was something poor kids seemed to have; the wealthier ones had parents who would take them to doctors, or even specialists, or for facials, or buy them the right kinds of magical products that would minimize the problem. Poor kids were left to comb our hair over our foreheads and put our hands up to cover our faces as often as possible. Yes, of course it was the worst possible thing to do, but try to tell that to someone who is interested only in hiding.

You've never seen a girl with rough skin in a movie; you've never seen any woman whose flawless, silken face is anything but perfect. It just doesn't happen. Guys who have rough faces are usually cast as the tough characters, mobsters or evil-doers, but at least they get roles and they are visible in some way. While it's true that physical perfection has always been at an absolute premium for women, a beautiful face is la créme de la créme --it is at once the most essential and it is the most valued element of loveliness. You can, after all, get a body double; there is no face-double to be used for the close-ups. You are your face. And when you hate your face, it's a pretty short step to hating yourself.

Okay, it sounds like I should be asking you to get out the violins. It's not a sense of adolescent whining I'm trying to convey, but instead to give a sketchy map of a real issue for a lot of girls and women (and maybe for men as well, although I imagine it would be slightly different). How is this different from worrying about weight, for example? For one thing, weight is (for better or worse) a topic the culture has supplied with a large vocabulary; giggling or weepy girls trade diet stories the way boys trade baseball cards.

The only girls who ever drew attention to one of their facial imperfections (a nice way of saying "zit"), however, were the ones who had skin like Glenn Close, just as the girls who usually shrieked about putting on a pound were usually the ones wearing the skin-tight jeans and looking good in them. And, yes, it is both true and tragic that eating disorders can destroy the lives of some young women, while in contrast few people have died from acne. But when it's your face you're trying not to look at, the pain is pretty real.

When did it get easier? My husband Michael made all the difference in the world to me when, very early on in our relationship, he wanted to stroke my face. Gently but unhesitatingly, I pushed his hand away and told him not to touch my cheek because I felt too self-conscious, too uncomfortably aware of my own unloveliness. He asked again, and kept asking, telling me he loved how I looked. I told him I was ashamed of the scars and he told me that it wasn't scars that he saw, that whatever scars I was talking about were the ones left inside, from a long time ago, not ones facing the world everyday.

Not to sound too corny or anything, but I took him seriously and spent time looking at what inside wounds needed healing and what inside work needing doing. And I started to be able to look at myself a little more steadily and to face the world.

across billboards. My answer to them is: yes.

Having said this, I do like make-up. I especially like those little, tiny sample supplies given out as "free gifts" (as opposed to those nasty "gift-with-purchase" offers where you have to do something to be given a gift. Let me put it this way: I deeply resent those bargains in life and so not surprisingly I can't abide them at the lipstick counter, either).

I have about seventeen hundred "free-gift" objects scattered throughout my bathroom, office, purses, and glove compartments. Just in my everyday bag, the one I carry with me at all times --in case I have to begin life anew in a different country without much notice--I carry a dozen teensie-weensy sample mascaras. Some of these I've had with me since the Carter administration; they're probably no longer fashionable. Actually, they are probably no longer viscose; by this time they've probably mutated into a geological formation. But I refuse to throw them away.

Make-up is one of the few things I'll hold onto until the very last smudge; I'll scoop out the last few molecules of a favorite lipstick by using a cotton swab. This is a sad act to witness, not because it is tragic, but because it is obsessional. I fell into this habit back in my student days, when the purchase price of a full-size lipstick took most of a week's paycheck. I persist in doing it, however, not only out of habit but because cosmetic companies inevitably decide to cease all production of my favorite colors ten minutes after I have purchased them.

Okay, I hear you: maybe I should take the hint. This is sort of what Sandy was gently trying to tell me over there under the shadows of Big Ben and St. Paul: maybe I should pay more attention to how I apply this paint.

Sandy began the process of showing me what to do, as we sat in twin robes in front of her mirror. Turns out that I should never, ever have been putting on mascara and eye-brow stuff first--you're supposed to do this last. Diane, another friend, had already explained this to me but I supposed I hadn't quite had the presence of mind to see it as the deep threat to my appearance as Sandy indicated it could be. I think I was supposed to put on lip-liner first.

I can't apply lip-liner; I've never been able to color inside the lines. Sandy tried to teach me. I tried to follow her instructions. Dutifully, I lined my lips. Yes, I looked like someone from a movie. Unfortunately, the character I looked like was Blanche DuBois from A Streetcar Named Desire; this was not the look I had hoped to achieve. Sandy tried to show me how to highlight my cheekbones and then to employ eye-liner. Simultaneously engaged in the same activities, Sandy began to look like a Vogue model; I was beginning to look like Tim Curry from The Rocky Horror Picture Show, only not as good.

Long story made short: I learned how it was supposed to be done, but I couldn't do it. After I'd adjusted the Sweet Transvestite look into something slightly more becoming a middle-aged professor, I was ready to go out. Michael liked how I looked, but then Michael usually likes how I look, which is--after all--one of the reasons we are married. The evening was wonderful, full of good food and good talk, and I forgot about what I was wearing and whether or not my nose was shiny. It was so much fun I didn't notice whether Sandy's lipstick needed touching up or wonder if the blush on her cheek came from the laughter or the brush.

And I bet that neither Michael nor Leonard noticed whether either of them needed a shave.

Domesticity

House Porn

On Sunday mornings Michael and I often find ourselves enthralled by a television program we refer to as "house porn." Before you avert your eyes and gasp in horror, please let me explain: this viewing experience has nothing to do with impropriety but everything to do with property.

The real estate company sponsoring and producing this half-hour show knows that the success of such videos (in your own home, please, and viewed by consenting adults) depends on an invariable routine: the viewer is exposed to quick and titillating overviews of a piece of property-- there's a shot from the back, a view from the side-- and then permitted to see a few close ups of the best, most sumptuous parts. This is perhaps followed by a couple of gratuitously artsy shots photographed through foliage and then the camera discreetly backs away.

Let's face it: after a certain age, real estate becomes sexy. I know that's not a nice thing to argue, either ideologically or politically but I still think it's true

So how is real estate like sex? You start to think about getting it, where it will be, what you'll do with it once you have it; you imagine its shape, texture, and impact on your life. You wonder what your friends will think. Some individuals become obsessed with it: they want it no matter where it is, what shape it's in, or even if it will cost them more than it's worth. Others are so committed to one and only one that they read endless articles about how to preserve it, how to jazz it up, how to up-date it so it doesn't go out of style, and how to tweak it here and there so it remains a source of delight. Real estate becomes sexy because it's about physical comfort and bodily pleasure, and it seems to create an appetite for itself. That's why it's fascinating to see what other people have and what they've done with it.

And that's why we call the Sunday morning show "house porn." Thank goodness it's made out of state and therefore deals with locations north of our fair community. This means we're not peeking into the homes of those we know, which would be perverted, after all.

Without a doubt, the best aspect of this "infomercial" is the use of language. My favorite comes from the very first broadcast we watched, drawn to the television set almost against our will: the house was described in the voice-over as "getting a great deal of bright light during the daytime hours." Michael muttered through the side of his mouth while sipping a cup of coffee, "What? No bright light comes in during the nighttime hours?" It was, I must admit, the beginning of a free-for-all.

"Situated in a natural setting" became a favorite phrase of mine. Having lived for several years on the Lower East Side of Manhattan I can, personally, vouch for the fact that there are indeed domiciles (mine was one) situated in unnatural settings. I'd just never heard it put that way before. Michael liked learning about a piece of property where "the living room opens to the dining room, which opens to the kitchen" ("Which opens to the garage so you can park your car right on your sofa," according to my husband).

Fireplaces are always a big deal. There is often talk about the possibility of a "roaring fire in the fireplace" (verses a "roaring fire in the linen closet," I presume) or the fact that "the bedroom contains one of the house's three working fireplaces," suggesting that there are seven or eight other fireplaces in the house which are seriously kaput. "The fireplace anchors the living room," we hear, which makes us imagine that the rest of the rooms all somehow float, like giant balloons from the Macy's Thanksgiving Day parade.

So we laugh. Haha.Yet we also watch, commenting on size and availability. Sometimes we sigh with the idea of possibilities missed, but mostly we have a second cup of coffee and are grateful for what we have.

Arguing About Money

Earlier in our marriage, we used to argue about money.

When I say earlier, I mean "about twenty minutes ago" because no matter how long or how successful your marriage, you never stop arguing about money. Money may not be the root of all evil, but it sure is at the root of a whole lot of slammed doors, tissue-use, ripped and crumpled pieces of paper with meaningless lists of figures written on them, and yelling. Yelling and money really go together in my experience, with partners switching over from the "yeller" to the "yellee" with surprising, not to say, harmonious, regularity.

For example, my husband Michael and I will have the Arguments of Doom about once every three to four weeks, or when any major purchase appears on a credit card, whichever comes first. Hints of the approaching storm will begin with a few grumbles about how come we stopped making sandwiches to take to work with us before we leave in the morning, thereby saving the expense of eating out?

I'll remind him of the primary reasons we stopped this delectable practice: 1). We used to squabble over whose turn it was to make lunch, with some of these particular disagreements beginning the night previous to the sandwich activity; 2). We disagreed over the merits of toasted vs. untoasted bread, the use of plastic vs. foil wrap, the application of paper vs. plastic bags for transport, etc.; 3). The sandwiches were dreary, soggy, and --despite this--we inevitably devoured them before ten-thirty a.m. because neither of us is

Coming Clean

When I'm rooting around in someone's kitchen, and just happen to look-
-very casually, you understand-- into their sink, I can't stand when I find
massive amounts of glubbage in their metal drain-strainer (or whatever that
thing is called which prevents the whole chicken carcass from being washed
into your septic system).

"Glubbage" is best defined as "Icky stuff accumulating after long term
inattention." This means, of course, that everyone has a different "glubbage
field" in one's life. My charming host's detritus-filled metal drain-strainer
obviously doesn't bother him in the least, whereas it causes a huge swelling
of anxiety within my soul. His spice rack, however, is not only accurately
alphabetized but the individual glass containers are shining with care. My
spices, tossed into a drawer, consist mostly of yellowing bottles, arranged by
astrological sign as far as I can tell, which I've been dragging around since I
left college. (Maybe the bottles of ginger, anise, and lemon zest were a
graduation present? Maybe I was given the nutmeg as a memento when I got
the job at UConn? Who can remember?) They're not pretty, but what do I
care? Yes, the tops are a little difficult to get on because of the glubbage
around the grooves. Does that mean I'm a lousy housekeeper?

Apparently, the short answer is "yes." At least according to Francy, a
southern friend from college who recently came up to spend the weekend.
She was glancing around my kitchen in an extremely--perhaps even
unnaturally--casual fashion if you can believe her, when she just happened to

How to Argue Bitterly Even When Nothing Is Wrong

Things going a little too well at home? Not enough domestic angst? Nobody in the house living on the edge of mania and depression?

Try cleaning out the basement. Try deciding what must be kept and what must be thrown away. This activity, within the first half-hour, is guaranteed to transform even the most enviably happy couple into a pair of cranky, disheveled, sullen combatants.

This works not only with basements, but with attics, with garages, and with sheds. It can work, if you're really desperate, with those storage boxes stuffed into the back of small closets ("I didn't know you kept pictures of your old girlfriend," "Well, I didn't know you kept letters from that weed you went out with before me," "At least he knew how to write a full sentence . The only reason you have photographs but no letters of that fool is because she could barely block-print her name," et cetera). Trunks of cars also work ("You haven't ever used this tire gauge. I might as well make an earring out of it or use it as a bookmark" "Why don't you use it to see whether the turkey is done and we can bury that crusty old meat thermometer?" "We're talking about the trunk, not the kitchen" "Yeah, well, you didn't have to throw away the picture of my old girlfriend"), as do the cabinets underneath the bathroom sink ("Why do you need seventeen bottles of nail polish when you don't wear nail polish?" "Why do you need an unsigned warranty card for the electric razor that stopped working on the day you bought it?"). Fun, fun, fun for the whole family.

We did this recently because we are (God help us) redoing the kitchen and making our at-home offices a little bigger. All I can say for myself is: I didn't know. I didn't know that the process of merely preparing for this event was the equivalent of moving to another country. We had to pack everything away.

Now, I understand that everybody out there is thinking, "Um, yes, okay, and your point is?" Everybody else old enough to cross the street by themselves would have anticipated the tiny state of crisis a little packing up would bring on. I didn't. I long ago faced the fact that I am not going to win the "Miss Domestic" award (pretty much about the same time I realized I wasn't going to win any awards except for "Most Likely To Antagonize Others Upon A First Meeting" and "Least Likely To Bake"). But I wasn't prepared for the heartfelt fury and rage over possessions.

I wanted to keep cute toys I was given (as an adult, mind you) to take on planes to keep me safe even though I'd kept them in the basement (the toys, not the Boeings) even after their non-flammable stuffing had become home for colonies of mutating insects whose only brain cells are bent on populating the universe with more of their kind (I also have cousins like this, but at least they don't live in our basement). My argument was that it was Bad Karma to throw them away. My husband suggested that perhaps I wanted to put them in a "self-storage" container so that the mutating insects could at least take over only one part of the world at a time. Given that I couldn't imagine myself ever opening this sort of container once I'd put a highly infested toy into it, because I'd watched enough 'Fifties movies about precisely this sort of thing, I decided to give up. Karma is not as persuasive as cinema.

But to be fair I made Michael throw out boxes of yellowed page-proof he'd been carting around for the last fifteen years without ever consulting. Under duress he jettisoned yellowed tee-shirts (I was a runner-up for the "Least Likely To Bleach" award), white jackets, hats he hadn't worn since 1971, and a stack of Consumer Reports so old they told the readers what to look for in an eight-track tape deck. (We also threw away the eight-track tape deck). I pried from his clutching hands a radio-clock so ugly it could turn those who looked at into stone. "It doesn't work!" I growled through clenched teeth. "But it's right twice a day!" he yelled back.

Then after a while we started talking again. Together we put in the "donations" box clothes we once loved but could no longer wear, record albums we once danced to but would never again listen to, sheets that fit a bed way too small for us now. We gave away months, years, whole sections of life, hoping that this will clear a place for what's ahead. Everything you give away makes room for something new; everything you put behind you clears your vision for what's ahead.

And if what's ahead is going to be as much of a mess as what came before it, then it's obviously best to start going through everything immediately. Anybody in the mood for a good, clean argument?

relationship during which neither participant emits any sounds or odors."

Let's put it as genteelly as possible: you don't need to be a (arghhh!) Rules Girl to know the way the wind shouldn't blow during an evening out; you don't need a dating manual to understand fully that a really fine lady doesn't belch with satisfying vigor even after a taco-and-beer binge. (To believe that really fine ladies don't indulge in taco-and-beer binges is so unrealistic we won't even bother to concern ourselves with the implications raised by this level of naivete.)

If the theory is that girls aren't supposed to do anything a Barbie doll wouldn't do, then this cuts down on quite a few physical options--positive as well as negative ones. Okay, Barbie never needs to use Beeno or take Tums, but then she never worries about STDs either because--and let us make this clear-- she is in possession of no functioning orifices. You take the bad with good; if all you want in a chick is somebody to look good in clothes, who never shuts her eyes, and who can float in a tub, then Barbie is fine.

(Warning: if you are a guy who in fact thinks, "Well, actually, at my stage in life that about meets my needs," please don't say it out loud to the woman sitting across the breakfast table. Not until you make sure you've got a reservation at the "Y" so that you can move out very, very quickly.)

Real men might not eat quiche, but if they eat peppers and onions on garlic bread, you better watch out. Why else do men like one particular scene in Mel Brooks' Blazing Saddles involving eight guys digesting food around a camp fire? Why do boys of all ages adore Jim Carey? Not because of the subtlety and finesse of his acting, that's for sure, but because if you met him, you'd expect Jim to greet you with the testosterone-linked line, "C'mon, pull my finger." Ever notice just how rarely women use that line when conversing with one another?

We can deduce from these observations that the culture has decidedly fewer problems with the public nature of men's bodily functions than it does with the idea that women have bodily functions at all. After all, that's why we each get our own little stall in a restaurant bathroom. We're neither competitive nor collective about what goes on in there. Proof of this, perhaps, is that no woman has ever written her name in the snow. Even if a woman were able to perform this task, she would not then want folks to be able to look up her name in the phone book.

Another curious example of the way men and women differ in terms of defining and displaying their intimate functions: you would not be shocked to see a man spitting--out of a car window, at a sporting event, after swimming, after hearing a really good story, while taking a walk--at almost any time, that is, except during the funeral of a close friend or a wedding ceremony.

His own wedding ceremony.

But it's rare to see a woman hawk one out a window or while standing outside the corner deli during her lunch break. And yet women, as far as I know, are not walking around with whole mouthfuls of phlegm. Does this mean that phlegm-production is also genetically linked to the y-chromosome? Or is it just that certain guys like to spit, in the same way that certain guys like to jump up to see if their fingertips can touch the awning?

I'm not suggesting that women practice burping or that men learn to suppress all physical displays of their ability to affect the environment. We are who we are. I am, however, suggesting that just because a woman snores every once in a while, she should not be made to feel this undermines her essentially female nature. Let's face it: once the courtship period is over, we're all down to our essential selves. And the most you can do in a marriage is poke the essential self lying next to you ever so gently in the ribs to turn over when the noise gets too much. Just don't hit rewind.

Lassie Stays Home

Deciding to leave was easy. Deciding which dog to take was hard.

For weeks she packed boxes in the cramped basement and drove her important clothes over to her sister's house. Her husband didn't notice but she hadn't expected him to; he was never the type to observe much or pick up on detail.

The dogs knew. They whimpered at the basement door and trotted nervously behind her as she hauled dresses in drycleaning bags to the car. Two mutts, one big, one small, both rescued from the pound, chosen on a day when life seemed as safe as slippers. Bowo, the little one, was all nose and ears, eyes squinted against what he figured would be the next blow. Lassie, the big one, didn't look like Lassie from t.v., that's for sure, what with a short shiny coat tipped with white and mottled pink ear. "Bowo" was named after an aunt's ancient poodle the wife had adored while growing up. "Bowo" was short for "bow wow" and she always thought that was cute. Her husband picked "Lassie" for a name. The four of them lived in a duplex condo. There were lots of other dogs and lots of other young couples in the complex so everybody had company.

Until now. She was leaving because she was sick and tired of everything around her. Her husband was annoying. His job, once promising, now bored her and she couldn't believe it didn't bore him. He ran one of the offices of a big commercial maintenance company but was no longer the ambitious guy he'd been six years ago when she met him. At that point he wanted to rise up in the company, become one of the real executives, one of those men who were part of contracts being negotiated and papers being signed. His current job was part of management, sure, but that was about the best thing to say about it. His big input was looking over the poor slobs being fired or hired, and even that was mostly decided without him.

Her job was even worse. As the buyer in housewares for a department store's local outlet, she was able to exercise what she thought of as her own unique talents in only a very limited way. Just last week, for example, she wanted to order a grouping of towels, bathmats, and shower curtains based on designs by a famous artist, but she wasn't given the go-ahead by her boss. Her boss was about fifty-five years old and her idea of taste was beige and black on white. "You can't go wrong with neutral tones" was her favorite saying. As if life itself couldn't afford style or color.

She'd furnished their condo in a southwest motif, with terra cotta colors accented by hints of turquoise and gold--very tasteful, but still special. Also the dogs couldn't really mess it up since they were sort of browny-terra cotta themselves--only the white tips of Lassie's fur were noticeable on the darker brown faux-suede love-seat in front of the television. She didn't mind and her husband didn't notice.

The two dogs faced her as she sat on the loveseat now. They were alert, ears forward, as if asking what they could do to make it all better. They wanted to help but they couldn't because they didn't understand what she was doing. If they did, she suspected they'd hide, like they did after they misbehaved, trying to fit under the entertainment center or behind the kitchen door but giving themselves away by sniffles and scratches.

She picked up Bowo and scratched him under the chin while he wiggled in her arms, trying to lick her face. Bowo wore a turquoise collar with a small silver design. She held her chin up and away from him while she spoke directly to Lassie.

She told Lassie it just wouldn't work. She was going to her sister's for a little while but pretty soon she'd be getting her own place and it would be hard to find somewhere that would welcome one dog, let alone two. Lassie looked at her, trying to translate but remaining bewildered.

She explained that she'd done her best to make a good home but it just wasn't working. "He's happy the way things are but I need more," she said. "He won't even notice I'm not here in a couple of months. Your life will stay the same. It's me and Bowo you should worry about." At the sound of his name Bowo stretched full length and licked her neck. Lassie sat still, head to one angle as if to catch words, like the RCA dog trying to hear every sound but still puzzled by the process. "I can't stay, sweetheart. If there'd been kids or a bigger place or a better job, maybe I could have stuck it out. But I got to go." At the word "go" Lassie lifted her paws, toenails clicking on the floor like a Geiger counter, thinking that "go" meant "let's go."

But it didn't. When she put the leash on Bowo's collar but not her own, Lassie knew what was happening. At least, the inexplicable events of the past few weeks now had an explanation. The important thing was that Lassie wasn't involved and wouldn't be punished. She was not a bad dog, but simply an inadequate reason to stay. Bowo was portable; Bowo had the ability to claim affection without taking up space.

Lassie had noticed different smells on both owners, and picked up the scent of impending change the way you'd smell rain in the air or know when it was about to snow. Chewing on her gray collar the way she'd chewed through all her previous ones, a nervous talent she'd picked up at the pound and never managed to lose, Lassie had been trying hard to get a sense of where things were going. Her chewing had escalated lately and she was sawing away with her teeth a mile a minute right now.

She saw Bowo's happy but nervous eyes, saw the bags piled up near the door, and figured out that she was staying home. Now that Lassie actually understood what was happening, she didn't really mind. She would be allowed to sit on the furniture and probably sleep at the foot of the bed. It wouldn't be too bad.

The woman had tears in her eyes. "Sweetie pie, I love you, but I need to do this." Lassie wagged her tail at "sweetie pie" and walked to the door, not to protest their exit, but to show them the way.

The Woman
Who Keeps Our Marriage Together

Heidi is here and so I am working, although it would be more accurate to say I am working BECAUSE Heidi is here. I always work when she's around because I am happy and content. Also because writing is how I remind myself of how Heidi came into our lives. A cross between a muse, a conscience, an inspiration, a guardian angel and a life-saver, Heidi takes care of my house, our house. When I am asked how I manage to write, teach, lecture, and generally make a public nuisance of myself, I am most honest when I reply "I don't participate in any sport and I don't clean my own house."

I used to clean other people's houses, back in my earlier days, and for years afterwards I announced in a particularly sanctimonious, lofty manner: "How any woman could employ another woman to complete her domestic tasks for her, well, I just don't understand." I said this, however, when I was living in a New York apartment boasting the size and ambiance of a Roach Motel. Then for a year or so after I moved to Connecticut full -time (having been tenured and married, indicating that CT would be my home for the duration) and we moved into a place with its own personal mailbox, I tried to keep our house looking nice. This, it turned out, was not possible. My husband did a great job of keeping the big yard, as well as the many trees, plants, and bird-feeders beautifully maintained, but then again he had a John Deere that he adored the way a kid adores a go-cart. Remember Roseanne's line, "When Sears makes a riding vacuum, then I'll clean my house"? That became my motto.

I didn't enjoy cleaning, not after the first ten minutes of pretending I was Donna Reed, charmingly dusting the furniture before the doorbell rang and today's adventure began (which would prevent me from doing the lousy part of the job, like scooping up the kitty litter from corners of the room where, somehow, they managed to fling it, as if they were participating in the finals of a Kitty-Litter Flinging Contest). And I didn't do a good job. I discovered that it was much easier to clean other people's houses than it was to clean my own in much the same way that it is easier to edit other's people prose than to write.

So I asked around and Heidi appeared one day. Smart, astute, energetic, delightful, and understanding, she was putting herself through college with assorted jobs. She sang as she worked (and not ditties such as "You Load Sixteen Tons and What Do You Get?" or "Nine to Five"). When she became an English major we had long talks about Hawthorne and Brontë; when she got her teaching certification, we had long talks about classroom behavior and course preparations. Throughout these demanding and complicated stretches of time, Heidi kept us on her agenda (perhaps from a sense of pastoral duty which prevented her from abandoning the domestically incapacitated). That was almost ten years ago. Since then she received her honors degree, got married, delivered and is busy raising two fabulously adorable children, purchased her own home. And, hallelujah, she is still in our lives.

And this is more than luck or friendship or loyalty: it is a blessing. When those pesky demands of life interfered (you know, stuff like childbirth), her gracious mother Paula arrived in Heidi's place. We've been adopted by Heidi's family. Those mornings when both Paula and Heidi were here together, with all of us laughing and telling stories, them making the bed and me filing my papers, were wonderful. Then Paula went to work full time (I still consider her a good friend and miss her contagious, generous laughter) and so Heidi, solo, is here today as I write.

Heidi has seen me through tearful, miserably anxious mornings before I have to begin a three-thousand mile plane journey, and she's given me the benediction of a prayer and a smile, thereby assuring a better trip. She treats the big and the small things of life with graceful affection, everything from looking after me when I recovered from my operation, to indulging our cats' need to play tag as she mops the floor. And she tells me that if I ever achieve fame, she won't sell stories to the National Enquirer. At least not for a small sum.

Fame, or lack of it, is not something that worries me. The only thing that worries me is the thought that one day Heidi will not arrive, having decided that the moment was right for her to give her energies and talents to a wider arena. Naturally it will be a busy time for us, since Michael and I will have to move, but of course we will applaud and cheer for Heidi. In everything she does, Heidi brings the song in her heart to a larger world. We are simply happy to be part of it.

Scratch and Sniff

I am trying to get the cats not to sleep on the furniture. There are only two cats but my husband secretly believes there are triplet versions of these creatures, feline body-doubles, so that these two are multiplied exponentially into dozens of cats which he pictures as all sleeping and deliberately, consciously, purposefully shedding pounds of fur over new sofas, tables, chairs, etc.. That is, he pictures them merely shedding and asleep when he is not actively imagining them tearing the couches into small tidbits for their amusement and delectation.

It's not that Michael doesn't like the cats--he does, really. He just wasn't brought up with cats the way I was. My father, brother and I can do the family chronology only by recalling which cat we had then: "Was that when we had the big orange cat or the small stray?" We don't refer to them by name because they were all called "Min," which I believe is the sort of French-Canadian generic equivalent of "Kitty," a legacy from my mother. Michael remembers what he was doing in his youth by recollecting what kind of car he was driving; his cars were his pets.

They still are, in a way. He bathes them regularly and takes care of them with sincere affection, evidence of a true bond. In contrast, I believe that washing a car in the winter makes as much sense as washing the bottom of your shoes. Michael doesn't mind cleaning up after his vehicles, getting the oil changed, for example, where the very sight of an unscooped litter box sends him reeling. I only remember to get tune-ups for the car because there is a big sticker pasted on to a highly visible part of my windshield telling me exactly when I need to stop driving it for fear of the whole thing blowing up.

This sign functions, I realize, in the same way that ones pinned to the sweatshirts or jacket-sleeves of small children, telling them to remember to blow their noses or keep their socks on all day. These devices, while not sophisticated, are nevertheless effective. I remember to get the oil changed (and blow my nose, too).

The cats don't offer quite the same reminders when they need tune-ups. The old cat, the current holder of the "Min" title, is as old as Methuselah. Her way of letting me know she needs to see Super-Vet, Dr. Todd Friedland, is to throw up repeatedly throughout the house in a random pattern, usually during the night so that it is difficult to discover until trod upon the next day.

I, in turn, call the Windham Animal Hospital demanding an immediate appointment because I am sure Min's taking her last breaths. I am folded into the calendar next to everyone else who is also certain their pet is scratching at death's pet door. Then comes the fun part: I catch Min and shove her into the carrier (a series of maneuvers that also helps to convince me of her will to live; no cat would protest this much if she'd lost her inner resources). This erstwhile alley-cat, adopted out of a gutter on Lafayette Street in 1981, then howls the whole way to the vet's in a way that makes it sound like the car is full of lost souls and not one vintage tabby.

Min should have bought the kitty farm a long time ago; there have been several times when I figured she needed an exorcist, not a veterinarian. But they always manage to save her and give her back to me. I bring her home, both of us enormously relieved, and she naturally wants to sleep on the new couch. How can I refuse her this?

In response to what I see as a purely rhetorical question, Michael points out, in perfect truth, that there are about seven hundred more suitable places for her to relax, such as one of the eight cat-beds I've purchased over the last few years in the vague and clearly deluded hope that she'd call one of these her own. The little cat, just under two years old now, tries them out every once in a while, just to keep us happy. I suspect she considers herself sort of like the vice-president here, the vice-alpha-cat, making sure that everything might be easily set up for her succession while not actually trying to kill off the current leader.

Before you offer advice, let me explain that I've tried almost everything: sprays to keep them off the furniture, water pistols (which I could not actually bring myself to use on anyone except unsuspecting guests, and that was during the summer, and was really fun), sprays smelling of cat-nip to get them onto places we wanted them to be, yelling, throwing wadded-up newspaper, the whole kitten-kaboodle. Even if they avoid Wickedness when we're around, we inevitably find them, snug and unmovable, on the new furniture when we get home.

I can think of only one solution: Michael and I should live in the cars, which are so nicely kept, after all. The cats can then have full run of the house. (I've just shouted this suggestion out to Michael, but for some reason he doesn't like it.)

Wish me luck.

Picture This

The other evening my husband and I were taken to a fancy concert by a friend who decided that her birthday celebration should include a grown-up's night out on the town, complete with a fancy restaurant dinner and a concert (the sort of concert where you dress up and applaud nicely, not the kind where you pass unknown people over your head in a crowd). This is a good friend, believe me. Looking for any excuse to dress-up while I'm still able to wear high-heels without toppling sideways and scraping my ankles on the sidewalk like my old aunts used to do, I insisted we accept.

My husband mumbled something to the effect that driving to the city on a Tuesday night might make teaching at dawn on Wednesday morning a bit of a trial, but I overruled his objection by pointing out that life was short, that we only pass this way but once, and that I wouldn't sleep at all on Tuesday night if we stayed home because I'd be bitter about life in the suburbs, etc., which meant that he wouldn't sleep either. Of that I was certain. So, if we were going to be up all night anyway, we might as well enjoy ourselves. He was persuaded, whether by the logic or the threat I'll never know (we've been married long enough for me to have learned not to ask such questions). By Tuesday afternoon he was genuinely happy that I'd nudged him into it.

The whole evening was terrific. We went out with a bunch of funny, smart, nice people, ate in a genteel manner (meaning not in front of the t.v. or while standing), laughed, and nodded at each other with delight at having been sophisticated enough to make such good choices. The celebration even included the tacky but nevertheless desirable option of having one's photograph taken with the star performer. This was one for the relatives, I thought, especially since the star performer resembled (and I mean precisely, sort of clone-like uncanny) every uncle in my huge Italian family.

I was all geared up for this event until they asked us to fill out little cards with the usual information so that they could mail us the photos when they were developed. No big deal, right? Heck, I've even memorized my social security number so am therefore usually confident, if not to say cocky, about filling out these cards. This stuff I'm good at.

But the form facing me that evening included a new little gem: "Please describe yourself briefly so that we can be sure we're mailing you the correct photograph." Perfectly polite, of course; after all, they're not asking for my sexual history or darkest secret (lots of overlap between those two categories, by the way). I saw my husband's handwriting move across the lines as if he were inscribing our destiny. Breathless, I watched while he was writing.

"Bald guy, white shirt, red tie. Wife: short, fuzzy hair, wearing scarf."

I was horrified. That's it? That's who we've become? "Bald guy, short wife"? Us? I thought we were this debonair duo, I thought we were part of this racy, lively, hip group of people just entering their prime. I didn't think of us as a cross between Archie Bunker and Edith on All in the Family and Homer and Marge on The Simpsons.

Not that anyone could argue with the accuracy of the description, although I might have substituted the term "curly" or even the slightly sexier-sounding "disheveled" for "fuzzy" which is a word best used to describe imperfect telephone connections. Granted, he lacks in hair what I lack in height, but I always told myself that we make up for that by our overwhelming sense of joie de vivre. At least we accessorize, for goodness' sake: at least he had the decency to put on a tie and I had the wherewithal (or, in this case, the wear-with-all) to wrap a scarf around my no-doubt very short throat. We stood next to the performer, we all smiled for the camera (with me trying to make my hair look shiny and stand on tip toes), and my husband and I started the long drive home.

We talked about the little white card as we drove through the familiar darkness of outlying towns. Talked, once that is, after I stopped biting my upper lip and sniffling in despair. After a sigh that indicated that he knew exactly what was ahead, he asked me what was the matter. He's a good guy that way.

I explained that I knew all too well that writing "joie de vivre" under "physical description" wouldn't have gotten us our pictures. Neither would "more or less happily married," "good senses of humor" or "gainfully employed for more than twenty years," which I would also consider to be accurate assessments of our selves. But I was worried that I'd dwindled into this generic middle-aged lady married to a generic middle-aged man without even the compensation of having our lives optioned for a sitcom.

My husband pointed out that we were pretty lucky to have friends who not only put up with us but who want us to celebrate their special occasions with them, lucky to have lives that permit us not to have to work a second-shift, each lucky to have a partner who could see the fuzzy hair or the shiny pate and still want to be photographed with their arms around each other. "Next time," he said, "I'll write under the category of wife: 'Looks like she deserves the husband she has."

I knew he meant it as a compliment, and I thought--to myself--that for a bald, middle-aged guy wearing a red tie, he wasn't bad.

Anxiety

The Holiday Impaired

The holidays make me nervous. They are a Big Deal. I can understand perfectly well that they hold a sense of overwhelming significance for those with religious convictions. (I've been arrested by religion but never convicted.) Those who celebrate the season because it actually coincides with an important spiritual moment for them are the ones whom I admire and wish well. Maybe they'll say a prayer for the rest of us.

Because the rest of us are definitely Holiday Impaired. We spend a month or more driving ourselves crazy trying to get everything done and trying to be all that we should be, as if Christmas were an exercise organized by a troop of invading Marines. We are trying to be Martha Stewart and Garrison Keillor and Frosty and Rudolph and even Bing. We spend our time frantically Making Crafts as if they were lifeboats, seizing upon Decorating Ideas as if our lives depended on them, and wildly embracing Seasonal Recipes as if we might never eat again after the third week of December.

We are making ourselves tense over the idea that someone might have the unbelievable audacity to be nice to us when we haven't been nice to them--i.e., they might send us a rogue greeting card or, worse yet, present us with a stealth gift. The very prospect of the generosity of others causes people (yes, yes, mostly women) to horde bundles of auxiliary gifts ready to be fetched out of the back of the closet and given to the stealth giver on astonishingly short notice.

Sometimes these gifts have been handed around various towns since the

'Thirties without anyone having made use of them except as a commodity to ensure that the ritual itself continues. I'm sure anthropologists have studied this process in great detail. What I'm not sure of, however, is why these anthropologists cannot therefore just write us one big universal note saying that you don't have to give anybody a gift unless you find something perfect for them. The note would go on to say that you, the giver, don't expect anything more than a verbal thank-you and the pleasure of having made the presentation. This note would also guarantee that the giver does not get to ask the receiver every time she sees her whether "you've had the chance to wear that charming hand-crafted ceramic ankle bracelet yet."

Perhaps most unnerving of all is our absolute certainty that every other family unit on the planet is having a better, happier, more peaceful, and more loving time than we are. Surely no other family unit is arguing bitterly over whether foil or plastic should be placed over the top of the bowls containing candied yams. Surely no other family is watching videotapes of This is Spinal Tap or early episodes of The X-Files during this time meant for emotional bonding, spiritual renewal and the sharing stories between generations (one of my aunts left the room when my niece put on the X-Files because she--the aunt-- thought they were dirty movies).

Nowhere else is one of the family members going around saying "You want to see my belly?" as proof of historic overeating (n.b.: the family member is over fifty but is in full possession of what are laughingly called his faculties). In no household but ours, we are sure, would the women be playing a noisy game of poker and the men all reading sections of the newspapers silently to themselves in different parts of the house. Everyone else is eating charmingly-prepared wholesome meals; we are eating mashed potatoes which have been prepared with cheese and butter and which, no question about it, taste great but are about as healthy as eating Drano.

In nobody else's house is a small child whining and rubbing her extravagantly running nose on the pink fur of her new plush toy; in no one else's house is the cat throwing up on the living room rug. In nobody else's house is anyone screaming silently at the spouse in the kitchen who has once again thrown the drippings down the sink; in no one else's house is the college student on the phone long distance for seven or eight hours with his/her significant other discussing how they will contrive to avoid this entire event next year.

When you drive past other people's houses, all the windows look brightly lit and all the faces look happy. But of course that happens when anybody drives past the houses of the Holiday Impaired, too; almost everybody looks good from far away when surrounded by a warm light within a frame of darkness. Let's face it: we--the best and the worst of us-- all tango through all these times as well as we can manage. Some years will be better than others, but all such days deserve recognition and, yes, celebration.

Why? Because, despite the fact that the holiday is not going to be perfect, not going to be like something out of a magazine (unless you count the official publication of the World Wrestling Federation), and not going to be everything you hoped, it is a chance to make what might be just another day a memorable time. All days are gifts and should be celebrated; the holidays give us a chance to do it together.

And they give us, if we allow ourselves to embrace the possibility, a chance to laugh out loud about the wonders and absurdities of life. And laughter, after all, offers a joyful sound unto world.

It can't hurt.

Guilt-Edged

Not much is immutable in life. Not many things can be counted on day after day. Guilt, however, is always there, the staunch companion of my waking and my sleeping, my childhood chaperon who's always by my side no matter how well-behaved I seem to outsiders. Guilt and I are (cross index finger over middle finger to indicate intimacy) like this .

I feel guilty when I don't return phone calls; I feel guilty when I don't write on both sides of a piece of paper; I feel guilty when I eat dessert. I feel guilty when I put on weight and then I feel guilty when I take it off (feeling guilty, you see, for caring about such frivolous matters when there are Big Things to worry about, as opposed to worrying about whether I myself will become a Big Thing).

I feel guilty for not doing more volunteer work and guilty for not having enough time to see friends I really want to see. I feel guilty when I hold one cat and not the other; I feel guilty for liking certain students more than others; I feel guilty when I think I'm having a better time than other people (how dare I?) and guilty when I'm unhappy (how dare I waste the precious gift of life on being depressed?).

Blame it on a grandmother who cried "I know what happened: you went outside with wet hair last week! Of course you got sick! Why do you always do these things to yourself?!" even as she ministered hot soup for a bad cold.

Blame it on boyfriends from high school who pouted handsomely even as they cooed threateningly "Are you really going to stay inside to do your homework and leave me to hang out all by myself at the park when I might run into Mindy?"

Blame it on the residual old-fashioned Catholicism which encouraged me to regard every single nasty thought--even those unuttered-- as a spear through the heart of the Virgin Mary. (Yes, I know: newer and smarter Catholics tell me I don't have to be this way anymore but for somebody who thinks she should still be eating fish on Fridays, it is unlikely that reconciliation will appear more desirable to me than absolution).

Blame it on my French Canadian relatives who invoked the cliché "Née pour petit pain"("Born for small bread") when you tried anything fancy, a phrase designed to keep you feeling guilty if you had ambitions above your station. Blame it on a lack of folic acid or blame it on El Nino, one thing is certain: half my life is spent feeling guilty.

And here's something that really makes me feel guilty to admit out loud: I think it's a girl thing. (Shhh, don't tell anybody). Guilt seems to me to be estrogen-linked. Wide-eyed and unhappy, I'll nudge my long-suffering spouse awake in the middle of the night to explain what's eating at me, what's consuming me with a sense of remorse, and he'll explain that the only thing I should be feeling guilty about is bothering him at four a.m.. He will then go right back to sleep.

He won't feel at all bad about not listening to me whereas I live in abject terror of being accused of not listening to someone--anyone--at any time. I am devastated by the idea that I might not be paying enough attention, or that I might not seem grateful enough, or that someone will feel left out.

For example, when I wrote a piece about having my wonderful fake fingernails refurbished on an hourly basis by a group of distinguished professionals, I inadvertently left out the name of one of the patient women who deals with both my nails and my neurosis. Diane didn't make it into the column.

The next time I walked into the salon, broken-nailed, I realized my mistake. Diane was laughing--since she is a mature and sensible women, to her it was no big deal -- but in contrast I was filled with contrition. I thought about it for hours. I considered buying her flowers. I apologized profusely every time I walked into Headliners. I became annoying in my contrition and then started feeling guilty about that. Oy.

My guilt didn't do Diane any good, except that we could laugh together about it. Lots of guilt goes nowhere. We should jettison the emotional baggage if it is only weighing us down. But some guilt is good: contrition that gets you off your couch and into the community to do something generous is useful; remorse that makes you change your ways for the better is constructive. Looking ahead with renewed sense of commitment to what's right certainly beats looking backwards penitentially.

And do you know how certain I am of this? I can say it without feeling guilty at all.

Miss (ing) Manners

I'm always wildly impressed by people with good table manners. This is because mine aren't so hot. Not only don't I know how to set a table properly--I find the placing of two forks next to a plate a challenge so genuine I believe I need a grant to overcome it-- but I don't even know how to eat properly once a table is set. For example, even when my tongue is in an almost biblical way cleaving to roof of my mouth from thirst, I always wait until someone else at the dinner picks up a water glass so I can see what side she's drinking from; I daren't choose a glass that might turn out not to be my own.

I get extremely nervous when accomplished, contentious hosts use linen napkins because I know, for a sadly non-negotiable fact that I, with my red lipstick and messy ways, will make this napkin see the last of its dinnertime usage. They'll use it to clean up after the cat, or to wipe juice from the baby's face in the minivan, or maybe they'll just bury it in the yard. I've tried asking for a paper napkin before we sit down for soup, but the request is usually regarded as a self-effacing and witty remark instead of a heartfelt plea, which is truly a shame because after this happens a couple of times my husband and I are usually invited out for a restaurant dinner, or else only permitted to attend outdoor functions, such as barbecues.

Often, of course, we dine informally at home. Now, growing up where and how my husband and I both grew up, the phrase "dining informal" usually connoted "without the bother of sitting down, using more than one utensil, or breathing between bites." So we're not exactly the Vanderbilts, the

Baldridges, or even the Flintstones. We're more like hunter-gatherers, let's say, happy to be eating at all and not paying too much attention to the niceties. For example, we rarely apologize for our bad manners when we're dining a deux ; instead, we usually compete, in rituals most often associated with twelve-year old boys or feral children, to out-do the other in terms of uncivilized behavior.

This is not pretty. We would be horrified to do it in front of anyone aside from ourselves, something we learned when Michael's sons, even as teenagers, would occasionally look at us aghast. This not how grown-ups are supposed to behave, they implied, and they were right. The little space on that DNA double-helix labeled for grown-up behavior kicked in for most things--paying bills, showing up for work on time, being unable to watch even good horror movies if they didn't come on before eleven p.m.--but not for table manners. We've been known to eat supper in front of the television (a meal which often includes macaroni and cheese) while still wearing our school clothes. We've been known to eat popcorn in bed. We've been known to have two desserts. We have been known to look at each other at one in the morning and agree that we need a snack, which we will also sometimes eat in front of the television. Granted, this gives us something in common with our students (at least the undergraduates) but I am hard pressed to figure out what else good it does.

Except that we enjoy it enormously. The script we both follow most of the time is scribbled over with serious suggestions, rigid rules, precise procedures, inherited policies, and whole other batches of adult-stuff. Even if we behave badly, therefore--meaning even if we break the grown-up code on our own time--I think it might do us some good. Yes, we burp and laugh and yell at one another to stop eating onions after eight p.m., but if you can't do that at home, why bother to live with another person? We're made up of bone and sinew and gas and fluid and all kinds of icky material; why pretend we're made of porcelain? Porcelain shatters; we bounce back.

At dinner parties, we count on the amiability of our friends to protect us from the contempt that surely could seep our way. When invited to Brenda and George's for a wonderful bouillabaisse one evening, Michael declined a second serving of this complicated dish because "If I have too much soup, I'll miss the main course." Given that what he was eating was the main course, I continue to be impressed by both George and Brenda for their patience, as well as impressed by Michael for his lack of embarrassment. Roaring at his own blunder, he dug in for another helping. Me? I ate with a fork and used the wrong water glass, but the conversation was good and the evening was a real pleasure.

And isn't the accomplishment of a wonderful evening the very reason good manners were invented in the first place?

Sleepless in Storrs

The two hardest things in life are falling asleep and waking up.

I'm not a good sleeper. As a kid I was a good eater and a good talker; anyone who has ever met me knows that those particular traits haven't altered one bit. But I was one of those radically annoying children whose eyes snapped open the moment their head hit the pillow. I asked for water, for more stories, for prayers, for the truth: I was sort of like Tammy Faye Baker. My parents, having worked hard all day, were daunted by my effortless energy but they never left me to cry it out on my own. They stayed with me until either I or they fell asleep. That I lasted longer than they did in the land of consciousness is no tribute. You try singing 1,117 stanzas to "Here Comes Peter Cotton Tale" and see just how long you want to remain lucid.

So of course I blame them for my current sleep dysfunction (I used to say "trouble" but now I say big words like "dysfunction" so that I don't get into trouble). I never learned (and I adore this phrase, too) to "self-soothe," meaning I never learned to fall asleep like a human being. Like a fox, I was alert; like a cat, I seemed to see in the dark; like a watchdog I was vigilant; I did everything except hang upside down like a bat and that was only because we had really high ceilings. Thank goodness we didn't have bunk beds. I would have made a cocoon.

But even kids who have trouble falling asleep--mostly because there might be something good on t.v. after nine p.m.-- usually turn quite happily into adults who fall asleep in front of the t.v. at nine p.m.. Not me. I'm like a nerdy vampire: up all night, no curfew, nothing to feast on, unable to contact the living, reluctant to look at myself in the mirror for fear of having disappeared altogether, and ready to kill anybody actually enjoying a good night's sleep. I think about sleep the way I used to think about sex ten years ago: everybody is getting more than I am, I'm envious, and it's all I think about wanting to have if I don't have it.

When I was in my late twenties and living in New York, this sleeplessness business was a really desirable trait. Other people paid actual money for drugs to induce the same state I'd been born into (and that state had no license plate, believe me). I could walk out of my apartment on Lafayette Street in Manhattan and immediately dive into the all night diner, or go to the Ritz club (closing time 4 a.m.) or visit a bunch of friends who also stayed up to finish their tragically long papers for graduate school and drink espresso.

In Storrs, Connecticut it's different to be up all night. For example, it is now four o'clock in the morning and I am deliriously awake. The radio is on and someone who I am sure is really a very interesting man is talking about the creation of the universe but my mind keeps reverting back to a single thought: if all of space is a vacuum, then why isn't my living room cleaner? It is indicative of my state of mind that while I realize there must be a flaw in my argument I cannot figure out what it is.

My hands clutch the cup of chamomile tea I made under the hysterical belief that it would help me sleep. The tea is now cold and looks more like something I should put into my hair (or into my my transmission) than into my mouth. I consider washing my hair. I consider the creation of the universe while pouring the cold tea down the clogged drain. I decide the creation of the universe might not in fact turn out to be the wildly terrific idea it seemed on the drawing board.

I will never sleep again. Having resolved this, certain elements begin to clarify. I should adjust myself to the advantages of being awake. What's on television?

An American in Paris? They Saved Hitler's Brain? (I actually watched that one the other night; they not only saved Hitler's brain, they saved his head and shoulders). Is there a round table discussion on the end of the universe? No, there is only a documentary on hoof and mouth disease. I watch this with a sort of eerie fascination. I decide that I have hoof and mouth disease. I decide to switch off the tv.

Then I really start to worry: given the fact that I will never sleep again, I have far too many sets of pajamas.

Dial "N" for "Nervous"

I spent my youth sitting next to telephones waiting for a call from The Planet of the Boys. Ma Bell offered an umbilical cord linking me to whatever poor soul was my true love that particular week; whether or not he was actually on the other end or not was immaterial. Nothing could tempt me away from the phone if I thought a call might come. Endless lush summer evenings when I was sixteen, eighteen, even twenty-two, I spent sweating next to the phone, feeling like a late-night convict waiting for the governor's reprieve.

I should have bought stock in the phone company. I most certainly should have bought stock in the first answering machines, and bought all the stock invested in the patent that developed "call waiting." I thought, personally, that I already had the copyright to "call waiting" since that was all I did--wait for calls. I didn't know it referred to a technological advance that would make it at least remotely possible to have a life (or at least have another conversation) without losing my signature sense of insanely focused anxiety.

What I was most afraid of, you see, was picking up the phone and making a poorly-timed call myself. I didn't want to seem overwhelming. Remembering what I was like in my twenties, my attempt not to appear "overwhelming" was sort of like RuPaul trying not to appear overwhelming. Shy and retiring I wasn't. Scared, yes, but not enough to rein myself in except when absolutely necessary.

Around that time a friend sent me a card that invoked a new service: "Call Thwarting." Call Thwarting would automatically block any calls to a man one was dating (but not living with) after midnight. "No more two a.m. calls to his apartment, with the promise to hang up if a woman answers. No calling just to see if anyone picks up. No continuous ringing and disturbing the neighbors." How about calling the operator to see if your own phone is working (just in case he's trying to call but can't get through)?   Call Thwarting: An idea whose time had come. I kept that postcard next to my phone for ten years.

Okay, so now I'm a happily married woman. No more phone neurosis, right? No more waiting for the call, no more checking to see if there's a message, no more repeatedly playing the messages for girlfriends to see if they can decipher the real, hidden meaning beneath the phrase "I'll call back later"? I got rid of the postcard, right?

Guess again. I've simply moved it to my office. I've transferred all that finger-chewing, lip-biting, mind-numbingly neurotic energy onto waiting for phone calls from The Planet of Professional Contacts.   This, as you might imagine, is a whole lot of fun. Instead of spending summer evenings wondering whether I should call a boy for a date, I spend summer days wondering "Should I call the editor now or wait until I know she's at lunch? Is it right to leave a friendly please-please-please-get-back-to-me-so-that-I-can-get-on-with-my-life message on her voice mail? Is this editor the one that has the sort of voice mail where you can listen to the message you've just left in order to check whether or not you sound as tragically insecure as you feel? Should I speak to her assistant to try to get a feel for how things are going, or should I try to call her early tomorrow so that she'll think I'm a bright morning person even though I am no such thing?"

I've called publishers at ten in the evening, figuring that I can safely reach someone's office machine only to have them beat me at my own game by having the nerve to answer the phone. That's when you begin to babble (saying things like "Oh, I didn't think you'd be in!" to which the only sensible reply is "Then why are you calling?") thereby forfeiting all possible points. Yet even this foolishness pales in comparison to the world's most embarrassing telephone routine: forgetting whose number you dialed. At these times you say cheerily "Hi! (pause) I'm just checking in. How's it going?" and hope the other party will give you enough information to guess their identity; when I can tell someone is doing this to me I occasionally disguise my voice or use a phony accent, proving that it isn't only editors who can cause deep anxiety.

Call me sentimental, call me neurotic, call me crazy, but call me. (Just try to remember whose number you dialed.)

The Next Bus Home

My father drove me to college in our cranky 1967 Buick Skylark, a long trip without air-conditioning and without the calming presence of my mother who had died the year before. I was dressed like I was always dressed back in New York--black denim skirt, black tee-shirt, black boots, long curly hair and kohl eye-liner--and I was terrified when I started to see the other students sauntering around campus in chinos and polo shirts. The few girls I saw were dressed languidly and casually in boy's clothes and resembled junior Katherine Hepburns. In my most generous estimation, I looked like a poor-man's Connie Francis, had a New York accent, and a voice like traffic. It wasn't a good match. No doubt I was visibly shaken.

My father, a man of few words, said the right thing that day. Without looking in my direction he observed lightly "You can always take the next bus home." It was better than magic. I grinned and we laughed and pulled into the ugly parking lot behind a pretty building. That phrase has been a talisman to me since 1975 because it's given me permission to take risks without worrying about the irrevocable. "I can always take the next bus home," I thought when I moved to England, or when I moved back to New York, or when I moved to Connecticut to begin teaching. Every time I think of that line I think of the airless drive in the Skylark, and to the beginning of my life away from home. Change is twinned inexorably in my mind with a sense of difference, of fear, and of limitless adventure.

I needed the courage to face my chosen college, a place where I felt as if

I were the only person whose last name ended in a vowel. I needed a sense of humor to face early fraternity parties punctuated by beery guys named Skip or Chip asking me where I went to school and then sneering when I replied "I go to school here." It was a year before I added "And where do you go?" which at least caught the attention of anyone who might also have trouble with the usual dating rituals. I can't imagine that freshman year anywhere is easy for anyone; surely the suave and sophisticated amongst us were driven by their own insecurities and worries. (But maybe not. . .). Nothing was as hard as social life. Compared to figuring out codes of behavior, classes and seminars were a piece of sweet cake. A freshman seminar may well have provided me with friends I have kept until this day even if it did ruin Milton for me for life.

And it wasn't all gruel and ashes. There were great teachers, great dances, great roommates and friends, and one infamous tea at the Hanover Inn where, unladylike as ever, I spilled Earl Grey down my one good dress. My pals, male and female alike, were also part of the dispossessed in some way. Too urban, too shy, too ethnic, too working class, too outrageous, too intellectual, too subversive to be accommodated by the mainstream, we formed our own gang. We went to the local diner and sang "You Picked a Fine Time to Leave Me Lucille" with everyone else in the joint when the song came out of the jukebox. We'd jog or walk by the river, slightly worried about the bats and the occasional stray dog, and talk about what we'd do in ten, twelve, fifteen years. We argued with each other and lambasted the system even as we found comfort and support in this place we made for ourselves. I never would have imagined in my freshman year that I would look back on those days as a crucial time in my life. I wanted to get through them and out of them as quickly as possible.

But there are lapidary moments, polished off by years of looking back over them. I remember a wonderfully compassionate and brilliant teacher who has since left the profession, telling me not to wish my life away. "These days, one by one, will be important to you in ways you cannot now imagine. They are the beginnings of things to come. Don't underestimate them." I wrote down those words, and next to them I wrote another line he gave me, one borrowed I now believe from Gertrude Stein: "If you can do it then why do it?" Up until that year I'd always figured that you did whatever came easily and whatever you were good at. This teacher, among others, gave me the chance to learn to take a risk for all it was worth. If there's one lesson from my freshman year, that was it. Risking loneliness, I found luxuriously lasting companionship. Risking rejection, I found an odd sense of acceptance. Risking failure, I found the confidence of some sort of native ability laboriously honed into skill. Risking unhappiness, I found at least measured and memorable joy. Risks are worth it.

After all, you can always take the next bus home.

What You Fear = Who You Are

I'm the first one to admit she loves Halloween, to dress up in a remarkably ridiculous outfit while sporting a feather boa, and to eat candy like a kid whose family works for the Fixodent company. But I still think it's strange that we agree to stage a celebration of fear at the end of every October.

As if we weren't scared enough the rest of the year.

Think about how we cherish these Kodak moments of fear: we dress our kids up as The Hunchback of Notre Dame or, far more terrifying, as Barbie. We go to grown-ups parties where women old enough to know better wear cat-suits, accompanied by otherwise emotionally and intellectually stable men dressed as 1) women; 2) bikers; 3) women bikers. We eat foods that scare us the rest of the year, buying bags of chocolate and peanut concoctions, then justifying the purchase by pretending that we'll give most of it away. Small strangers ask for food by saying "Trick or treat!" offering the tiniest of threats in this ritualized chorus, and laughing, we offer handfuls of caramelized sugar or money for the poor. Most odd, perhaps--and thinking about it might make you shudder--we open our doors to strangers after dark. Has that gesture become the scariest part?

Or is the scariest part that we willingly open our doors to strangers who knock after dark only one night a year?

An after-sunset knock on the door in our neighborhood, for example, usually means that a student new to campus is pathetically lost and needs directions, or that one's cat has been discovered yet again on the neighbor's porch chomping on his geraniums as if they were part of a salad bar. It took me quite a few years, however, to realize that the knock-after-dark could be so benign.

As a recovering New Yorker, I regularly panicked at every noise for a full three years or so after moving to Connecticut. This made getting to sleep as difficult as finding a decent onion bagel. I kept thinking of Jack Nicolson in The Shining. A tree branch falling outside my window meant that an axe-murderer was near. (Why always "axe-murderer"? People in the city always fear that the country is full of this particular kind of homicidal nut. When did we first embrace the equation of "rural life= danger of axe murderers" in the public consciousness?) The creaking of wood as the house settled meant that we were on the verge of being devoured by a sink-hole. The cat's meowing meant there were mice (that much turned out to be true, but the blue-eyed mouse was too cute to be scary).

Not that I wasn't also scared of the quiet. Quiet in my old Lower East Side neighborhood meant that the customary buzz and spin of activity stopped for some reason, and that reason more often than not would involve the use of the word "felony" when described later on. But I've become accustomed to this Connecticut blend of silence and sound after nine years, and am grateful for the ability to trust that every night doesn't have to hold massive amounts of anxiety, not even Halloween.

There's something delicious about indulging in terror a very little bit and that's why Halloween is fun. It turns the world into a controlled chaotic environment and so paradoxically makes us feel safer. If we control what and how much frightens us we can convince ourselves that everything is okay. Alfred Hitchcock argued that folks liked horror movies because "They like to put their toe in the cold water of fear." A little bit of what scares you can act as a sort of inoculation against what really horrifies you in the same way that a controlled dose of an illness can build your resistance to its full onset. Watch a little Fatal Attraction and you'll not need to ask that new colleague out to lunch; watch a little Psycho and staying at a Motel 6 or any other nationally recognized chain starts to seem like a really good idea.

Perhaps I should confess that I still watch most of these movies with my eyes hidden behind my hands, as if peeking at something gruesome doesn't count. I recall that Alien, for example, starred my index and middle fingers, which were busy framing my left eye as Sigourney was out there in the slime. When I was in high school guys invited their dates to scary movies so that the girls would snuggle up to them in fear, but that strategy didn't work on me. I would be so terrified I'd end up clutching my date's wind pipe or removing bits of his forearm with my nails. On second dates I'd be invited to musicals or films with a religious message.

But when I think about the role of fear in everyday life, I think about how pervasive it is, and how little we consciously acknowledge it even as fear shapes our thoughts and behaviors. What does fear do? Fear fidgets by the phone until the call comes, fear hides jewelry in paper bags underneath the sink, fear rehearses every word of a conversation with a sister that ended coldly, fear counts calories, counts pennies, counts a partner's nights away from home. Fear wonders about a child's friends, a child's grades, a child's future. Fear looks both ways but still refuses to cross; fear looks twice and still doesn't leap. Fear believes that the early worm gets caught by the bird, and sympathizes with the worm's regret at being punctual. Fear usually arrives late, inevitably leaves early, and ends up never going out of town at all. Fear is the phantom hand on the back of the neck and the sound of a door opening downstairs when no one is coming home.

Fear does everything except go out and buy the groceries.

Fear grows poor because it watches others gain wealth but cannot enter the fray; fear grows sick because it eats away at health even as it fears its diminishment; fear grows old watching others live in ways that seem to threaten--but in reality only enhance--life. You become afraid to bicycle because you might fall, but you in fact become less healthy for lack of exercise; you become afraid of the water and so avoid taking a cruise that would relax and refresh you. "Life shrinks or expands in proportion to one's courage," counseled Anais Nin. Courage is especially necessary when facing one's own invented demons: our own nightmares can become overwhelming because of our skill in constructing them.

Too often fear is regarded as a failure of intelligence or will. Someone scared might be reprimanded by a companion, and told to "Get a grip-- anybody with sense can see that there's nothing to worry about." But fear is paradoxically often a product-- not a failure-- of being both astute and perceptive: the most fearful are often those with the most imaginative intelligences, the most self-determining ways of life.

A good friend of mine, a woman otherwise admirably courageous, won't drive on the highway. She can imagine too clearly the scene of an accident, imagine how she would lose control and cross a barrier, imagine how she would be at fault. Someone else in precisely the same situation merely picks up the keys and heads out the door.

You might fear applying for a promotion because you can imagine in excessive detail how the insecurities of your supervisor will be brought to the surface by your request; someone with less insight might just submit an application and get the job.

Understanding fear is a crucial dimension of self-discovery: What you fear, why you fear it, how it affects you, and what you do about it is the key to how you live your life. We inherit many of our fears; others are formed during our childhood without our knowledge or consent. Fears influence our behaviors and choices as we grow up; fears seep into the water table of our emotional, psychological, intellectual and spiritual lives just as some barely traceable toxin can poison the well. All experiences of fear are intensely meaningful. Fear leaps over the domestic and familiar world of what is known and lands in the apocalyptic landscape of our imagination. The subtleties of these unmapped territories can lead us to truths about our visible lives.

Although fear in the right dosage and under the right circumstance protects us --survival and success depend, in part, on being afraid of life's real dangers-- the intimate fears of our imaginations can paralyze us. Healthy fear can galvanize us to action-- making us run when we need to, or stand

and fight when it's necessary-- but imaginary fear offers straitjackets instead of lifejackets, nooses instead of safety nets.

Fear is an especially embarrassing emotion because what we fear often seems petty. The big worries seem noble--fear of nuclear annihilation, of environmental destruction, of human suffering-- but everyday personal fears (fear of elevators, fear of embarrassment,fear of French poodles) creep around coveting the nobility of "real" fears but never quite making it. Insecurity about the details of life causes excessive concern for them in the lives of many women, who then permit their fears about the details to obscure genuine threats to their well-being.

There are women with immaculate houses who refuse to go to the doctor for mammograms; they are apparently more worried about their bedspreads than their breasts, but surely this isn't the case. Displacement of fears from the large to the small leads not to reassurance but to a distorted sense of protection from danger.

Fear is familiar to me; it has circled my ankles since childhood, its soft tail brushing against my skin almost imperceptibly. It's strange how scared a woman can be and still be thought of as courageous. I traffic in risk-taking, advising the students I teach and the readers I write for to embark for deep waters only, risking the ship, themselves, and everything they've ever known as safe. I tell them the truth: the most important thing in life, without exception, is to step out of the magic circles of safety we create for ourselves. Tapping the same lever to get the same pellet day after day, safe as it is, is for the birds; security isn't the best thing life has to offer and habit dulls both desire and imagination. We need, deserve, hunger for more adventure, but it's difficult to move ahead when you're afraid to step on cracks in the sidewalk, or travel after dark.

My fears wouldn't have lasted this long unless they met some emotional and psychological need. Just as a religious woman might say her prayers every evening, I rehearse my fears before I sleep. Why didn't she return my phone calls? Why did he put off our meeting? Why haven't I heard the results from that annual physical yet? Who will take care of me if I get sick? Pretty soon I'm worrying whether the national blood banks have my particular blood-type in good supply, how many people value me enough to donate quarts, and whether it would be embarrassing to ask them, while simultaneously feeling guilty for avoiding the last blood-drive at UConn. Sometimes it seems as if I embrace my fear as transcendental experience, as an act of moral redemption. I'm not just going over old material, I'm performing a rite of atonement for the sins of survival and success. I am reinforcing lessons learned at an early age: not to count my blessings, but instead to consider how high the odds are against my luck holding out.

It's not just for me that the world of fear exists--all you have to do is move to the margins, go underneath the world considered normal, or wait until what's normal turns out the porch light and there it is, what is feared, scratching at the glass behind a dark window. The darkness is the same, the metallic taste of fear is the same for everyone but the individual causes for fear-- the shape of the windows framing the darkness-- are wildly different.

My deepest, most gut-searing fear, was once also a safe fear--if you can have a safe fear-- but it is no longer possible for me to live with it. I am afraid of airplanes. I can imagine disaster perfectly, with much more clarity than I can imagine serenity or success. Unlike ordinary life, which flows along without much detail, disaster is drenched in detail, filled with exclamation points and dashes. I can tell you all about what it will be like when disaster strikes, tell you about the yelling, smoke, and the lack of oxygen. I can also tell you what I'd be wearing and how I would react. Such detail is not healthy; such flights of imagination are bound to be expensive when it comes time to pay for the indulgence of fear. They are not first class. I am afraid they will cost me the world.

Fear has kept me very busy. I've been reassured, been informed, and have had airline safety demonstrated to me on countless occasions. I've listened to tapes meant to relax me and read books meant to answer every question. I've done breathing classes, desensitization, self-help programs, in addition to taking enough prescription medication for Blue Cross to give me a Gold Card.

Everybody has shown me why my fears of flying are groundless. Demonstrations of safety offer nothing, I am convinced. I once asked a pilot (my panicked voice pitched so high that I was afraid only bats could hear me), if he thought the flight would be free of turbulence. I expected the usual reassurance, but this nice young man with the crew-cut instead showed me the print-out of the weather map. By way of demonstrating how safe we would be, he showed me how we would avoid the worst of the thunderstorms ahead. I hadn't known there were thunderstorms up ahead, but now that I did I thought of nothing else the entire trip.

By flying I encroach on a domain unwelcoming to me: I push myself into the sky and expect winds and lightning--I see meteorological events as metaphoric.

People have talked sense to me. When you're frightened everybody tells you things that make perfect sense. That's when you realize it isn't sense you're looking for. We search for reassurance and compensation and are handed platitudes and statistics, sort of along the lines of asking for bread and getting stones.

Terrified as I am of airplanes, now I must travel if I'm to make a life for myself as a writer and lecturer. As an adult.

I once sat next to a poor soul, a pilot from a cargo company flying home on a passenger airline, and for eight hours he answered my questions about the details of why people don't usually die on airplanes. "Count to seven after take-off," he advised. "If you make it through the first seven seconds, and then the first seven minutes, you're home free."

So I've counted at every take-off, moving the moments from one side of my mind to the other like colored beads on an abacus, counting with the seriousness and precision of a child for whom numbers are new. I've survived every flight, but I secretly know that counting won't help me if the wing flaps aren't working. But I count, nevertheless, every time.

The primary quality of what we fear, the thing which ensures for our fears a convincing and permanent presence in our lives and the power to survive in our memories is their very limitedness. They are fixed, static. Their presence in our lives is unfailing; their fidelity to us is assured. No wonder we embrace them. When you can't count on being happy or being loved, at least you can count on being able to terrify yourself at a moment's notice.

Fear is sometimes familiar, sometimes appropriate, sometimes inherited, sometimes lifesaving. Fear and pain are danger signals, letting us know there's trouble ahead and telling us that we should either stop short or speed up--and telling us we need to do something now. But when fear is a constant feature it becomes like sirens threaded through the background noises of every city: ordinary and expected, although no less invasive. Fear is also exhausting, confusing, disruptive, painful, seductive, and dangerous. Perhaps the most interesting thing about it is that fear comes in far more than 28 flavors: because everything is so dangerous we play a version of the children's game "duck-duck-goose," picking and choosing our nightmares in order to avoid total paralysis.

Women have a particular and complex relationship to fear because they have for so long been barred from acting on their ambitions or rebellions that they have learned to turn to fear as a way of dealing with and influencing the world. Women's fears, however, are often misdirected. I know women who are terrified if they can't fit into the bathing suit they wore when they were eighteen; I know men who don't find it a cause for concern that they're too fat to fit into a Geo.

Their fears confirm their existence, and, if the dreadful thing actually comes to pass, their instincts, intelligence, and importance. That fear can sometimes smooth a pathway on which disaster arrives more quickly is a terrifying but nevertheless possible outcome of many scenarios: the husband, repeatedly and without cause accused of infidelity might decide to a commit a crime to fit his punishment; the teenage daughter constantly fretted over by a too-anxious parent gets pregnant as if to cry out "See, Mom? You're right, I'm no good. Now are you happy?"

Many women are afraid to relinquish their fear, even when they understand intellectually that it hinders them and in no way helps them. They fear security, and by extension, success, because it appears like hubris, and so invites defeat and humiliation. They wait for the next shoe to drop, the disaster that inevitably follows in the wake of good news. In other words, they believe that those fools who consider themselves safe are actually in danger. If they get a reassuring diagnosis, they seek another physician, believing more strongly that the risk and consequence of false security can be grave. It's tough to be happy when you're waiting, like Henny Penny, for the sky to fall.

And that's the scariest part of fear: being frightened can eclipse some of the possibilities of happiness. I've spent some beautiful flights too frightened to look into the lapidary blue sky; I spent those early years of my time in Connecticut waiting for Norman Bates. What a waste of perfectly good days and nights, I think now; how I wish I could have that time back. What's frightening is that there's little enough time for pleasure and joy: why use it up by giving into fear?

Maybe this year my real fears will show up in costume at the door. Instead of adorable miniature witches and gleefully greedy ghosts, I'll find Incompetence, Futility, Anger, and Mortality standing there. I'll know what to do with them, as I see them coming up the walk. Oh, I'll open the door and let them in all right. But I'll invite them into a bright house full of laughter and love, pile on the sweets and the soda, and tell them to make themselves at home.

Facing them won't be as bad as worrying about their approach; acknowledging them will be better than desperately pretending they don't exist. Maybe they'll unmask themselves and turn out to be perfectly ordinary parts of the everyday world. But even if they're the nightmare figures I've always feared, at least I'll have made their acquaintance. I'll know how to deal with them. I'll know what makes them appear strong, what makes them feel unwelcome, and maybe I'll even learn how to ask them, politely, to shut the door behind them when they leave.

Stop Trying to Tie the Perfect Bow

Let me make your day easier by revealing the truth: nobody is dealing with the holidays any better than you are. Relax, take a deep breath, and stop trying to tie the perfect bow.

We're all in a state of frenzy. You see us at the malls? We look like a combination of characters from The Stepford Wives and The Rocky Horror Picture Show. There's a wild and primitive glare in the eyes of some. Others, sniffling in despair, are reduced to picking up and putting down the same object, wondering if their brother-in-law could learn to like a tie that chimes. Picking it up, putting it down, looking around, picking it up again. It's not a pretty scene.

We're driven nuts by the idea that every other human being is handling the stress, pressure, and needs of her loved ones more effectively. Sure, some of the sneakiest are quiet. Some are knitting adorable scarves and making braided challah bread. They look peaceful--now. But when they realize that sixteen OTHER pals will be expecting loaves of challah bread once they hear challah is hitting the streets, they'll turn into Tasmanian Devils, whipping around the kitchen and swearing in a very un-Betty-Crocker-like manner.

And while hand-knit scarves are occasionally and truly appreciated as the works of art and love they actually are, such complex concepts are not celebrated by most children under age eighteen. Children under age eighteen want items with a minimum of twelve-thousand individually moving parts. They want to create empires, complete with diverse educational systems and industrial military complexes. Scarves have few moving parts.

Of course, if you love to knit, great. But please don't be like one of one of my aunts who knit me a thing that itched, tickled, and somehow made my head look like it was being served on a platter. In order to prove I wore this garment, I was forced into it every time my family went to see her. This was not a gift; it was penance.

I call Bonnie. She's neck-deep in negotiations with her sisters concerning what time will be spent with which part of whose families. The morning will be here, the middle of the day there, the mid-to-late afternoon elsewhere. She gets the relatives in Brooklyn and Queens while the others flank north to spend time with the elderly relations in Yonkers. They'll make plans to reconnoiter late in the day and see what territory is left to cover. It's like establishing the Treaty of Versailles.

I call Amy, who explains that her family will fly to Chicago on Christmas Eve. Aware that airports put up banners in December announcing "Abandon Hope, All Ye Who Enter Here," Amy, her husband, and their three children are flinging themselves into the worst travel day in history because if they don't, her mother-in-law will construct the emotional equivalent of an Iron Maiden for Amy to inhabit for the next millennium. Amy will spend hours sitting in airport lounges while the smaller of her children gnaw on the ankles of strangers and the eldest practices flirting with boys. Amy's husband will say he is just going to get a paper and he will come back with representative journalism from diverse nations. Amy's husband will construct a tent out of these, shielding himself from all annoying interaction. Amy will fret, believing she has lost control over her life and assuming that Everyone Else Gets The Holidays Right Except For Her.

She will be incorrect in her assumption. There is no exactly-perfect-one-right-way to "do" the holidays. If we're honest with ourselves and with each other, we'd admit it is all improvisation. The fun parts, actually, are the purely serendipitous moments, those times of laughter not caught on videotape but recorded, indestructible, in our hearts. There is no script for seasonal cheer any more than there is a guarantee for daily happiness. We all know that everyday we should be thankful for what we have, bask in the affections of those we love, do what we can to help those who could make use of us in their lives. Holidays are important because they help us highlight our blessings and our connections to other people. When they start making us whine, cry, despair, or run shrieking through a store in order to be first in line at a newly opened register, however, it is time to lighten up on the seasonal spirit. Tying the perfect bow is not worth tying yourself in knots.